A Clinician's Guide *to* Teaching Mindfulness

The Comprehensive Session-by-Session
Program *for* Mental Health Professionals
and Health Care Providers

CHRISTIANE WOLF, MD, PhD
J. GREG SERPA, PhD

New Harbinger Publications, Inc.

Author's Note

Writing this book together has been a true collaboration. We have typically used the pronoun "we" to share information or a story. While it is our pleasure to teach together often, some of the stories here are from one or the other of us. Some examples we offer are composites to make a point, and all names have been changed to ensure our participants' confidentiality.

Publisher's Note

"A Story on Kindness" from THE WISE HEART: A GUIDE TO THE UNIVERSAL TEACHINGS OF BUDDHIST PSYCHOLOGY by Jack Kornfield, copyright © 2008 by Jack Kornfield. Used by permission of Bantam Books, a division of Random House, Inc. Any third party use of this material, outside of this publication, is prohibited. Interested parties must apply directly to Random House, Inc. for permission.

Distributed in Canada by Raincoast Books

Copyright © 2015 by Christiane Wolf and J. Greg Serpa
        New Harbinger Publications, Inc.
        5674 Shattuck Avenue
        Oakland, CA 94609
        www.newharbinger.com

Cover design by Amy Shoup
Acquired by Jess O'Brien
Edited by Marisa Solís

Library of Congress Cataloging-in-Publication Data on file

FSC
www.fsc.org
MIX
Paper from
responsible sources
FSC® C011935

Printed in the United States of America

19   18   17

10   9   8   7   6   5

To Bert and our amazing children, Lynn, Tristan, and Antonia.

—CW

For my boys, Jeff and Logan. The joys of my life.

—JGS

May we always live in the full embrace of our loving hearts.

"A 'must-read' for anyone who wants to teach mindfulness in groups. The authors' experience and talent shine through every page. They spell out for readers what is often implied in hands-on teacher trainings. A special bonus is how mindfulness and compassion are seamlessly woven together. Highly recommended!"

—**Christopher Germer, PhD**, author of *The Mindful Path to Self-Compassion*, coeditor of *Mindfulness and Psychotherapy*, and clinical instructor in psychology at Harvard Medical School

"What a beautiful, wise, and user-friendly handbook on how to teach mindfulness. I also appreciate how the authors provide clear directions on how to support the clinician's ability to sit in the mindfulness teacher's seat with greater wisdom and humility."

—**Bob Stahl, PhD**, coauthor of *A Mindfulness-Based Stress Reduction Workbook*, *Living with Your Heart Wide Open*, *Calming the Rush of Panic*, *A Mindfulness-Based Stress Reduction Workbook for Anxiety*, and *MBSR Every Day*

"I can't imagine a more ideal how-to-teach-mindfulness manual! This book offers clear and comprehensive support in learning to lead meditations, offer beginners classes, and respond to the natural challenges and questions that arise in introducing mindfulness to clients. Keep this guide close at hand—it will enable you to bring your full intelligence, heart, and confidence to sharing these life-transforming practices."

—**Tara Brach, PhD**, author of *Radical Acceptance* and *True Refuge*

"What a practical, thorough, extraordinary book. Wolf and Serpa give a crystal clear road map for any professional wanting to teach mindfulness in clinical settings. Their detailed lesson plans and voice-of-experience guidance are infused with their own deep practice of mindfulness, encouraging support, and clinical acumen. Highly recommended."

—**Rick Hanson, PhD**, author of *Buddha's Brain: The Practical Neuroscience of Happiness, Love, and Wisdom*

"Broad in scope, yet practical, *A Clinician's Guide to Teaching Mindfulness* can serve as a resource for secular mindfulness teacher training programs. Clearly the result of years of experience, this book provides especially good support for new instructors, while those with experience will appreciate its clarity and fresh perspectives."

—**Sharon Salzberg**, author of *Lovingkindness* and *Real Happiness*

"Wolf and Serpa have given us a wonderful gift—a clear, complete, and inspiring guide for teaching the basics of mindfulness. The authors' deep understanding of this topic from both Buddhist and psychotherapist perspectives is evident throughout, and helps to make this book not only a very practical manual, but also a succinct and direct guide for how to become a more effective and comfortable teacher or facilitator of mindfulness. This book will be highly valuable for anyone interested in this area, regardless of prior experience. Absolutely the best book on this topic I have encountered."

> —**Bruce D. Naliboff, PhD**, research professor of medicine and psychiatry, and biobehavioral sciences director in the pain research program at the Gail and Gerald Oppenheimer Family Center for Neurobiology of Stress at the David Geffen School of Medicine at UCLA

"*A Clinician's Guide to Teaching Mindfulness* is a wonderful guide for far more than only clinicians! There is no one on this life's journey who cannot deepen their experience and their joy through understanding and practicing mindfulness. When we as clinicians, in the broadest sense of the word, advance our capacity to understand and teach these fundamental concepts, this way of being in the world and in our lives will take root more organically. It will become a fundamental way of being. I would highly recommend this book as a guide to all of us who would like to better help ourselves and others discover, understand, and integrate this way of being."

> —**Tracy W. Gaudet, MD**, executive director of the Office of Patient Centered Care and Cultural Transformation, US Department of Veterans Affairs

"Thorough, practical, and full of heart and integrity. I highly recommend this book for anyone who is looking to get started or enhance their ability to teach mindfulness individually or in groups."

> —**Elisha Goldstein, PhD**, author of *Uncovering Happiness*

"This is a book that is really more like a kind and trusted mentor to guide you through the wonderful and rewarding journey of sharing mindfulness with others. Written with a warm and engaging style and informed by deep wisdom and long experience, Wolf and Serpa have found a way to support new teachers in a systematic yet personable way on the path toward teaching mindfulness. The twin threads of solid clinical experience and deep reflection on the dharma provide a unique, complementary, and informative perspective on something that is hard to skillfully put into words. If you seek to teach mindfulness in any sort of setting, you will find this to be a valuable resource that you will refer to often in your journey. You'll be glad you have this resource at each step along the way."

— **Steven D. Hickman, PsyD**, executive director of the Center for Mindfulness at the University of California, San Diego, and associate clinical professor in the UCSD department of psychiatry

"Teaching and guiding mindfulness requires a mindful practice. As with any skill, the more experience one has the more effective they will be. I have found that there is tremendous variance in teachers of mindfulness and some are much more effective than others. This book is the guide I would recommend for anyone who wants to be an effective teacher. It provides strategic tips and supports how your own practice can be authentically shared with others so we can all walk together on a more mindful path. I highly recommend it!"

— **David Rakel, MD**, founder and director of Integrative Medicine at the University of Wisconsin, and associate professor at the University of Wisconsin School of Medicine and Public Health

"Here is a book that actually delivers on its promise. *A Clinician's Guide to Teaching Mindfulness* provides a structure and detailed instruction for new teachers of mindfulness that is without parallel. This practical and inspiring book provides both the information for structuring a mindfulness class and numerous examples of how you can improve what you are currently doing in your teaching. Whether you teach mindfulness in schools, health care settings, mental health services, or businesses and nonprofits, this is a book you must have."

— **Phillip Moffitt**, mindfulness teacher and author of *Dancing with Life* and *Emotional Chaos to Clarity*

"A *Clinician's Guide to Teaching Mindfulness* offers a wise and practical immersion into the nuts and bolts of guiding others, and oneself, into the daily practice of mindfulness meditation. Christiane Wolf and J. Greg Serpa build on their years of experience to create this useful, scientifically grounded, step-by-step manual for understanding, planning, and implementing a didactic program to create more well-being in our lives. Take in their sage guidance and the world will be a better place for us all!"

> —**Daniel J. Siegel, MD**, author of *The Mindful Brain*, *The Mindful Therapist*, *The Developing Mind*, *Brainstorm*, and *Mindsight*; executive director of the Mindsight Institute; founding codirector of the UCLA Mindful Awareness Research Center; and clinical professor at the David Geffen School of Medicine at UCLA

"This guide is a warm welcome to clinicians who have seen the benefits of mindfulness around them and may have a personal practice, but don't have the proper tools to share it with others. With true generosity, the authors provide these tools, leaving no stone unturned in terms of the practical details of teaching an introductory mindfulness course, while also sharing their wisdom on the theoretical underpinnings of mindfulness. This book should be required reading for trainees in medicine and nursing as well as psychology."

> —**Kirsten Tillisch, MD**, associate professor of medicine and director of the mind-body research program in the Gail and Gerald Oppenheimer Family Center for Neurobiology of Stress at the David Geffen School of Medicine at UCLA, and Chief of Integrative Medicine at the VA Greater Los Angeles Healthcare System

Acknowledgments

We are indebted to Jon Kabat-Zinn for seeing the potential of the Buddhist practice of mindfulness and for starting the "Mindful Revolution" (cover of Time magazine, June 2014), and to everyone at the Center for Mindfulness at UMASS Medical School for their part in implementing that vision. It has deeply touched and influenced our lives and our work.

We are grateful for Sandy Robertson, chief of Patient Centered Care at the Greater Los Angeles VA. Her energy and commitment to healing practices is an inspiration. We have been enriched personally and professionally for our collaboration. Donna Beiter, former director of the Greater Los Angeles VA, has provided the leadership and vision that has allowed much of our work to take place. To our VA-CALM colleagues, Wendy Schmelzer, Paloma Cain, Joni Cohen, Linda Good , and Trudy Goodman and InsightLA: thanks so much for your efforts and kindness, as we have all worked to bring mindfulness to the VA. Thanks to the VA Office of Patient Centered Care and Cultural Transformation for supporting our work and distributing our Mindfulness Toolkits throughout the nation and on YouTube (find our videos by searching our names or at http://www.sharingmindfulness.com). It is a great joy to work with partners who share a vision for whole-person health.

We are deeply grateful to every person who has ever taken a class or trained with us and allowed us to witness, support, and grow from his or her personal unfolding.

We are grateful to Carol White for her suggestions during the contract phase of the book. We want to thank our talented editor, Marisa Solís, for her great editing skills and organizational talents. We appreciate all the professionals who guided us along the way including the amazing team at New Harbinger Publications: Jess O'Brien, Jess Beebe, Jesse Burson, Vicraj Gill, Michele Waters, and anyone else we may have inadvertently omitted, thanks for believing in our vision for the need of this book from the beginning. And we are especially grateful to Jon Kabat-Zinn for reading the final draft of the manuscript and providing invaluable feedback, particularly about the misnomer "secular mindfulness" and the importance of letting poetry live inside of you by learning it by heart.

Great thanks to everybody else who read the whole or parts of the manuscript and gave much-appreciated feedback, especially Lisa Hills, Jill Shepard, and Laura McMullen.

Christiane's Acknowledgments

I'd like to acknowledge my deep love and gratitude to my husband, Bert, my favorite grown-up, and to our three wonderful children, Lynn, Tristan, and Antonia. I also want to thank my mother, Anne Wolf, for instilling a strong sense of what is right and wrong in me as well as an unshakable trust in gender equality.

I'm deeply indebted to my Dharma teachers and guides over the years: Amaravati (Oliver Katz) and Aryadeva (Michael Petersson), Jack Kornfield, Jon Kabat-Zinn, Sharon Salzberg, and, more recently, Phillip Moffitt and Kate Lila Wheeler.

Most credit, deep gratitude, and appreciation is due for my heart teacher Trudy Goodman, who showed me how much I needed and appreciated a female teacher and fiercely supportive mentor who is not only a dedicated Dharma practitioner but also a professional and a mother. Without her we would not have stayed in Los Angeles, and I wouldn't have changed my life from being a dedicated physician to being a full-time Dharma teacher and helping to build InsightLA.

Thank you to all my friends and colleagues at InsightLA, especially to our Teacher Development Group and Beth Mulligan. And thank you to my Dharma friends and colleagues at the Center for Mindfulness at UMASS Medical: Bob Stahl, Florence Meleo-Meyer, Saki Santorelli, and Lynn Koerbel.

Thank you to Babette Rothschild for seeing and believing in my abilities to write and encouraging me to start.

And of course a big thank-you to my dear friend and colleague Greg Serpa, whose big heart, professionalism, and silliness when needed helped us through the ups and downs of writing this book.

Greg's Acknowledgments

It has been my great fortune to have mindfulness teachers who have taught and encouraged me for years; first among them are Trudy Goodman, Jack Kornfield, and my inspirational partner in this writing venture, Christiane Wolf. I truly am grateful for your generosity of spirit, keen intellects, and passion. I am also indebted to many other teachers including Sharon Salzberg, Wes Nisker, Christopher Germer, and Kristin Neff.

As a psychologist, it has been the highlight of my professional career to be affiliated with two outstanding organizations: the VA and UCLA. At the Greater Los Angeles VA, my first chief of psychology, Gary Wolfe, and my current chief, Peter Graves, each supported the creation of innovative mindfulness programs. I am indebted to you. Susan Rosenbluth is my partner in our Interprofessional Integrative Health Fellowship program; I would be lost without you. All of the psychology interns and fellows I have trained throughout the years have certainly given me just as much as I had to offer them. You all have my deepest thanks. And for all of my psychology colleagues at the VA, you inspire me and make me proud of our profession. At the UCLA Department of Psychology I am grateful for Jill Waterman, Danielle Keenan-Miller, and all of my colleagues throughout the department as well as the many wonderful graduate students I have supervised across the years. And to my research colleagues at the VA and at the David Geffen School of Medicine at UCLA—including Kirsten Tillisch, Bruce Naliboff, Stephanie Taylor, Milena Zirovich, Jean Stains, Suzanne Smith, Tiffany Ju, and many others—I am grateful for your commitment to our shared research and for simply being so wonderful.

The time and commitment it takes to write a book, while working full-time and engaging in research, has been daunting. It couldn't have happened without my husband, Jeff Giordano, who supports our family in every way imaginable. And to my son, Logan, the light of my life, I thank you for your enormous zest and for your understanding when I missed your soccer games.

Contents

Foreword

One of the most revolutionary of human gifts is our capacity to see clearly and to be present, interested, and connected to our own lives in a wise and compassionate way. We come alive when we mindfully eat an avocado, look into the eyes of a child, or see the apricot sunset reflected in rain puddles after a thunderstorm. Ancient wisdom and modern science teach us that the capacity for presence can be developed. Research now shows that the practice of mindfulness is profoundly healing, allowing us to tend wisely to the body, to listen carefully to the heart, and to bring a compassionate understanding to our mind and our world.

For those wanting to teach the gifts of mindfulness and compassion, this book is a treasure. It will support you, offering thorough and practical guidance and step-by-step direction. It is filled with specific instructions and great examples. All the tools you need are here: guided meditations, a summary of research, group development, an excellent clinical overview, class outlines, rich stories, compelling cases, and support for the critical development of your own practice.

With Trudy Goodman, Christiane developed InsightLA, her primary place of practice and teaching. Greg has been spearheading mindfulness groups at the Los Angeles VA years before mindfulness became so popular. The longtime dedicated practice and clinical skills of both Christiane Wolf and Greg Serpa shine throughout this guide, making it both accessible and deep. We have known Christiane and Greg for years, and we can say with confidence that they exemplify, both personally and professionally, the qualities of healing presence and compassionate wisdom their book helps you embody in your own teaching.

A Clinician's Guide to Teaching Mindfulness is an encouragement to teach the skills of well-being, mindfulness, and compassion, offering and spreading blessings—to which we add our own.

—Jack Kornfield, PhD, and Trudy Goodman, PhD
Los Angeles, November 2014

Introduction

It seems that wherever you turn these days, *mindfulness* is there—or people want it to be there. And for something *this* amazing, many good teachers are needed. Each day, we are approached by people who want to teach mindfulness and wonder how to best go about it.

Maybe mindfulness has deeply touched your own life. And now you want to start sharing that.

Or maybe you have been asked by your institution or clinic to start a mindfulness class. You know what mindfulness is—kind of.

Or perhaps you have taken some trainings and classes, and have a solid personal meditation practice, yet you still don't feel like you have the exact tools to get started as a mindfulness teacher.

Maybe you have looked into how to become a teacher of the gold standard for mindfulness programs, mindfulness-based stress reduction (MBSR), but you're not (yet?) ready for a multiyear training program to teach this intensive class. In fact, you are pretty sure that your clients or patients would be more compliant with a sixty- or ninety-minute class compared to one hundred and fifty minutes, and with a fifteen-minute daily home practice compared to thirty or forty-five minutes. And you're wondering what curriculum to use instead.

If you fit these scenarios, or any situation resembling them, you've come to the right book.

Why This Book?

A Clinician's Guide to Teaching Mindfulness is a hands-on manual to get you started as a mindfulness facilitator or to deepen and fine-tune your skills if you already have some teaching experience in this field. Whether you want to teach a multiweek Introduction to Mindfulness class, adapt mindfulness practices into an existing group program, or use short practices in one-on-one sessions, we've got you covered. This book provides you with practical and easy-to-implement tools and techniques for mindfulness facilitation, while at the same time supports you in deepening your own mindfulness practice.

Another unique aspect of our program is that it's not only meant for a health care setting. Our Introduction to Mindfulness course can be easily transferred and adapted to any class or individual practice, whether it takes place in a community center, business office, or a university classroom.

To make this book easy to navigate, it's structured into three distinct parts:

Part I: Mindfulness and Compassion gives an overview of mindfulness and compassion, as well as its roots in Buddhist philosophy, in chapter 1. In chapter 2 we provide a summary of the most salient research on these subjects.

Part II: Teaching Essentials provides the fundamental preparations advisable when first starting out, as well as effective techniques for teaching in a group setting. Chapter 3 focuses on the importance of a personal practice and how to go about that. Chapter 4 gets you ready to teach with in-depth descriptions of the different aspects of leading a class. This chapter also introduces the particular language of mindfulness facilitation and helps you with confidently leading any mindfulness practice without a script. You will get the nuts and bolts of launching a mindfulness class in chapter 5, with all you need to know about getting referrals and finding the right space. For therapists, we provide suggestions for working with specific diagnostic presentations in clinical settings. We also go into more depth with the distinction between a mindfulness class and group therapy, differences in facilitation between a therapist and a mindfulness teacher, and common therapist pitfalls.

Part III: The Core Program walks you step-by-step through the six-week curriculum of our Introduction to Mindfulness program. Provided are outlines for each session, meditation scripts (and links to downloadable audio files), tips for transitioning and keeping track of time, advice on how to answer common questions, and practical, effective solutions for managing a range of participant experiences. We also share two complete bonus sessions on compassion and resiliency, to either add on to the six weeks or to teach separately.

For years, we have taught this six-week program in adaptations and in all of its individual components to populations as diverse as homeless veterans, those in inpatient drug-abuse-recovery programs, cancer survivors, hospital clinicians, and to everyday stressed-out professionals and parents, leaders in nonprofits and businesses, and more.

After reading this book you will know:

- How to deepen and support your own mindfulness practice

- How to set up and start a six-week Introduction to Mindfulness class for your group

- How to teach the class and the individual components with confidence

You will know exactly how to prep for leading a particular practice and what are the most common issues and questions you can expect from your students. And our proven Teaching Tips, based on our many years of experience and sprinkled throughout this book, offer insightful pointers for successful facilitating.

We want to support you to start teaching or, if you're already teaching, to deepen your understanding and instruction skills. At the same time we want to emphasize that this book is not a substitute for professional training; rather, it's meant to complement, support, and strengthen it. And to get you started—*now*. We wish for this book to be your constant companion while sharing mindfulness with others, well read with earmarks, highlighted sections, and many sticky notes.

Who This Book Is For

While the title of the book includes the words "clinician's guide," and we cover in depth how to introduce mindfulness to various clinical populations, it is by no means exclusive to clinicians.

We, the authors, are both clinicians: one a physician (Christiane Wolf) and one a clinical psychologist (Greg Serpa). We have trained and mentored many clinicians and want to share what we have learned with you. This book is for mental health clinicians such as psychiatrists, psychologists, social workers, marriage and family therapists, psychiatric nurse practitioners, and psychiatric nurses. But it's also intended for clinicians and professionals not in mental health, like physicians, nurse practitioners, nurses, occupational therapists, physical therapists, midwives, osteopaths, and acupuncturists, as well as yoga instructors, health coaches, and nutrition coaches.

We have also taught this material with great success to facilitators new to mindfulness in the fields of business, law, education, and religion, to name just a few. Keep in mind that when we use the word "clinician" throughout this book, we're speaking directly to you.

No matter what your background is, this book is the right place to plan, set up, and start teaching mindfulness and compassion.

The Benefits of Mindfulness and Compassion

During every participant's first class, we ask, "Why are you here?" Some seek help with anxiety, insomnia, depression, an addictive disorder, or deep heartache after a breakup. Others come for help with chronic pain, hypertension, skin rashes, or a host of other physical manifestations of the stress in their lives. We have even had a student report, "I want to downregulate the activity of my amygdala!" Many will say, "I have too much stress in my life" or "I feel like my to-do list is running my life." As a facilitator, you will hear many different reasons for what brings an individual to class. But most reasons can be distilled to a simple and profound wish: "I want to be happier."

"Happiness" is a complicated and not-easy-to-define word. Yet people know what it means to them. It's usually not the hyperexcited kind of happiness but more the calmer, kinder, and more peaceful happiness. A kind of "deep down inside" happiness.

How do they get happier? We can look to symptom reduction (physically and psychologically), stress elimination, a better quality of life, better coping skills, and a greater sense of connection or enhanced self-acceptance.

How does this happen? By experiencing a greater sense of control and ease over how we relate to or cope with what is happening in our inner and outer experience. We also learn to relate to what is happening with more kindness. This, in turn, will also lower our physiological stress response. We like the metaphor *learning to surf life's waves*: You can't control the waves, but you can learn how to surf. And you have to be very mindful and in the present moment to watch each particular wave and then decide if you want to catch it or let it pass.

The Clinical Psychologist and Dharma Teacher Perspectives

At different places in the book we offer different perspectives on the same topic. That's because we come from different traditions. Greg Serpa writes the "Clinical Psychologist Perspective" sections, which include his direct clinical work with patients (at the Department of Veterans Affairs, at a university hospital, and in private practice), his role in training and supervision, and work as a clinical scientist. Greg has experience with diverse mental health populations. He had been a meditation practitioner for decades when, in 2011, he became the federal government's first full-time mindfulness teacher and teacher trainer at the VA Greater Los Angeles Healthcare System's Center of Innovation.

Christiane Wolf, on the other hand, has focused her own training in the last decade on deepening her understanding of the Buddhist teachings, including of long silent-retreat practices. She writes the "Dharma Teacher Perspective" sections. Christiane became fascinated with *Vipassana* (insight) meditation after finishing high school in Germany. The practice helped Christiane greatly through medical school and later during her residency in gynecology. She trained as an MBSR teacher and also to teach dharma, the Buddhist teachings, in the Vipassana tradition. Christiane likes to say, "When I was working as an OB/GYN I sometimes would save lives, but I would rarely change them. I might for example do a C-section to save the baby's and maybe also the mother's life. Of course the family would be grateful, but what I did would hardly change their lives. But with teaching mindfulness, I witness pretty much every day how people change their own life through the practices I teach them. That is such gratifying work."

The overwhelming majority of participants in mindfulness classes come for stress reduction and more ease of living, while in the traditional Buddhist setting the focus is more on spirituality and the attainment of liberation (often used synonymously with "enlightenment"). Since mindfulness practice stems from Buddhism, we find it of utmost importance that mindfulness facilitators are not only aware of this background but also know about the basic concepts from which mindfulness and compassion are taken. Otherwise mindfulness can be taught in an overly simplified and reductionist way, which conceivably cuts down on its life-changing potential.

And while Buddhism is not a proselytizing religion and everybody is welcome, there is a difference between Buddhist classes and what we are offering here. That's why we find it helpful to give the Buddhist and the psychologist angles on the same topic, particularly when teaching new mindfulness facilitators. These perspectives don't contradict each other but usually enhance the understanding for both sides, which is why we offer them in this book.

Formal and Informal Practices

Throughout this book we refer to two main ways to practice mindfulness and compassion: formally and informally.

Formal practice: A formal practice is what is traditionally called "meditation." It entails setting aside the time to do nothing but meditating, for example, by doing a Body Scan. A formal meditation can take take between one minute and many hours. Traditionally, a formal practice can be done in four body positions: sitting, standing, walking, and lying down.

Informal practice: We practice informally when we apply mindfulness or compassion fully to something that we are already doing in our everyday life. Mostly we focus intensely on the sensations that arise within the situation. For example, eating: We focus on sight, smell, taste, touch, and maybe even sound to anchor us in the present moment. We might also become aware of emotions or thoughts arising in the moment.

The basic instructions are the same for both formal and informal practices:

1. Become aware of the present-moment experience ("to know that you know").

2. Once we notice that our attention has wandered off, gently redirecting our attention to the *new* present moment.

Look for our fail-safe Practice Tips, sprinkled throughout this book, for helpful pointers on establishing a successful and ongoing meditation practice.

Secular Mindfulness? Mindfulness!

Over the past few years the term "secular mindfulness" has been used by some as one way to denote the use of mindfulness practices in nonreligious contexts and differentiate it from more traditionally Buddhist contexts in which mindfulness is taught and cultivated. At times a special term seemed—and still seems—to be necessary to allow these teachings to enter settings like universities, hospitals, and all other organizations in which teaching explicitly religious practices would not be welcome or appropriate. However, we feel that use of the term "secular" in the context of mindfulness is inappropriate, as the word itself suggests a differential split away from what we think of as its opposite, namely the "sacred." It thereby introduces a fundamental dualism that undermines the essentially nondual essence of dharma wisdom upon which mindfulness practices are based, whether framed within classical Buddhist teachings or in a more universal idiom. The doctor/patient or teacher/student relationship, for example—and really, each person's willingness to relate to the fullness of life through this path—has a sacred quality to it that we are unwilling to give up.

In this book, we have chosen to simply use "mindfulness." In rare cases, we use the term "mainstream mindfulness" with the hope that, over time, even this distinction will no longer be necessary as mindfulness becomes more deeply understood, embodied, and integrated within mainstream society and its institutions.

What This Book Is Not

While we want this book to be your "security blankie" as a new mindfulness facilitator, and a go-to guide for ongoing teachings, it is not a replacement for your own regular practice or for professional training. And while we can't meditate for you—we wish!—we share a list of helpful resources online at http://www.sharingmindfulness.com: where to find classes and additional professional trainings, books to deepen your understanding and teaching skills, online support, and more.

PART I

Mindfulness and Compassion

CHAPTER I

Mindfulness and Compassion: The Basics

What study after study show is that meditation and mindfulness training profoundly affects every aspect of our lives—our bodies, minds, physical health, and our emotional and spiritual well-being. It's not quite the fountain of youth, but it's pretty close. When you consider all the benefits of meditation—and more are being found every day—it's not an exaggeration to call meditation a miracle drug...

—Arianna Huffington, *Thrive*

"Mindfulness" is on the cusp of becoming a household word. It's not only entering hospitals and clinics, but major organizations and businesses are training their leadership or even all employees in mindfulness and stress reduction. Books on the topic make it onto the *New York Times* and Amazon best-seller lists. It is covered extensively in the popular press, it's on talk shows and magazine covers. One could say that it enjoys quite a celebrity status these days. Why is that? What is the promise of mindfulness that makes it so attractive?

So What Exactly Is Mindfulness?

Mindfulness is a common English word that simply means "paying attention." But the act of paying attention isn't what everybody is so excited about it. "Mindfulness" in this context means paying attention in a particular way. We like the working definition of Jon Kabat-Zinn, the founder of mindfulness-based stress reduction (MBSR):

> Mindfulness is awareness, cultivated by paying attention in a sustained and particular way: on purpose, in the present moment, and nonjudgmentally. It is one of the many forms of meditation, if you think of meditation as any way

in which we engage in 1) systematically regulating our attention and energy, 2) thereby influencing and possibly transforming the quality of our experience, 3) in the service of realizing the full range of our humanity, and of 4) our relationship to others and the world." (2011, 1)

Another definition we really like is from the work of Scott Bishop and colleagues (2004), a group of psychologists and mindfulness researchers:

> We propose a two-component model of mindfulness. The first component involves the self-regulation of attention so that it is maintained on immediate experience, thereby allowing for increased recognition of mental events in the present moment. The second component involves adopting a particular orientation toward one's experience in the present moment, an orientation that is characterized by curiosity, openness, and acceptance. (232)

These are just working definitions, because in the end mindfulness is something that needs to be practiced and experienced in order to really understand it. It's a complex felt and known experience that scholars and practitioners alike have found hard to put precise words to for literally thousands of years. Whatever description is used will always be reductionist. It's a little like defining love, only more people already know what love feels like than what mindfulness feels like; we can read about it all we want, but we don't really know it until we have experienced it over a period of time. And just as with love, we will probably regard other things for the "real stuff" before we get it right.

Where is mindfulness experienced? In the present moment. Where are most of us, most of the time? *Not* in the present moment. Where are we instead? Usually we are on autopilot going through the motions of whatever we are doing, such as eating, driving, even talking. At the same time, we are lost in thoughts, and the mind is busy with either rehashing the past or rehearsing the future. In this way, we are missing our life as it unfolds moment by moment.

Until we become skilled at mindfulness, we don't fully understand the possibilities and power that lie within each moment. But being present in this moment is not enough. Meditation teacher Joseph Goldstein quips that a dog is totally living in the moment yet is actually not mindful—since he is not aware of it. In order to be mindful, we have to be conscious of our awareness.

Here are some possible consequences of *lacking awareness* in the present moment:

- We are not aware how our mood colors our so-called objective experience. When we are in a bad mood, we will be more likely to hear a comment more critical than it was said or meant.

- We might not be aware of how desire and aversion influence how we respond to our environment. Or as an Indian proverb goes: "When a thief sees a saint, all he sees is his pockets."

- We tend to carry tension and stress in the body without realizing it.

- We miss a lot of potential positive and pleasant moments, like the smile of our kids or spouse, how nice the wind feels on our skin, or that we really like the landscaping of the house we drive by every day.

- We might miss crucial information we need to make a good decision, like how we actually feel about a potential business partner.

- We tend to hold on to unpleasant moments and experiences in our mind long after they are over, even if the present moment could be pleasant or neutral again.

While mindfulness is about directing and sustaining attention to the present-moment experience, it is not only about the fact *that* we are paying attention, but also about *how* we pay attention.

Directing one's attention purposefully is just one aspect out of the many present in every given moment. We don't pay attention in a vacuum. In fact, our perception is influenced by many different details: needs at the moment of perception, values, memory, cultural background, intention, and the emotional state, to name a few.

Some mind states stand out for their support of mindfulness. The more we get familiar with the following attitudes in our everyday life, as well as in our meditation practice, the more they will co-arise with mindfulness—and the more we will deepen and accelerate the transformational process. This is of particular importance for a teacher of mindfulness. The more these attitudes are understood and embodied by the teacher, the more they facilitate a student's understanding and learning at the nonconceptual level.

Foundational Attitudes That Support and Strengthen Mindfulness

Practicing mindfulness—nonjudgmental moment-to-moment awareness—isn't easy. We can force ourselves to pay attention for a moment, but we can't force ourselves to be nonjudging. Yet we can enlist other qualities of the mind that support and strengthen mindfulness. Jon Kabat-Zinn calls them *attitudinal foundations of mindfulness.* He first named seven of them in his best-selling book *Full Catastrophe Living* and has since added and elaborated more on the list: acceptance, nonjudging, nonstriving, letting go/letting be, patience, trust, beginner's mind, and gratitude and generosity. We recommend that you watch the excellent short video series on it (available on YouTube).

We have added three more that we have found helpful: curiosity, kindness, and humor.

All these attitudes can be practiced and strengthened in many situations during the day: at work, with our children and partners, with ourselves. We cultivate them very much like we cultivate a garden.

They are all interconnected. When focusing on one attitude, often others will arise as well. We encourage giving attention to one attitude per week for eleven weeks and seeing how they are interconnected. But deepening any of them will greatly support your mindfulness practice.

Curiosity

Mindfulness without curiosity is impossible. When we turn toward our present moment experience we do that in order to learn about it, to perceive it fully. When we are on autopilot there is no space for curiosity. We can explore how being curious changes our perception of the moment. It's the antidote for autopilot and boredom. We can become curious about anything if we choose to, asking questions like: "What is here that I'm not yet aware of?" or "What *is* this?"

Kindness

The attitude of kindness can act like fabric softener for experience. When kindness is present, judgment and harshness will recede. We see what happens in a different light. Kindness often arises from a deeper and more complex understanding of how the heart and mind work—not just for ourselves but for everybody. We learn to see not only the behavior but also what might have spurred it. For example, if we don't just see the angry behavior but also the hurt and confusion that caused the anger in the first place, we are more likely to respond with kindness.

Gratitude and Generosity

Generosity and gratitude are closely interlinked. Gratitude has the attitude of "I have…" instead of our often automatic "I don't have…," or "enough" instead of "not enough." It shifts the attention to peace, contentment, and calm instead of being driven, in need, and discontent. Since the brain will focus more automatically on what's missing, starting a gratitude practice actively helps to counterbalance this. Research (Emmons & McCullough, 2003) backs that something as simple as writing down what we are grateful for will not only elicit more positive emotions and more well-being but can even translate into benefits like more exercise and fewer visits to the doctor. The practice and attitude of gratitude will shift the sense of "not enough" to "there is enough" and "I have enough," which in turn will elicit more spontaneous generosity. It is easier to give from a place of abundance than from scarcity. Generosity also deepens the understanding of the interconnection between the givers and the receivers.

Acceptance

Acceptance might be the attitude that new students of mindfulness struggle with the most. It is hard to understand why you would even want to accept the hard or negative thing in your life. Isn't this why you are learning mindfulness in the first place? To get rid of pain or negative moods?

As we start to see how much the struggle against the challenge adds to the suffering, we might be willing to test acceptance. And then we notice that it's not that easy. We can't simply wish acceptance into existence in our lives. We can only invite it in and learn more about the conditions it needs to show up more regularly. Acceptance requires an active turning toward a situation and realizing that it really *is* the way it is right now. Acceptance does not require that we like what we're accepting, but it asks for the honesty to say, "Yes, I don't like it *and* this is the way it is right now." Until we can do that we will continuously try to force things into the way they are not, which in turn is the cause for a lot of tension, stress, and often suffering. Acceptance is different from resignation. Acceptance doesn't mean that we stop trying to change a situation or to make the world a better place, but the force behind it is much healthier and often wiser.

Nonjudging

Nonjudging is such an important aspect of mindfulness that Jon Kabat-Zinn even put it into his working definition of mindfulness: "the awareness that arises from paying attention, on purpose, moment by moment and nonjudgmentally." As we begin to practice mindfulness, we will quickly notice that nonjudging is pretty much impossible because we have an opinion about everything. No matter what arises in our experience, be it internal or external, we have an opinion about it. Actually, chances are that if you don't have an opinion about what's going on, it probably won't even register as a thought—because, why bother? Have you ever wondered why you don't think about things that are meaningless to you?

But what do we do if we start noticing the constant onslaught of opinions, judgments, assessments, and evaluations? We simply notice them—and not judge the judging. To set ourselves in relationship to anything that is arising in our experience is a natural habit of the mind. But in mindfulness, there is no need to stop it—even if we could—but to observe it and see the effect of it instead. Can we suspend judgment at times? Can we see that our opinions are often just products of a habit that we don't have to reinforce?

Nonstriving

Nonstriving is one of the core principles of mindfulness. It means being fully present in this moment without the need to change it—actually being present without *any* agenda. Even without the agenda to relax or to feel better. And surely not with the agenda to reach a special meditative state. Nonstriving is moving from our constant, habitual *doing mode* into the more open, receptive *being mode*. Being mode allows this moment to be "good enough"—again, not perfect, and sometimes even stressful or painful. But we learn that *letting go* of striving will often open a sense of ease. As we practice nonstriving, over time we learn that the being mode is deeply healing and restorative.

Letting Go, or Letting Be

Letting go or letting be: These attitudes are the opposite of clinging or grasping and also the opposite of pushing away. When we have thoughts, emotions, and sensations that we like, we naturally want to hold on to them, to prolong them and to have them again. There is nothing wrong with that—except if they are not aligned with reality: the relationship is ending, the plate is empty, the deal we had hoped and worked for isn't coming through. Then holding on creates stress and pain.

The opposite is true for the sensations, thoughts, and emotions we don't like: we try to push them away or pretend they don't exist. Again, there is nothing abnormal about that, but in an interesting way the pushing away causes stress and pain just like the grasping. In both cases we are in conflict with how things really are. With practice we learn to hold them more lightly. We learn how to let go in small moments of both desire and aversion. With practice we grow our ability to see where we are caught *and* to let go or leave it alone. When we are paying close attention to what grasping and aversion feel like, and what letting go or letting be feels like, we can discover which brings more or less tension, which offers more or less spaciousness.

Breathing is a great example of letting go. At the end of each in-breath we need to let go, as well as at the end of each out-breath, in order to make space for the new out-breath and the new in-breath. It doesn't make sense to hold on. With small examples like this we can turn our attention to the felt experience of letting go.

Patience

Many of us are habitually impatient. With our busy schedules and long to-do lists, pretty much everything can feel like it's taking up too much time. We notice that it is often impatience that pushes us on to the next thing. To get to *there*. Which is one of the reasons why we are so rarely *here*. *Here* doesn't feel as good or rewarding as we expect *there* to feel, so we miss *here* altogether. As we rush through this moment we miss a lot of the detail and also the potential joy of this particular moment—only to do the same thing once we are *there*. If the mind isn't trained to be patient and to stay *here*, how can it do it once you are *there*?

The good news is that the times we are impatient are the best (and really, the only) times we can practice patience! We can make the decision to allow it to be part of our experience—and not do anything about it. Simply notice the way impatience makes you feel, the way it colors the experience of this moment. Interestingly enough, patience is heralded as an important virtue in all major religions. Why do you think that is? It might be around the universal understanding that often things will and need to unfold in their own time. We try to move them along, but that might not be helpful. That might be like the child who pulls up the carrot to see if it's ripe yet.

Humor

Humor is a wonderful support for a mindfulness practice. Jon Kabat-Zinn says: "Life is way too serious to take too seriously." Humor allows us to take a step back from a particular situation, to see our habits of mind and find the amusement in our all-too-human foibles. Sometimes the way the mind behaves is hilarious. We laugh a lot in our classes. We laugh the laugh of recognition: "Me, too!" We can laugh at how petty and stubborn the mind can be. When we do this, we step away from being overidentified with the situation and are able to create space.

Trust

You are the expert on yourself. In the end nobody knows you as well as you do, and nobody can make better decisions for you than yourself. We often believe that wisdom, authority, and knowledge are outside of ourselves. A mindfulness practice brings us back to the simple truth that we *can* trust ourselves and that trusting ourselves is mandatory if we ever want to live a meaningful life. We start by trusting the body with practices such as Mindfulness of Breathing or the Body Scan (see Session 1). As we start to pay close attention to our body, we become aware that we can trust it to breathe by itself, to digest, to move, to heal, and so on. Often, we only start paying attention to a body part or a function of the body when its function is impaired. Mindfulness practice changes that. We can deliberately pay attention to all that does work well (miraculously well), and we can learn to appreciate it while learning about trust.

It would be so much easier to have another person make decisions and tell us what's best for us. Finding our own answer is often hard and takes time. But we have found that trusting ourselves to find the answer brings about the "right" solution far more often than not.

A Beginner's Mind

A beginner's mind allows us to see a situation or a person—or ourselves—with fresh eyes. We so often go into a situation thinking we know all about it. Our mind is full of preconceived ideas, concepts, and opinions. But we often overlook what is right in front of us. Maybe the situation has changed. Or the individual isn't the same person on whom we had based our opinion. How can we really see a person if we make him or her something from our past experience? A beginner's mind can help us see a stuck situation in a fresh light. This is *not* about giving up all discernment but allowing new information in that might have been overlooked or received in a biased way.

A beginner's mind can also bring back a sense of wonder and awe to situations we usually don't think are worth paying much attention to anymore, like eating or driving or hugging a loved one we see often. As the Zen master Suzuki Roshi says: "In the beginner's mind there are many possibilities, but in the expert's there are few."

What Is Compassion?

Put simply, "compassion" means "to sympathize," or "to feel with," especially to feel the pain of another. We might have a sense that a person is innately compassionate or not, or we might choose not to be compassionate if perhaps we have enough of our own pain to deal with. Over the last few years, compassion as it is practiced in the Buddhist traditions has moved into the spotlight for researchers and meditation teachers alike, as it promises more than just "to sympathize."

Compassion in this context is defined as the wish or impulse to alleviate suffering in another living being (which is different than to just "feel with"). If the suffering is in oneself, we call the wish *self-compassion*. Compassion arises out of the foundation of a general well-wishing and benevolence toward all living beings; this is called *loving-kindness*. Compassion arises out of loving-kindness as a natural response to suffering or pain.

Throughout the book we sometimes use "loving-kindness" and sometimes "compassion." Please keep in mind that the source of the feeling is the same, but the expression depends on the situation (e.g., if suffering is present or not).

Compassion, like mindfulness, is a capacity that we are born with and all know how to access to various degrees, but it can be enhanced, deepened, and strengthened through specific meditation practices and reflections (see also chapter 2 for the latest research on compassion).

The Difference Between Compassion and Empathy

Recently, terms like "compassion fatigue" or "vicarious or secondary trauma" have become mainstream, especially in health care and caregiving circles. In everyday language, "compassion" is often used synonymously with "empathy." But empathy is more of a reaction to witnessing pain in another being: the "I feel your pain" response, which is commonly how compassion is defined in mainstream English.

There is evidence that empathy is transmitted automatically through *mirror neurons*. Mirror neurons are a network of neurons in the brain that fire upon observing a behavior or emotion in the same area as the neurons in the person or animal expressing the emotion or behavior. They were accidentally discovered by a research group in Italy (Di Pellegrino, Fadiga, Fogassi, Gallese, & Rizzolatti, 1992) when a monkey, who had electrodes placed in its brain to study movement, watched a researcher eat a peanut. The motor neurons in the monkey's brain correlating to hand and arm movement fired as if he had moved the arm himself.

The working group around Tania Singer in Germany is doing some fascinating research around the difference between empathy and compassion. Empathy is feeling the pain of another without any protection or buffer. It can easily overwhelm us and lead to emotional shutdown. Compassion, in comparison, is the protection against this overwhelm and shutdown. Singer's group likens empathy to the currency in an electric pump and compassion to the water in the pump. If there is only empathy, the pump will easily run hot and burn out. The presence of compassion (i.e., the active wish to ease the suffering) will buffer the pain and make it tolerable. Dr. Singer's team states that "compassion fatigue," a recognized phenomenon in caregiving contexts, is a misnomer and that it should be called "empathy fatigue" instead (Klimecki, Ricard, & Singer, 2013). Compassion can be taught and will protect from burnout, which is one of the reasons for the increasing interest in the subject. (See our online resources list at http://www.sharingmindfulness.com for a link to Singer's work, including her free compassion guide.)

What's the Difference Between Mindfulness and Compassion?

Jack Kornfield, Trudy Goodman, and some other senior mindfulness teachers now use the term "loving-awareness" when they talk about mindfulness. Buddhist monk Ajahn Brahm calls it "kindfulness." Why? Because kindness is the most important quality to be cultivated together with mindfulness. Strictly speaking, mindfulness and compassion (or kindness) are not the same. But to wed them in the terms "loving or friendly awareness" or "compassionate awareness" makes sense, as we know that the easiest, least painful way to hold our experience in awareness is in the presence of kindness or compassion. And the more the better. This is particularly true during difficult moments.

To quote Jon Kabat-Zinn: "In Asian languages, the word for *mind* and the word for *heart* are the same. So if you're not hearing mindfulness in some deep way as heartfulness, you're not really understanding it. Compassion and kindness towards oneself are intrinsically woven into it. You could think of mindfulness as wise and affectionate attention" (Szalavitz, 2012). These definitions of the terms also help practitioners and teachers alike understand that we are not just talking about attention skills (like the attention needed to solve a math problem or to finish homework). So while we like to marry these to the qualities of the heart and mind, we also want to help you understand the differences.

Here are some basic differences between mindfulness and compassion:

Non-Doing vs. Doing

Mindfulness entails uninvolved receptivity of experience in a non-doing mode. Loving-kindness and compassion, on the other hand, are actively directed practices: radiating out or embracing. The deeper understanding that all beings want to be free from suffering transforms into the wish to alleviate this suffering (in others and in ourselves). We desire to do something, even if it's as small as a kind word, a loving smile, or a hug. We could also call it *"resting with* experience versus *embracing* it."

Cool vs. Warm

Mindfulness is often described as having a cool or cooling—but not cold— quality. Observing, witnessing, and resting with experience all allow for the reactivity, aversion, or desire to cool down. Common idioms express "the heat of the moment," "making one's blood boil," or "a burning desire"; we know from experience that it is hard to stay cool or rational in these situations. Mindfulness helps with that.

That said, we associate kindness and compassion with the heart (or qualities of the heart) and some heat, as in "she is a warm person" or "he has a warm smile"; this warmth describes a kind and friendly person.

The Traps of Detachment and Sentimentality

Mindfulness and loving-kindness are traditionally described as two wings of a bird: With the wing of mindfulness, you develop the capacity to observe nonjudgmentally and allow things to be as they already are. With the kindness wing, you cultivate a friendly and compassionate stance toward what is happening. And you need both wings to fly.

When mindfulness encounters suffering and sees it clearly for what it is, compassion will naturally arise. The same is true with compassion: compassion has the seed of wisdom built in. But the natural balance can get uneven at times: unbalanced mindfulness without kindness can become detached and cold. And unbalanced compassion that is void of "seeing things as they really are" can become sentimental and too soft. We can train them separately or together. But together they balance each other out and allow us to fly.

> **Example.** Lin struggles in her relationship with her partner. During meditation she can be mindful of sadness. She can feel the sensations of being sad in her body: the tightness in her chest, her body feeling heavy and pulling her down. With mindfulness, she can softly name it "sadness, sadness." And she can feel that while she is sad right now, that doesn't make her a sad person. She can observe the thoughts that come with being sad. She can be sad without judging herself. When Lin can also access self-compassion, she can feel or picture a warm, inner embracing of herself that includes the sadness. She might also offer some words to herself, like "This, too shall pass," or "It will all be okay." This also helps her connect more to her partner's struggles and pain.

The Origins of Mindfulness

While all religions have contemplative branches and often practices that are quite similar to mindfulness, its roots as we teach it lie in the Buddhist tradition. The program presented in this book is based on mindfulness-based stress reduction (MBSR), which is based on *Vipassana* or insight meditation, which is based on the larger teachings of Buddhism. It is helpful to have a basic understanding of where these teachings stem from and their sources in Buddhist philosophy.

The Buddhist Background

Mindfulness as taught in MBSR or pretty much any mindfulness class stems from the tradition of Vipassana, or insight meditation. During the last forty years, three main strands of Buddhism have gained massive popularity by Westerners in the United States and other Western countries: Zen, Tibetan Buddhism, and Vipassana, the latter sometimes used synonymously with another form of Buddhism, Theravada.

Zen originates in China, Korea, and Japan; Tibetan obviously in Tibet, with His Holiness the Dalai Lama as its spiritual leader; and Vipassana stems from Southeast Asian countries like Thailand, Burma, and Sri Lanka. All three are monastic traditions.

As with most religions, there have been dogma splits throughout the centuries. Two main schools have survived into the twenty-first century: Theravada and Mahayana. Mahayana split off from the main school of Buddhism in the first century BCE. Zen and Tibetan Buddhism are Mahayana schools. Vipassana is a practice form of Theravada. The Theravada traditions claim to teach from the direct words of the Buddha, the Pali Canon. Theravada Buddhism is still the main religion in South Asian countries like Thailand, Sri Lanka, Laos, and Burma.

There are other Buddhist traditions in the West that are mainly practiced by "born" Buddhists, mainly Asian American groups.

Zen

Zen is mostly known in the West for its minimalistic Japanese aesthetics and succinct teachings. The word "Zen" has found its way into the vernacular of many Western languages as a synonym for "cool, laid back, and relaxed."

Zen, like Tibetan Buddhism, is a Mahayana school. It was brought to China in the sixth century CE as the Ch'an school and exported first to Korea in the third century and later to Japan in the twelfth century CE.

In Zen, the focus is not on the study of the scriptures and doctrine but on a meditation practice in every moment of life. It focuses on the attainment of enlightenment and realization into the truth of the teaching through direct insight and through the connection with a realized teacher.

The main meditation practice in the Soto school of Zen is silent illumination—close to "choiceless awareness" in Vipassana, often also called "just sitting," "open awareness," or "Dzogchen" in some Tibetan schools. Zen is famous for its cryptic stories and *koans*. A koan is a word or a sentence that seemingly doesn't make sense or contradicts itself, like "What is the sound of one hand clapping?" or "What was your true face before you were born?" These koans are encoded "pointing-out instructions" meant to point out the true nature of reality. They confuse logical thinking and stop the mind so that insight can arise in a direct, nonconceptual way.

Tibetan Buddhism

Most in the West are familiar with Tibetan Buddhism through the teachings of His Holiness the Dalai Lama. This tradition is an extension of Mahayana Buddhism known as Vajrayana. It first made its way to Tibet in the eighth century CE when it merged with the indigenous Bon religion that proliferated the region. The goal of Tibetan Buddhism is for the practitioner to attain enlightenment for the benefit of all beings. Although this goal is not foreign to other forms of Buddhism, Tibetan Buddhism is known for its unique methods of practice, which range from elaborate visualizations and rituals to devotional chanting and mantra recitation. To most people it is known for its colorful statues of various deities, temples, and prayer flags. And, of course, for the Dalai Lama.

Vipassana

Vipassana translates into "clear-seeing" or "insight." The focus of Vipassana is to gain deep, transformative insight or wisdom into "seeing things as they really are," which will lead to freedom from suffering. The core teachings of Vipassana are spread throughout this book in the sections of the "Dharma Teacher Perspective."

Vipassana stems from the Theravada monasteries in Southeast Asia. There are slightly different opinions in the different schools as to what Vipassana is, but for our purpose we keep it simple and call all the formal practices we offer in a mindfulness class as stemming from Vipassana.

How Vipassana Buddhism Made It to the West

In the late 1960s and early seventies, many young people in the West were disenchanted with the politics of their countries, the cultural heritage of their parents, and the predominant religions. Some made the trip to India and other Asian nations to find a new meaning of life over there. While many influential teachers returned, three stand out as having had the most influence in bringing the Vipassana practice to the West: Jack Kornfield, Joseph Goldstein, and Sharon Salzberg.

In their early twenties they studied and practiced Buddhism and meditation for years in India and Thailand with different teachers. When they came back to the United States, Boulder, Colorado, was the "it" place to be for young people fascinated with meditation. The charismatic Tibetan Buddhist teacher Chögyam Trungpa Rinpoche had started Naropa University there in 1974. It's where Kornfield, Goldstein, and Salzberg teamed up and started teaching longer silent Vipassana retreats. It was on one of these retreats that Jon Kabat-Zinn had his epiphany about MBSR (see "How MBSR Started").

The Vipassana movement grew, and the group founded the Insight Meditation Society, in Massachusetts. Kornfield moved on some years later and started Spirit Rock Meditation Center, in Northern California. Both centers are still the go-to places in the United States for Vipassana retreats (see also a more extensive list online at http://www.sharingmindfulness.com).

How MBSR Started

Jon Kabat-Zinn was a young molecular biologist with a PhD from MIT in Boston. He started his Buddhist practice in the tradition of Korean Zen in the early seventies but soon began to also attend Vipassana retreats with Kornfield, Salzberg, and Goldstein. He was also an avid yoga student and teacher, and practiced aikido, a martial arts form. What he was learning and discovering changed his life. He clearly saw that much of our suffering is mind-made and unnecessary. And that it was eased by paying attention to the simple, repetitive practices of feeling one's breath when sitting and one's feet when walking. During one of the retreats he attended, he had the vision to take elements from what he was learning and to merge them into a class. This way, ordinary people from all walks of life could benefit from these practices, not just people who identified as Buddhists or were open to Buddhist practices.

Kabat-Zinn approached the hospital at the University of Massachusetts and was given permission to use the cafeteria in the basement for his first classes in 1979. He invited all department heads of the hospital to send him their most difficult patients: the ones with cancer, chronic pain, depression, insomnia, and other chronic diseases that led physicians to inform them that they had to "learn how to live with that." The people who took Dr. Kabat-Zinn's class got better. They actually did "learn how to live with that." Sometimes their problems would completely disappear; other times people simply felt more content, happy, and positive, even though their physical symptoms didn't change in a significant way.

Being a researcher by training, Kabat-Zinn knew that if he wanted this class to gain any traction in the field of medicine and beyond he had to conduct vigorous research to show its efficacy. Word of the class's success began to spread and led to its being featured in Bill Moyers's *Healing and the Mind* series in 1993, as well as detailed in depth in Kabat-Zinn's own book *Full Catastrophe Living* in 1990. The class became a center, and its success brought in more researchers and those from other fields interested in the topic. Soon the growing center started to train teachers.

During the last fifteen years, other meditators and researchers from around the world have started to adapt and change MBSR to make it more accessible to their specific populations.

You could say that MBSR is the stem cell for mindfulness classes in the West. Our curriculum is no exception to that. There are mindfulness-based classes for specific conditions like depression or childbirth, as well as compassion-based trainings and therapy interventions with essential mindfulness components. For a more in-depth listing of those, please visit our website at http://www .sharingmindfulness.com.

Dharma Teacher Perspective: The Four Foundations of Mindfulness

One of the core texts or teachings in Vipassana is the *four foundations of mindfulness*. The four foundations lead, when properly practiced, to "liberation, to the end of suffering." You could also phrase it as: this practice leads to increasing moments of freedom from suffering. Mindfulness students in clinical settings don't typically join a class for the kind of "enlightenment" the foundations point toward. Yet competent facilitators in such settings should be familiar with these foundations.

All the main mindfulness practices in this book can be categorized into these four foundations.

1. **Mindfulness of the body:** Mindfulness of the body is the first foundation of mindfulness. It is our starting point and our anchor to the present moment. We practice this first foundation with the Body Scan, Mindful Eating, Mindfulness of Breathing, Mindfulness of Sound, and Mindful Walking (see Sessions 1 through 3) when we notice the direct sensory experience of the body.

2. **Mindfulness of feeling tones:** By being mindful of the body we start noticing that all experience can be categorized into three distinct "feeling tones": unpleasant, pleasant, or neutral. While the two are easily confused, feeling tones are not the same as emotions rather, they actually accompany them. For example, while we usually think sadness is unpleasant, it can also be experienced as pleasant, or not really register at all if the feeling tone is neutral (see also Session 5).

3. **Mindfulness of the mind:** In the third foundation, we turn the attention to mental activity like thoughts or emotions as mere objects that can be observed in a nonreactive way (see Session 3's theme, "Our Storytelling Minds").

4. **Mindfulness of how the mind operates:** In the fourth foundation of mindfulness, the focus is on the classification of related experiences into specific categories or lists (starting out as an orally transmitted tradition, Buddhism is full of lists). For example, see the "Dharma Teacher's Perspective" on the Five Hindrances (Session 2), the Five Precepts (chapter 3), or this list here, of the four foundations.

Summary

Mindfulness is present-moment nonjudgmental awareness, while compassion is an active and kind turning toward suffering—one's own and that of others—with the aim of relieving it to whatever degree possible. We learned about other supportive atttitudes that support mindfulness practice as well as the origins in the Buddhist tradition—both in the East and in the West.

We hope the foundational skills presented in this book are helpful to you both personally and professionally in all the work that you do.

CHAPTER 2

Mindfulness and Compassion Research

Science cannot solve the ultimate mystery of nature. And that is because, in the last analysis, we ourselves are part of nature and therefore part of the mystery that we are trying to solve.

—Max Planck

Prominent meditation researcher Richard Davidson was always interested in meditation and the brain. But all of his career advisers signaled more or less clearly that this would kill his career. So he studied the brain and emotions while being a self-described "closet meditator." This changed in 1992, when he met His Holiness the Dalai Lama, who urged him to explore the effects of long-standing meditation practice on the brain.

Since these first steps of research, mindfulness research has picked up exponentially during the last decade. And the results are very promising—as you will see in this chapter. Science may not have all the answers into the mysteries and importance of mindfulness, but the modern tools used in research are starting to explain some of the passion associated with the ancient practice.

Empirical Evidence Is Not Enough

We hear about the profound impact of mindfulness teachings on our students nearly every day. Paul, a young combat veteran recently returned from the conflict in Afghanistan, came to our program after a series of unhelpful medication trials for post-traumatic stress disorder (PTSD) and related insomnia. His first day of class he shared, "I just haven't felt right since I came back. I'm either jumpy and angry all the time or drugged up and numb."

Paul had heard from another young combat veteran in the waiting room of the clinic how much mindfulness had helped him. Yet Paul was reluctant to join our class due to the group format and his pattern of avoidance behaviors. When he finally started the group, he never smiled, rarely talked to other class members, and was heel tapping throughout the entire first class, which is a common behavior for somebody suffering from PTSD. But week by week, Paul began to soften—to smile—and the hyperarousal symptoms completely disappeared. After our last class together, Paul stayed behind to share with us his experience of the class. He told us, "I was completely skeptical, but I haven't felt this good since before my deployment." He added while laughing, "My girlfriend wanted me to tell you 'thank you' because I'm back to normal and I'm not such an asshole anymore."

Over time, mindfulness teachers gather their own case examples of transformation and renewal. But these stories alone are insufficient, as they still can (and often will be) exceptions—exceptions that stay with us because we personally believe and are invested in the great outcomes of mindfulness practice. This can skew our perception and make us potentially blind to clients who are not helped by mindfulness—who need more support either one-on-one with a skilled clinician or with more or different medication (or both). A competent mindfulness teacher in a clinical setting should be familiar with mindfulness research; this gives her an idea what to expect in a particular setting in terms of outcome. She will also have the ability to quote salient research, which can provide motivation for class participants to continue with their formal practice.

The Importance of Having a Handle on Research

It isn't necessary to know every study—there are far too many for that—but familiarity with research supports the teachings. The reason for this is twofold:

1. A mindfulness teacher's awareness of research can be a reflection on perceived competence.

2. Most people coming to you to learn mindfulness have heard or read some research results in the popular press. They might expect that taking a class will make their symptoms disappear. The research will be partly why they feel inspired to practice and why they will keep practicing over any bumps. You as their teacher have to meet them there. As a facilitator, you should know the research well enough to effectively negotiate the middle path between the alleviation of a condition or set of symptoms and the transformation that can take place simply by relating to your present-moment experience differently and letting things be just as they are.

For example, chronic pain is one of the most common symptoms that drives participants to join a class. Some chronic-pain sufferers have tried just about every medical intervention and come to mindfulness with an expectation that the practice will help them to "feel better" and make the pain go away. While it is true that mindfulness is an effective approach for chronic pain, the relief comes about in a very different form than the participants might expect. They will realize that they have to accept the pain (or anything unpleasant that we can't make go away in this moment) in order to be able to cope better and to feel more moments of joy. A good teacher will gently question a participant without pulling the rug of wrong expectations out from under him.

Mindfulness teaches us how to relate to our experiences differently. Even our pain. We learn to live around the edges of our pain without being overwhelmed or bothered by it so much. And, interestingly, as we will explore later in this chapter, though we aren't trying to change our experience specifically, our practice paradoxically changes our brains in a way that mediates and downregulates the pain signals coming in from the peripheral nervous system. So mindfulness practice helps with chronic pain not by getting rid of it but by letting it be just as it is and relating to the pain differently. But after months of practice, brain changes occur and the perception of pain can diminish. You as a facilitator must erode any participant's expectation of yet another quick-fix notion; instead you must lead him toward relating to the present-moment experience, whatever it might be. This takes time and sustained practice on the participant's side. He will come back to his experience over and over again. And through what he shares in class, you can gently question and guide him more into the foundational attitudes of mindfulness. Mentioning study results, summarized in sentences like "the wandering mind is an unhappy mind" can be of great support for this.

Using Mindfulness Research as a Teaching Tool

A comprehensive review of the mindfulness evidence base and research findings would require a multivolume book. Our goal here is to provide mindfulness facilitators with the framework from which to teach. While there will no doubt be many new and exciting findings, we find it useful to conceptualize the research into three general categories. The first category is *symptom reduction*, which is typically measured by a self-report rating scale. This could be a reduction in anxiety symptoms or an improvement in psychosocial and quality-of-life outcomes among cancer patients. The second category includes *biological markers* in the body. This is a diverse collection of findings, from changes in cortisol measures in those with high levels of stress to immunological markers such as increases in antibody titers for the influenza vaccination to cellular findings such as positive changes to rates of cellular aging. The third category of research is *neuroplasticity*, which is simply the brain's ability to change in response to life circumstance and learning, or to a mindfulness practice. (Certainly, brain changes are biomarkers, but we find it useful to separate these findings into their own category.)

A mindfulness facilitator with an understanding of these categories of research findings can skillfully answer questions from class participants without having to know every recent study.

Improvements in Symptoms

Our first category for reviewing mindfulness research relates to the improvement of symptoms reported in a wide variety of both mental and physical conditions. Primarily, these outcomes report improvements in psychological functioning such as decreasing depression, anxiety, pain, and illness-related distress, as well as increases in quality-of-life measures, sleep, and functional status. One large meta-analysis that caught our attention is from Stefan Hofmann's lab at the Center for Anxiety and Related Disorders at Boston University. Dr. Hofmann is a well-regarded cognitive behavioral therapy (CBT) researcher and author who was a bit skeptical about some of the research findings for mindfulness-based interventions. In a rigorous meta-analytic review of thirty-nine studies with patients with a variety of medical and psychiatric disorders, Hofmann, Sawyer, Witt, and Oh (2010) found mindfulness interventions had a moderate *effect size* (meaning the strength of a relationship between two things) in improving anxiety and depressive symptoms. In patients with co-occurring anxiety and mood symptoms, the mindfulness intervention had an even larger effect size. These effect sizes are robust and were maintained over time.

Another recent large meta-analytic review of mindfulness-based interventions (Goyal et al., 2014) showed improvements in depression, anxiety, and pain with similar effect sizes. In our own recent work (Serpa, Taylor, & Tillisch, 2014), we have found that mindfulness reduces depression, anxiety, and suicidal ideation in veterans in a naturalistic setting. This is significant, as we had a "take all comers" approach. Our seventy-nine participants included veterans with active substance use disorders, serious thought disorder spectrum illness, severe personality disorders, and suicidal ideation. And in this population, likely to better reflect the real-world clinical setting, our findings were consistent with those of more restrictive clinical research populations.

Mindfulness interventions have also been very effective in addressing the psychological stressors and coping in chronic and life-threatening illnesses (Carlson, 2012). Mindfulness has been very well studied in oncology, with noted improvement in mood and a reduction in levels of stress (Speca, Carlson, Goodey, & Angen, 2000), for improvements in quality of life (Lerman, Jarski, Rea, Gellish, & Vicini, 2012), and in reduction in fatigue with improvements in sleep (Carlson & Garland, 2005). Research also supports the use of mindfulness for coping with rheumatoid arthritis, cardiovascular disease, diabetes, HIV/AIDS, irritable bowl syndrome, organ transplant, chronic pain, and fibromyalgia (Carlson, 2012).

Interestingly, the benefits of mindfulness interventions have also been studied in healthy populations. In one meta-analytic review (Chiesa & Serretti, 2009), mindfulness was found to reduce stress and trait anxiety while increasing empathy in those without a medical or mental health diagnosis. Even in presumably healthy psychotherapist trainees (Shapiro, Brown, & Biegel, 2007), mindfulness helped to reduce stress, negative affect, rumination, and anxiety while increasing self-compassion and positive affect. Across a wide spectrum of physical and mental health issues, including in healthy populations, mindfulness improves psychological measures.

Improvements in Biological Markers

The second conceptual vantage point from which to review the evidence base for mindfulness is the domain of biomarkers. These findings are truly fascinating. With mindfulness, we are not introducing a drug or performing surgery. We are simply teaching someone to pay attention with kindness to the present moment. This small and low-risk behavioral intervention has a profound impact on how the body functions and, ultimately, on our lives. Many researchers across a variety of disciplines explore the intersections studied in the field of *psychoneuroimmunology*, or the study of the complex relationships between our behavior and our psychological, neurological, and immunological functioning. For example, *cortisol* is the primary stress hormone from the adrenal glands and has long been associated with immunosuppression (Spiegel, Sephton, Terr, & Sittes, 1998). Changes in salivary and serum cortisol levels are an effective biomarker indicating a reduction in stress from a mindfulness practice (Matousek, Dobkin, & Pruessner, 2009). Yet cortisol is only the beginning.

Other studies are measuring diverse immunological biomarkers. One classic study randomly assigned healthy volunteers to an MBSR group or a wait-list control while measuring electrical brain activity and immunological response to the influenza vaccine (Davidson et al., 2003). Stressful life events are known to decrease immune titers to the influenza vaccine, which is a measure of a downregulated immune system. The meditation group demonstrated significantly greater left anterior frontal lobe activation, a region of the brain associated with positive mood, compared to the control group. Additionally, the meditation group also showed a stronger response to the influenza vaccine. Further, there was a relationship between left anterior activation and immune response. Those with the largest magnitude of left anterior activation also had the largest titer response. So the greater the shift in the brain, the larger the immune response to the vaccine.

Recent biomarker studies have begun to explore the relationship between mindfulness and *genomics*, or the interaction between our genetic makeup and the environment. We all understand that our genes establish not only the color of our eyes but our underlying vulnerability to certain diseases. Yet genetics is not destiny; one identical twin can develop cancer and the other can be healthy for years. Genes can turn on or off based on behavioral or environmental triggers. *Epigenetics*, or "around" genetics, is the study of gene changes caused by things other than the genes themselves, or how genes get turned "on" or "off." Genes related to the inflammatory process are thought to play a big role in the establishment and progression in many of the chronic, late-in-life diseases resulting in mortality.

One fascinating study (Creswell et al., 2012) randomly assigned a group of older, lonely adults into a meditation intervention or a wait-list control, as loneliness is thought to increase the genetic expression of pro-inflammatory genes. All the participants had their blood analyzed by a genome-wide transcription profiling procedure to examine known markers for pro-inflammatory genes both pre- and posttreatment. There was a clear relationship between the level of loneliness reported and the genetic expression of pro-inflammatory genes. Further, those in the meditation intervention experienced measureable epigenetic changes in their genome. Eight weeks of meditation training was sufficient to see a change in how their genes were expressed. This has implications for a wide variety of diseases.

Yet another area of compelling biomarker research in mindfulness is in the area of cellular aging. The 2009 Nobel Prize in physiology of medicine was awarded to Elizabeth Blackburn, Carol Greider, and Jack Szostak for the discovery of *telomeres*—the caps on the ends of chromosomes where our genes reside—and the protective enzyme *telomerase*. Telomeres keep our chromosomes from aging, much like the little plastic bits on the tips of a shoelace keep it from unraveling. Cognitive stress and constant rumination on potential threats creates a stressful environment that, in turn, shortens telomere length. Mindfulness, however, can have a beneficial impact on telomere length by reducing the cognitive stress and arousal that can decrease cellular aging (Epel et al., 2009). The first study to document how meditation can change telomere length and therefore cellular aging recruited thirty participants who spent three months on meditation retreat and were compared to matched wait-list controls. The results indicated that decreases in negative affectivity and other positive psychological changes were linked to increased telomerase activity, telomerase being the enzyme responsible for telomere production (Jacobs et al., 2011). The meditation retreat changed cellular aging.

Research into the changes in biomarkers as a result of mindfulness meditation is diverse and includes stress-hormone markers, immune and endocrine system markers, and even changes in cellular aging. Sort of makes you want to go meditate right now, doesn't it? But wait, there's more.

Mindfulness and Neuroplasticity

Neuroplasticity is the third area of essential research with which an effective mindfulness teacher should become familiar. This is an exploding topic that is fascinating to neuroscientists, clinicians, and the general public alike. Headlines in the popular press tout things like, "Rewire your brain for happiness in just eight weeks!" This certainly has everyone's attention. But what exactly is *neuroplasticity*? Can we rewire our brains and become happier? We all understand that cautiously stated scientific findings can easily get distorted when simplified for mainstream media. So a bit of restraint may be warranted; let's not get too far in front of the science. Yet, each year the research grows, and there is certainly a sense that much more is on the way.

"Neuroplasticity" is a blanket term used to describe how the brain changes based on our experiences. These experiences may be our mental habits, behaviors, even physical injury.

Back in 1949 in the book *The Organization of Behavior*, Donald Hebb, a psychologist considered the father of the field of neuropsychology, wrote "When an axon of cell A is near enough to excite a cell B and repeatedly and persistently takes part in firing it, some growth process or metabolic change takes place in one or both cells such that A's efficiency, as one of the cells firing B, is increased." That mouthful is now reduced to the phrase "cells that fire together, wire together." And this is the fundamental teaching point for a mindfulness teacher to understand conceptually and present to the class. This is why a daily or near-daily mindfulness practice is recommended. It isn't the concepts of present-moment awareness that rewire the brain but the actual practice of coming back to the present moment with kindness over and over and over again. We literally are rewiring our brains with our ongoing practice of kind attention.

When we were undergraduates some time ago, it was generally understood that after the synaptic pruning of late adolescence, neural connections were largely unchanged. Advances in neuroimaging, along with advances in a variety of fields, have shifted this faulty notion. Neuroplasticity has been widely documented in acquired brain-injury cases (Rossini & Dal Forno, 2004). Daily navigation of the maze of London streets resulted in gray matter volume difference in the hippocampi in taxi drivers, the hippocampus being an area of the brain critical for spatial navigation (Macguire et al., 2000). The first study to explore the brain changes in meditators found that experienced meditators had cortical thickening in areas related to emotional, sensory, and cognitive processing when compared to nonmeditators (Lazar et al., 2005). Subsequent studies have found a wide range of structural brain changes. This includes changes in the white matter or neural tract in the anterior cingulate, responsible for self-regulation, after only four weeks of daily practice (Tang, Lu, Fan, Yang, & Posner, 2012). These changes to neural tracts are the "rewiring" of the brain. Other studies have found changes in the gray matter density, or the actual number of brain cells in the hippocampus, after eight weeks of MBSR (Hölzel et al., 2011). Another study (Luders, Toga, Lepore, & Gaser, 2009) found that experienced meditators had greater cell volumes in the right prefrontal cortex, an area responsible for emotional regulation, than nonmeditators.

The neuroplasticity findings with mindfulness are wide ranging and intriguing, yet the challenge remains in how to summarize these findings when teaching mindfulness to a general audience. As a mindfulness teacher, you will need to understand and explain some key concepts without losing the class in unnecessary details.

Teaching Tip: During class, use the analogy of exercise or physical training to illustrate how the brain can be changed.

It is helpful to adapt any explanation of neuroplasticity to your particular audience. We find that a biceps metaphor is particularly effective with groups of veterans. It goes something like this:

If you want big biceps what do you have to do? You have to put the time in doing arm curls. You do this week after week, one rep after another. You don't notice too much at first, but over time your biceps start to get bigger and stronger. It isn't enough to understand that working your arms makes them bigger; you actually have to put in the time. It takes commitment.

So what do you need to do if you want to be more joyful and feel at peace in your body? Through neuroplasticity, your mindfulness practice can change your brain. The saying in neuroscience is "Cells that fire together, wire together." Regular meditation produces structural changes in the brain. These changes not only impact your mood but also influence the way signals from peripheral parts of the body, such as pain, are interpreted. So each time you come back to the present moment with kindness, or repeat a loving-kindness phrase such as "May I be safe," you are doing a rep. This opens up the possibility of strengthening the "feel-good" circuitry in your brain, and this has a direct impact on your life. But it takes commitment and patience.

Explanations such as this should inspire students to practice rather than try to be comprehensive in nature. The goal is not to review an entire body of research. Our goal is to support students in their personal practice.

Using Compassion Research as a Teaching Tool

After many decades of research into mental disorders and the particular circumstances of human suffering, new research is exploring the area of compassion. Compassion, as we have reviewed in the previous chapter, is our wish to relieve the suffering of others.

Compassion Research

"Compassion" is defined as what we feel—our emotional response rather than a cognitive response—when we recognize suffering in another and have an authentic wish to relieve this suffering. There are two important elements to recognize in the area of compassion research. The first is a bit surprising: it appears we are hard-wired for compassion, and it is not solely a learned response. This wiring has been called the *compassion instinct* (Keltner, Marsh, & Smith, 2010). It is supported by wide-ranging research from a study into the helping behavior and neurophysiology of rats (Decety, 2010) to the examination of behavioral and pupil responses in human infants too young to have learned the prosocial rules of politeness (Hepach, Vaish, & Tomasello, 2013). So there is an innate capacity for compassion built into each of us.

The second notable set of research findings is that compassion is so essential for our social connections—and both physical and mental well-being—that it has been an essential feature for the survival of the human species (Seppala, Rossomando, & Doty, 2013). Compassion has been linked to lower levels of inflammation (Fredrickson et al., 2013) and also linked to longer life (Brown et al., 2009; Konrath, Fuhrel-Forbis, Lou, & Brown, 2012). All of this research work is summarized beautifully by His Holiness the Dalai Lama, who said, "Love and compassion are necessities, not luxuries. Without them, humanity cannot survive."

Self-Compassion Research

Self-compassion is the same as compassion but the recipient is yourself. It is an emotional response to recognizing suffering in ourselves. According to Kristin Neff, self-compassion entails three components: mindfulness (being aware of the pain), shared humanity (recognizing that suffering is a part of being a human), and self-kindness (being kind to oneself).

Western research in self-compassion began to explode after Neff defined self-compassion as a research construct (2003a) and introduced the Self-Compassion Scale (2003b). To establish an effect size between self-compassion and measures of psychopathology, one group (MacBeth & Gumley, 2012) combined the results of twenty other studies together in a meta-analysis. This project found a large effect size between self-compassion and depression, anxiety, and stress. This negative relationship indicates that when self-compassion goes up, depression, anxiety, and perceived stress go down.

Research suggests that self-compassion also supports health, health-related behaviors, and coping with illness. Self-compassion has been related to stopping or reducing tobacco use (Kelly, Zuroff, Foa, & Gilbert, 2009) and reducing alcohol use (Brooks, Kay-Lambkin, Bowman, & Childs, 2012). Self-compassion also predicts positive responses to the aging process in the elderly (Allen & Leary, 2013) and can be a buffer against negative outcomes in those with chronic pain (Costa & Pinto-Gouveia, 2011; Wren et al., 2012). And self-compassion defends against the emotional impact of illness in people infected with HIV and is related to lower stress, anxiety, and shame (Brion, Leary, & Drabkin, 2014).

Recent findings suggest self-compassion training has a positive impact on biomarkers in the body associated with aging and disease. In one study in women (Arch et al., 2014), self-compassion training not only changed anxiety and cardiac responses in a stress situation, it also decreased the body's stress activation as measured by alpha-amylase, an enzyme in the saliva. Another study (Breines et al., 2014) compared a stress-induced inflammation marker (interleukin-6) in the blood in forty-one healthy adults after exposure to a standard laboratory stressor. Those with higher levels of self-compassion had significantly lower levels of inflammation markers, which suggest self-compassion may protect against the many inflammation-related diseases.

Overall, while self-compassion is a new target of research in Western science, it is related to well-being, decreases in psychopathology, increases in coping, and improvements in biomarkers related to stress. Given these findings, it is likely the interventions designed to increase self-compassion will produce meaningful health outcomes in clinical populations in the years ahead. One such random controlled trial study for mindful self-compassion (Neff & Germer, 2013) demonstrated that not only can self-compassion be enhanced, but, compared to the control group, participants in the compassion intervention increased mindfulness, compassion for others, and life satisfaction while decreasing depression, anxiety, and stress. For an ongoing review of self-compassion research, go to Kristin Neff's website at http://www.self compassion.org.

Summary

The research literature for mindfulness, compassion, and self-compassion is expansive and growing every year. The important point for a skilled mindfulness facilitator is to understand enough of the science to skillfully answer questions and integrate material as needed into the class to inspire students. But be cautious about creating an expectation of transformation or "getting rid" of unpleasant symptoms or experiences. Creating expectations and a sense of striving for things to be different than they are is a barrier to the unfolding of the practice.

PART II

Teaching Essentials

CHAPTER 3

Supporting Your Personal Practice

What lies behind us and what lies before us are tiny matters compared to what lies within us.

—Oliver Wendell Holmes

The most important quality a mindfulness facilitator brings into the classroom is the embodiment of mindfulness and compassion. This comes partly out of a person's character and also out of his or her life experience. But mostly—in this setting—it comes out of a regular, dedicated personal mindfulness practice. So in this chapter we focus on why personal practice not only helps you in your work and private life but how it also is the key element of becoming a great mindfulness teacher.

We present an introductory mindfulness approach in a somewhat manualized fashion in this book for the purpose of dissemination, knowing there is an inherent risk. Some people may simply start a group and follow the outline, mechanically reading the scripts with minimal presence while providing intellectualized explanations about the practice. In our view, this does little good and diminishes the role and potential of the teacher greatly; it can potentially harm the students, as they might take this for "real mindfulness" and check it off their list as another thing that's not working. Facilitating mindfulness groups from a place of authenticity, from an established personal practice, will inform your teaching and serve to offset this risk.

The Importance of a Personal Mindfulness Practice

The transformational possibilities mindfulness has to offer will reveal themselves in repeated application and in inspiration through the modeling of the teacher, not in reading about it or in listening to a lecture. Trudy Goodman says it's called medita-tion *practice* because, well, we need to practice it! Or to give another example: You wouldn't teach exercise if you don't actually work out yourself. Nor would you want to take a class from somebody who is just talking about the benefits of exercise and then asking you to do it.

Why would people even think about teaching mindfulness without a regular practice? Because it seems to be so deceivingly simple.

Don't be tricked by this apparent simplicity. Mindfulness teacher Sharon Salzberg traveled to India on a quest for special instructions to learn the secrets of deep peace and happiness (yes, it was the 1960s after all). When her teacher gave her instruc-tions for a breathing meditation, she thought: "What? I came all the way to India to focus on my breath? This must be the preparation for the more advanced teachings." And then she thought, "Focusing on my breath—how hard can *that* be?" Whenever she tells this story during a workshop, she laughs. And those in her audience who have ever tried to focus on the breath for even just five minutes are laughing right along with her.

Jon Kabat-Zinn calls mindfulness the "applied art of conscious living." The emphasis lies on being *applied*. Mindfulness seems to be so simple—just pay attention to this moment, such a no-brainer. When people first hear about the idea of "being in the moment" they often feel that it sounds very familiar, and they might say, "Oh, I've been mindful all my life." And yes, it's true, they have. To some extent. If asked for more detail they might say, "I love the taste of food. I love watching beautiful sunsets. I love feeling the grass under my feet on a summer morning. I'm completely mindful in those moments." While this is beautiful, it is only a small fraction of what a mindfulness practice actually is.

Mindfulness invites us to open to a moment-by-moment awareness. Now...and now...and now. Which also means being as nonjudgmental as possible while present with our not-so-great moments—being present with the pain, the fear, the pettiness, the jealousy. Mindfulness doesn't care what it is mindful of. We usually don't like to be mindful when we are impatient with our partner. Or when we get drunk or feel disgust for the homeless guy at the corner. Mindfulness is not an experience enhancer for the pretty moments in life, like a fabric softener. But it's not like a self-improvement project, either, finally getting a grip on those pesky thought patterns. It's the willing-ness to be present, to invite *every* moment into our awareness, be it pleasant, neutral, or unpleasant. This takes a lot of patience and practice—as well as the support of a teacher to inspire us to keep on coming back to *this* moment, because we see from her example it can be done.

How Much Mindfulness Experience Does One Need to Teach?

The best answer we can give is: it depends. Here's a story to illustrate our point: Susan Kaiser Greenland trains elementary-school teachers to teach mindfulness in

the classroom. One trainee told her that she was not a trained piano teacher b
she could play "Baa, Baa Black Sheep" on the piano and had been teaching th
cessfully to her preschoolers. Was that the same with mindfulness? Could she start
teaching mindfulness to her class even if she had only started practicing herself a
couple of months before? Greenland's answer was yes, absolutely, she could certainly
teach the mindfulness equivalent of "Baa, Baa Black Sheep" to her students—because
teaching "Baa, Baa Black Sheep" to preschoolers is totally appropriate for their devel-
opmental stage and the teacher knew just how to do. It was a fine fit.

What is the equivalent of "Baa, Baa Black Sheep" for you? What do you know in
your bones to be true about the teachings? And is that enough to meet the people in
your class with where *they are* at and what *they need*? This is an inquiry we do with
participants of our mindfulness facilitator training, and you might want to ask this of
yourself.

Teaching Tip: The closer you stay to what you know through your direct
experience, the better.

Here are some concrete starting points: Ideally you have taken some mindfulness
classes (MBSR if possible, since it's the gold standard for mindfulness courses). This
way you can get a firsthand experience of how a class format works and exposure to
the modeling of a good teacher (check our online resources at http://www.sharing
mindfulness.com to find classes close to you). We recommend that you have a regular
practice (most days of the week) for at least six months and have participated in at
least one full-silent daylong practice.

Practice Tip: If you have attended a weekend (or longer) retreat, even
better. The recurring feedback we get from those doing mindfulness facilitator training is that multiday silent practices are one of the most transformational tools for really "getting" mindfulness.

You don't have to be perfect and you don't have to get all tied up about being
mindful every minute. Don't even try—it won't work. If you love teaching and you
love mindfulness, the combination will support your commitment to your own practice. It helps to deepen your own understanding of what you teach and to refine the
ways you explain it. Teaching is also a way of accountability: you do what you ask
your students to do—and more.

Teaching Tip: You need to do at least what you ask your students to do,
better even if you do a little bit more. If you ask them to practice ten
minutes every day, we recommend that you practice at least fifteen to
twenty minutes. If you ask them to practice loving-kindness every day for
a particular week, that's what you would do as well, even if your favorite
meditation might be a different exercise.

You Are Not Only Practicing for Yourself

The beautiful news is that we do this practice for ourselves *and* for our students. The transformation that we have experienced ourselves, along with our active, regular practice, is something that class participants can pick up on, even if they can't put a finger on it.

Trudy Goodman tells the story that whenever she taught an intensive weekend Zen retreat, where she would practice alongside her meditation students, inevitably her therapy clients would have a major breakthrough in their session with her the following Monday. She wasn't teaching her therapy clients mindfulness, and most didn't even know that Goodman was a meditator. But her intensive practice of opening up space and becoming less identified with her "self" allowed her clients to move into this receptive space with her and see their own patterns and afflictions more clearly.

A fascinating study from Germany found that clients of meditating therapists get better faster than clients of their nonmeditating counterparts, even when the clients are unaware of their clinician's personal mindfulness practice. This was the case even when the clinicians didn't teach mindfulness. Practitioners bring specific qualities into the therapy, qualities of attention that are not attached to outcome—compassion and acceptance. And these qualities have an impact on the well-being and symptom reduction of the other person (Grepmair et al., 2007).

In the early 1990s, a group of psychologists—Zindel Segal, Mark Williams, and John Teasdale—set out to find a better treatment for recurring depression. They had heard about the benefits of MBSR and sat down to design an intervention that included some mindfulness practices: the playing of recorded tapes in class and some guided home practices. The clinicians teaching the class didn't feel the need to practice mindfulness on their own or lead the group practices themselves. The results of the pilot study were disappointing. The research team was puzzled and then decided to take an actual MBSR class.

They discovered what they had missed before: Students of the MBSR class did not only learn mindfulness through their own practice but also through the example of the teacher, who embodies the practice for the students.

> *Teaching Tip:* The teacher is an important model, demonstrating to the student how to gently be with everything, including difficulties, just as it is.

The researchers started practicing mindfulness themselves and noticed how challenging it was to make time for a daily practice, let alone to "invite in" all of their experiences. They went back to the drawing board and redesigned the intervention. They stayed very close to the MBSR curriculum, they led the meditations in the classroom themselves, and, most important, they did the home practice just like they asked their students to do. This time the results were astonishing. This eventually led to the creation of mindfulness-based cognitive therapy (MBCT), which is now taught all over the world and has been widely recognized as an evidence-based practice for depression relapse prevention.

Practice Tip: Our own sustained, continuous effort and practice of mindfulness is a nonnegotiable prerequisite of our being "good enough" mindfulness facilitators.

The Practice Will Do the Teaching

What is it we are doing when we teach mindfulness? How do you teach somebody how to meditate "correctly"? From the outside it looks pretty much like we are doing nothing at all. You ask people to sit up straight and still and to focus on the sensations of their breath. But of course that is not the point. It's not about the breath. And it's not about sitting still for increasing lengths of time. The meditation master Ajahn Chah says, "If you believe that sitting motionless for long times brings you closer to enlightenment, I have to disappoint you. I've seen chickens sitting on their nests for days on end."

Which is, of course, why court-mandated mindfulness training wouldn't work. How will you know what is going on inside a participant who is sitting there with his or her eyes closed? There is a gap between telling someone how to do something and experiencing it for yourself. Let's not forget, after all, that a map of the territory isn't the territory itself.

There's a classic story that beautifully captures this:

A student asked the meditation master about the meaning of a text. And the master replied, "Truth has not much to do with words. Truth can be likened to the full moon in the sky. Words, in this case, can be likened to a finger. The finger points to the moon's location. However, the finger is not the moon. To look at the moon, it is necessary to gaze beyond the finger, right?"

In the end, all we do in class is just point a finger at the moon. We point in the right direction, but we have to make sure that we never confuse the finger with the moon. What we are teaching can only be experienced by doing it. And sometimes this doesn't even happen immediately but unfolds slowly. You sit there and all you notice is how your mind races around like a crazy chicken or the much-quoted monkey. How is that supposed to get you more peaceful, less stressed, kinder?

And then you can have a physical sensation in the body of "getting it." It feels like your vision just got wider, your world bigger. It can be an elevated feeling, even a feeling of joy. People in a mindfulness class will often have a similar aha moment of insight as they deepen their understanding of what the practice is really about. We need to understand mindfulness from our own felt experience—or, as Saki Santorelli, the director of the Center for Mindfulness at the University of Massachusetts Medical School, says: "Let the practice do the teaching."

Practice Tip: Model yourself after a mindfulness teacher who inspired you or is still doing so. Ask yourself, "What is it about him or her that inspires?" Is it her intimate knowledge of the teachings? His enthusiasm and kindness? Her deep trust in the transformational power of the practice? His "walking the talk"? A true mindfulness teacher wouldn't even need to teach mindfulness in order for people to pick up on these qualities.

Modeling the Teaching Through Ethical Integrity

Just like kids learn much more from what their parents do than what they say, the students in our mindfulness class learn a lot more from what we do and how we do it than from all the words and theory we can offer them. Over the years we have learned a lot from watching our own mindfulness teachers. We look closely to see if they walk the talk. Are they able to stay centered and kind in the face of life's storms? We watch how they respond to students, especially the challenging ones. Can we feel that they are nonjudgmental and that they don't feel like they need to fix the participant's problem or to make it right? Or do we see that they're just paying lip service?

This doesn't mean that as teachers we have to be perfect and never fall into our patterns. But what do we do when that happens? Here is where it gets really interesting. Can we be nonjudgmental and compassionate with our own imperfection? Can we own that we did hurt somebody (or ourselves)? Can we say it out loud and make amends if necessary? Or do we try to hide it and cover it up? Maybe our working edge is that we can be nonjudgmental with others but not with ourselves. How do we work with that? How transparent can we be with that?

Dharma Teacher Perspective: On Ethics

You might find it strange that we even bring up the topic of ethics or integrity in a book about mindfulness. Isn't that the realm of religion? Yet we find it way too important not to mention it.

Sharon Salzberg says that you do your students a disservice if you don't let them know how taking a close look at ethics will help them move along on the path of wisdom and compassion. It might not be obvious, but, in the big scheme of Dharma, ethics play a prominent role in our lives as practitioners.

Buddhism has an interesting expression for ethical behavior: "the bliss of blamelessness." What this means is that whatever we think, say, or do (or don't do) has an influence on our state of mind in meditations and in life in general—and how we progress on the path of insight. If we act against our values this will reverberate in how we feel. We might harden against feelings of regret, guilt, shame, or self-loathing. Jack Kornfield puts it nicely by often saying, "It's hard to sit down for a peaceful meditation after a day of stealing, lying, and killing."

We call an action "skillful" or "wholesome" if it leads to more happiness in ourselves or in others, "unskillful" or "unwholesome" if it leads to more suffering.

Teaching Tip: If the goal is to be happier or feel more at ease, it important to know about the effect of behavior on happiness or suffering.

The Five Precepts

All religions, just like all civilizations, have ethical systems. In the Buddhist system this manifests in what are called the *five precepts*, or *five ethical guidelines*. These precepts are suggestions, not commandments. They can be viewed as guidelines for behavior. They reflect values and make sense—and over time one will become more skilled in acting from this place of integrity. It can be very interesting to ask the question: "How does this behavior affect my meditation? My peace of mind?"

The five precepts are phrased in the negative form (imagine what a place the world would be if people would just abide by these alone!). But since each of the guidelines represents a spectrum, we also provide the positive form. Keep in mind that there is a kind of neutral middle ground between the two points of each precept:

1. Not killing or harming—developing loving-kindness

2. Not stealing—developing generosity

3. Not harming anybody (including oneself) with sexuality or strong desires—developing contentment

4. Not lying—developing speech that is true, helpful, kind, and appropriate (This includes the written word, since we communicate so much through e-mails, texting, and so forth.)

5. Not intoxicating the mind (with anything that intoxicates and potentially leads to addiction, drugs and alcohol being just two examples)—developing mindfulness

By working actively with these five precepts we also become safer for our students (and for everybody, including ourselves), because we can be trusted to not harm, to not steal, to not lie, and so forth. The Buddha actually said that the biggest gift we can give is the gift of fearlessness, to be somebody who can be trusted. Or as the print of a T-shirt we've seen stated: "Entering a zone of peace." We all want to be around people like that.

Clinical Psychologist Perspective: On Ethics

Psychologists, physicians, social workers, nurses, and those in all clinical disciplines are steered by specific ethical guidelines. The Ethical Principles of

Psychologists and Code of Conduct, which I know best, is aspirational in nature and meant as a guide rather than an exhaustive compendium of enforceable rules. The guidelines are drafted broadly to capture the varied roles psychologists may take in science, education, and professional practice. But whatever your discipline and code of ethics, ask yourself this: Would you be drawn to a teacher who you know has serious ethical impairments? The teacher who commits fraud, beats his or her spouse, or allows his or her dog to starve in the backyard with an absence of concern? I imagine not. There is an understandable gap between the principles and ethical requirements of our various disciplines and our individual commitment to right action in all spheres of our life. Who you are as a person, not only a clinician, impacts who you are as a teacher.

Embodiment and Resonance

In this section we cover in more depth two characteristics—embodiment and resonance—that are essential for any mindfulness teacher. They can be deepened through personal and interpersonal mindfulness practice.

Embodiment. In the teacher who embodies the practice, there is a consistency of qualities such as calm, kindness, and nonreactivity. These are part of a professional skill set that is not just utilized in the classroom—it's integrated into the facilitator's very being. You could say that such a facilitator is "being" the practice instead of "doing" it.

This facilitator brings more than just a conceptual understanding of the practice of mindfulness. His mindful awareness practice is grounded in the foundational attitudes of mindfulness, and the class feels that. Because of the depth of his own practice, he knows, understands, and can point out the subtleties of the workings of the heart and mind in a way that resonates with his students. The recognition of his own vulnerability and yet the trust and faith that everything that comes up in the heart and mind is workable—will inspire his students to open to their own experiences in a new way.

Resonance. Resonance serves as an example for how ancient practices are increasingly understood through modern neuroscience, how attending to the present moment with loving-awareness connects to the neurobiology of attachment. In the 2000 book *A General Theory of Love*, a group of University of California, San Francisco psychiatry professors proposed the concept of *limbic resonance* to describe not only the capacity but also the mechanism for deep emotional attunement or sharing of an experience that occurs in the brain's limbic system (Lewis, Amini, & Lannon, 2000). This occurs on both the verbal and nonverbal level and is considered a core mechanism for healing in many psychotherapy approaches. We tune in to those around us through the function of our mirror neurons and neurotransmitters like dopamine that result in feelings of pleasant connectedness. This is a point of confluence and mutual enrichment between ancient teachings and modern neuroscience. It's a delectable moment when appreciating both perspectives results in a richer synthesis and understanding of each individually.

Jack Kornfield describes this meeting of ancient practice and modern neuroscience beautifully in his book *The Wise Heart*: "Each time we meet another human being and honor their dignity, we help those around us. Their hearts resonate with ours in exactly the same way the strings of an unplucked violin vibrate with the sounds of a violin played nearby. Western psychology has documented this phenomenon of 'mood contagion' or limbic resonance. If a person filled with panic or hatred walks into a room, we feel it immediately, and unless we are very mindful, that person's negative state will begin to overtake our own. When a joyfully expressive person walks into a room, we can feel that state as well" (2009, 17).

Your Personal Practice: How to Begin

Perhaps you already have a regular personal meditation practice. Or maybe you have a semi-regular or now-and-then practice. Or maybe you, like the students you may soon be teaching, don't have a personal practice—yet. Here are some common questions and answers about starting a personal practice that apply to teachers and students alike. As you read our answers, keep in mind that we are all different. What works great for one person might not work at all for another.

How do I start a regular practice? Begin with a practice time period that feels achievable and realistic. This can be just five minutes starting out, or perhaps ten or even twenty minutes. For most people (teachers and students alike), listening to guided audio is a big help in the beginning. Using guided meditations is not a crutch you have to wean yourself off eventually—some use audio tracks indefinitely, or go back to audio whenever they feel a slump in motivation or have a hard time staying focused. There are many free online resources for audio meditations available, including at our website, http://www.sharingmindfulness.com.

You might want to ask yourself: Is every day realistic? If not, consider incorporating your practice into your workday Monday through Friday and give yourself the weekend off. Or is the weekend when it works best for you? You might have some extra-busy workdays, when a longer practice feels too much as you are starting out.

Where are there pockets of time during the day that you could use? For example, one teacher at the VA stops by a park on his drive home from work every day. He sits under a favorite tree to meditate for twenty minutes, then he drives home to his wife and two young children.

When making time for your practice, be cautious about "fitting it in" your day. This can be impossible to do when your days are already packed. Consider instead "building it in." No matter how busy you are, you still find time to brush your teeth. Make your practice just as important.

> **Example.** Claire commits to twenty minutes of meditation practice five days a week. On Wednesdays, however, she practices just five minutes of meditation

before she goes to lunch, because she goes to a salsa class after work. Finally, she gives herself one flexible ain't-gonna-happen day per week.

I meditate daily. How do I keep it going? A practice community is helpful for most people to sustain a regular practice. In the bigger cities you should be able to find a weekly "sitting group." Sitting groups are drop-in groups, often hosted by an Insight Meditation or Zen Center, where there is a longer silent sitting period, sometimes a shorter mindful walking period, followed by a short talk by the person leading the group, followed by a Q&A or sharing. If there is no such group in your vicinity, you could start your own with a couple of friends or acquaintances who are also interested in meditation. These peer-led groups usually sit for thirty minutes followed by a discussion or a shared reading.

There are also online communities. Some host daily online live meditations, whereby people call in to a conference number and are guided through a meditation, sometimes with a Q&A afterward by a teacher. Some online communities give support through chat rooms. You can also check out various meditation apps (see our online resources). Some will let you know who else in the community is meditating at the same time. For some people this is inspiring; for others it's more a social-media-type distraction. Reading books, articles, and blogs on the topic is very helpful. There are many free and low-cost resources online, such as talks by renowned teachers in the field.

Being part of a live community gives you the advantage of being able to share your practice and experiences with like-minded people. It also gives you access to a teacher or practitioners who are more experienced than you and who can answer questions and help you deepen your practice and understanding.

Do I have to practice daily? Yes, this is the goal. We all have days when we just don't get to it, but it's very helpful to know this as an exception. We also might want to deliberately take one day off per week—if that makes it easier for you to stick to the routine the rest of the week. Meditation teacher Joseph Goldstein took the vow to sit (meditate) at least ten minutes every day. He says that often the hardest part is getting to sit down. Once you have started, you will often go longer, but you also know that ten minutes is enough. (Also see "How do I start a regular practice?")

Which time of the day is the best time to practice? That depends a lot on your personality. Are you a morning or a night person? Many people practice the first thing in the morning and they feel it changes the way they move through their day. We both prefer to practice in the mornings, before the kids get up. Other people love to practice right after work. It helps them to unwind and set a different pace for the rest of the day. We also know of many people who use their work breaks during the day for a shorter practice. Some people meditate in their car before they get to the office and then again before they go home. Be creative.

Usually, sticking with a regular time works best.

What is the optimal length of daily practice? The longer, the better, of course! Most of the research has been done with thirty to forty minutes of daily practice. But as with everything that you do on a regular basis, the most important thing is to do *something*. Just like with exercise, it's more effective to do ten minutes every day than one hour once a week. The changes probably won't be as pronounced as when you do longer periods, but never underestimate how small amounts of practice add up over time. We know many people who were only able to start with five minutes, because they were so restless or busy or convinced that this was all they could do; more often than not this helped them to gain confidence and stamina to sit for longer periods as their practice unfolded.

Jon Kabat-Zinn, when asked about the benefits of a longer daily practice, answered that if we only sit short periods of time we might never get to be really restless or really bored. We might never have to "be with it" for an extended period of time, which means that we lose the opportunity to deeply experience all the movements of the mind and how often these states will disappear by themselves—if we give them the time and space. Which in turn will give us the trust and confidence that a) things will change without our doing anything, and b) that we can allow this to happen.

Our general standard is that, as a teacher, you do more than your students or what you ask your students to do.

Can I practice once a week? While we have many students who only practice once a week—when they come to class or sitting group—and still gain from it, this is not what we recommend for teachers.

Do I need to get a meditation cushion? We always stress in our classes that nobody ever has to sit on the floor with his or her legs crossed. However, as a teacher you should be familiar with the four classic meditation postures so you can teach them comfortably: sitting (on a chair or on the floor cross-legged or kneeling, using a meditation cushion or a meditation bench), lying down, standing up, and walking. It is helpful to own the equipment and props to demonstrate these postures if they're not available where you teach. Your students don't need to get a cushion if they don't sit on the floor; in fact that might be contraindicated in some settings, like with geriatric patients.

It's also good to share sources from which your students can buy equipment.

Which practice is the best? Regular practice! Doing your practice on a regular basis is more important than what type of practice you do. In our class people learn different meditation practices, and while we encourage people to gain familiarity with all of them by adhering to the homework schedule, once the class is over we want them to stick with what works best for them or what they feel drawn to the most. As a teacher, it's important to feel at ease and comfortable with all of the practices you teach. This doesn't mean that you yourself won't feel drawn more to one or two. We also recommend that you do all practices periodically to "stay nimble" with them.

I'm really mindful throughout the day. Isn't that enough? No. An informal mindfulness practice without a formal practice is absolutely not sufficient for teachers. And we don't recommend this for students either. Formal and informal practice support and enhance each other but are not meant to be practiced exclusively. Formal practice has no substitute for a number of reasons:

- In formal meditation, you can watch your heart and mind and how they move very intimately. This is often the first step to seeing where we get stuck and how we are more likely to fall into habitual patterns from there. It's a lot easier to do that in formal meditation when there are not many outside distractions.

- All the relevant positive benefits of meditation were discovered in studies with formal meditation practice.

- Formal practice is like a laboratory for your own heart and mind. It's often helpful to start your explorations in the lab before you experiment with behavior changes in your everyday life. You start working with your mind in a "controlled environment." You practice things here, like tolerating something unpleasant, such as an itch. From here you generalize the acquired skill to your everyday life.

- Formal meditation calms the mind (and the nervous system) in a way informal doesn't.

- You need to be able to answer the questions in this section from your own experience.

- You don't want to ask your students to do something you don't do yourself.

- And last: Do the math. Add up the time during the day you are really mindful. For most people it's moments, meaning seconds or maybe a minute here and there. For the majority of people, informal practice is actually not a lot of time.

Do I need a teacher to keep going? We strongly recommend that you find a teacher. We are all on the path, and our practice is always evolving and changing. It's easy to get lost or to stagnate in one's practice. We can also be easily off about how the practice is going. You would want somebody who knows you and your practice and with whom you can be totally honest, so a colleague or your supervisor might not be the best person for this. And it might take some searching to find a teacher when you have learned mindfulness in mainstream setting, like in a hospital. But your teacher doesn't have to be a local, and you might not need to touch base with him or her more than once or twice a year. Many Vipassana teachers or other senior teachers are open to do short practice check-ins with people over the phone or via Skype. To be part of a group of mindfulness facilitators is also very beneficial. A lot of questions can be answered among peers and don't require a senior teacher. We also find that it helps our inspiration and clarity of intention to be part of a teacher group.

What about silent retreats? Are they necessary to keep my regular practice going? Yes. Retreats give your practice a boost and a deepening that is hard to impossible to find elsewhere. A silent teacher-led retreat can last from a day to many months and is one of the core elements to deepen one's practice of mindfulness. A day spent in silence with like-minded people can allow us to drop deeper into our own experience.

The time is spent with alternating sitting and walking meditations. On longer retreats there are also check-ins with a teacher to make sure one's practice is on track. We can listen inside and learn things about ourselves that are usually hidden. We practice alone but with others, which is an inspiration and a tremendous help, especially when we struggle. As we go on longer retreats (a common time spent on retreat for mindfulness teachers is five to ten days every year) the mind will quiet down considerably, so that we can learn in more detail how the heart and mind work, a process often called "having insights." (See the resources at http://www.sharingmindfulness.com for a list of retreat places.)

Most people are ready for a five-day retreat after they have participated in a couple of one-day retreats.

> *Practice Tip:* It is helpful to book a retreat like you would a conference or a vacation. Check retreat calendars of different organizations ahead of time and get your reservation in.

For people with very young children, longer retreat practice can be out of the question for a number of years; yet we still encourage parents to do two to four daylong retreats annually. We have found in many professionals a willingness to do many multiday professional trainings or conferences a year but a strong sense that a silent retreat is somehow "for fun," as if it would count for a vacation or as something self-indulgent. We strongly disagree. What you learn on retreat you will learn nowhere else. Once the mind quiets down, other learning than our regular "knowledge acquiring" can emerge. We see the silent retreat as a kind of mandatory continuing education.

Summary

We can't emphasize enough the importance of a regular personal meditation practice. Your full embodiment of the practice serves as a model for your students. Your willingness to show up for your own experience moment by moment will help you to be fully there—for yourself and for the participants. We hope that after reading this chapter you feel more clarity and inspired to give the core program your all. And when you get stuck, refer back to the Q&A.

CHAPTER 4

A Quick Start for New Teachers

Awaken curiosity. It is enough to open minds. Do not overload them.
Put there just a spark. If there is some good inflammable stuff, it will
catch fire.

—Anatole France

In this chapter we define the hands-on skills of the teacher. In the previous chapter
we looked at the bigger-picture qualities, mainly embodiment and resonance, which
rise out of the learning from your own personal practice. Now we cover the nuts and
bolts of the different aspects of leading a meditation; what to focus on in a big-group
discussion, including inquiry and disclosure; and how to inspire your class to practice
at home. Let's begin with overall competencies.

Mindfulness Facilitator Competencies

There is an ongoing discussion in the mindfulness community about identifying the
specific competencies of a mindfulness facilitator and describing the optimal path by
which these skills can be acquired, appropriately demonstrated, and externally evalu-
ated. What we call "mindfulness-based interventions" encompass a variety of
evidence-based approaches, each with some unique features and needed skills.

In the UK, two universities (Bangor and Cambridge) offer a postgraduate program
in mindfulness-based interventions. The team around Rebecca Crane from Bangor
University developed, implemented, and published the "Mindfulness Teaching
Competency Domains." They articulate well the great opportunity for healing made
possible by the broader spread of mindfulness-based interventions as well as the
inherent risk that the spread of mindfulness itself leads to a "dilution of its integrity."
We fully agree with many others who suggest that the quality of a mindfulness class
is only as good as its instructor. Provided here are their six domains for mindfulness
teaching. (See our resources at http://www.sharingmindfulness.com for a link to the
full criteria and assessment document.)

- Coverage, pacing, and organization of session curriculum

- Relational skills

- Embodiment of mindfulness

- Guided mindfulness practices

- Conveying course themes through interactive inquiry and didactic teaching

- Holding of group learning environment (Crane et al., 2012)

At this point, there is wide consensus that competencies are needed not only to operationalize and standardize the research into mindfulness but to ensure that the heart of the teachings is left intact. The competencies offered here are, we believe, among the best suggested to date.

A Unique Skill Set

We expand upon and add to the above competency domains with our own list. The following skill set is based on the blending of two discrete disciplines in addition to the embodiment of mindfulness. The mindfulness teacher needs to bring into the room the skill sets of a traditional teacher of any subject and of an effective group facilitator.

Inspiration to practice. You already know now that the main role of the mindfulness facilitator is to inspire the students to practice on their own. If the students don't practice, they will miss the point of mindfulness entirely. They might gain some intellectual understanding of definitions and some nice ideas, but there will be no lasting stress or symptom reduction, or behavior change; nor will they gain a greater sense of ease and freedom in their everyday lives. Inspiring participants to begin their own practice at home is an important step. This is how we shift the locus of control for health and healing from something done *to* patients in a medical setting into a doorway to healing that comes from *within*.

Embodying the teachings. This includes exemplifying compassion, equanimity, and acceptance. See chapter 3.

Creating a safe learning environment. As with any group, establishing a safe, respectful, and nurturing environment is essential. And this is your specific job as the facilitator from the very first moment of the group. Mindfulness facilitators with training and experience leading group psychotherapy will need little guidance here, but a brief review may be helpful for those facilitators and clinicians who do not have group experience. There are a number of different approaches to creating safety, but a common element is to establish age-appropriate rules and to consistently enforce them. In Session 1 we have provided a list of safety rules that might be helpful to establish. Feel free to adopt what works for you and your population and setting as needed. And, just to make it fun, another rule—don't have too many rules! Don't get bogged down in details. Rules are in place to support safety for everyone present. And group members understand this. Everyone will be relieved when the facilitator clarifies the rules and holds to them.

Connecting authentically to students. Do this in a human way. (More on this in chapter 3.)

Teaching. Actually, everything you do as a facilitator falls under the classification of didactics, or the theory and practical application of teaching. But another distinct skill of the facilitator is to present the thematic material of the class, what we might call the "lecture" portion, in a clear and engaging way. Everyone will have his or her own style. If you have experience with your particular population—say, teen girls with eating disorders, or perpetrators of domestic violence, or members of a religious community—you likely already understand how to speak to your group so they will "get it." How much humor and irreverence will you use? What will work best, a formal presentation on the whiteboard with bullet points or a more casual conversation? We suggest thoroughly reading and understanding the material for each class and then trusting your experience and instinct on this.

> *Teaching Tip*: Keep in mind that people make use of multiple channels of learning, as some individuals are auditory learners and some are visual learners. For some, the use of a whiteboard can help make a concept stick. Some students might remember a handout on research, while other times a story or a poem helps to bridge the more intellectual with the emotional learning (see also "Poems and Stories" in this chapter).

Guiding and leading practices. Practicing together in the classroom under the guidance of the teacher is the core element of the class. Each class is started, after some welcoming words, with a guided practice. This emphasizes its importance and centrality, and it helps the participants to settle and to get in touch with their individual truth of the moment. And a guided practice opens them to learning.

The Basics of Leading a Meditation

There are numerous factors to consider when leading a meditation practice. We list the most common here, along with our tips. Keep your particular population in mind as you go through this section; you might have valid reasons to adapt or change our guidelines to suit the needs and experiences of your participants.

Guiding with Eyes Open or Closed?

You should meditate along with your students and lead the practice from your own present-moment experience. At the same time, you have to be attuned to your class and what is going on in the room. We recommend that you have your eyes closed most of the time while leading meditations, but open them occasionally to look around the room. You would also open them if you hear sounds that are not obvious (no need to check the fidgety person to your left if you already know who it is).

Meditation Posture

A rule of thumb: as you practice with your students, model "good posture" with the posture that most students in your class will hold. That usually means sitting in a chair for sitting meditation. You do all mindful movements with them and all walking meditations.

One exception: if you lead a longer Body Scan and it's appropriate to invite your students to lie down, you should gauge if you want to lie down with them or stay seated in your chair. The common instruction for a long Body Scan is to lie down with your class and guide them through it lying down yourself. In our experience, especially in mental health, but also in some general-population class settings, many people have a hard time feeling safe—especially when lying down and closing their eyes. If you as the instructor stay in your chair, it can offer your participants a sense of support, a kind of watching out for them (and keeping an eye on the door). Of course, you should do the Body Scan yourself, just not lying down.

Teaching Tip: Please don't make yourself special by sitting on your meditation cushion—even if that is how you meditate at home—when nobody or hardly anybody in your class can do that. It's fine to sit on your cushion on the floor once you have introduced that in the class—if that is even appropriate for your setting—and a good number of your students can and will do it as well.

Before you move into the meditation, reinforce the extra support they can experience from their posture. It gets more important the longer the practice period is. Here are a few pointers for facilitators and class participants alike:

FOR MEDITATION POSTURE IN GENERAL

- Do what works for your body. Every body is different, and every body should be comfortable (but not slack or slumped over).

- Sitting still helps the mind to calm down. But if you feel you need to move, do it purposefully. Try to play with not moving and see what happens.

- Find a posture of "dignity and ease."

- Tuck the chin slightly in, or imagine that you are being pulled up at the crown of your head by an invisible string—this relaxes the neck.

- The position of your arms and hands is not so important, but make sure that your shoulders are not pulling the arms forward in the seated posture. Try hands folded in your lap, or one resting in the other, or just resting your hands on your thighs.

FOR SITTING IN A CHAIR

- Dining hall–style chairs work best. Couches make us slump. Your hips should be at the height of your knees or slightly higher (sit on an extra cushion, or put a cushion under your feet, depending how tall you are).

- Sit with an erect upper body, feet firmly on the ground, chin slightly tucked in, hands either on the thighs or folded in the lap, eyes closed or half closed.

- Maybe use a cushion or rolled up blanket in the small of your back for lumbar spine support.

FOR LYING DOWN

- If the body allows it, lie on your back, feet falling away from each other, arms at your sides (palms up or down is a personal preference).

- A bolster or rolled up blanket under the knees supports the lower back and helps with sciatica. It is also great to simply put the legs up on the seat of a chair ("astronaut's pose") for the same reason.

We won't cover the kneeling or cross-legged sitting postures in this book, as most beginning classes don't need it.

Offering Participants Options and Autonomy

You want your students to be active participants in their growth and healing. In order to do this, encourage them to listen to their internal voice for what is "right" for them. You want to be as inclusive as possible without being too permissive. Let your class know that there is no one right way to meditate, and invite them to either ask in class or talk to you after class to get more individualized instructions as needed. There are many options you can offer:

- *Eyes closed or open*: If open, participants should be looking down at their cheeks or with a soft gaze at the floor in front of them. This will diminish the amount of visual input and help the mind to calm down. It can be helpful to open the eyes for periods of time during the meditation if one is sleepy, restless, or very caught up in the internal dialogue. Eyes open can also help participants to feel safer.

- *Meditation position*: Some meditations require specific postures, but, in general, feel free to have participants make adaptations as necessary. Also, see "Meditation Posture" earlier in this chapter.

- *Type of meditation:* To some extent, the specific type of meditation can be an option. You want to invite participants to give all meditations a fair try, but eventually people may settle into those that they feel most drawn to (which makes it more likely that they will actually continue the practice after the course is over).

- *Length of meditation:* While in general the rule is "the longer the better," this only works if participants actually do it and not get entangled in (and discouraged by) their expectations. Also, for people with highly activated nervous systems (for example, those who suffer from post-traumatic stress) longer meditation can be destabilizing or lead to dissociation.

Language

Mindfulness has a very particular lexicon. By familiarizing yourself with different wording options and tone, you will make the experience for your participants a lot easier. All of them might feel unfamiliar in the beginning.

Teaching Tip: Practice guiding all of the different meditations with another new teacher. Afterward give each other feedback on language, voice, cues, space, and so forth. Please practice with all the different elements until they become second nature.

Use of the Present Participle

A prominent feature in guiding a meditation is the regular use of the present participle. All the *-ing* words, like *noticing, allowing, sensing,* and *breathing,* represent things happening right in the present moment. This allows for the language to be inviting. For example, notice the difference between the following two sentences: "Close your eyes" and "Closing your eyes." The latter invites the listener right into the action of the present moment. It is allowing and reduces the potential for resistance related to perceived hierarchy between the teacher and the participant. Closing the eyes is not an order; it's a suggestion or the description of something happening in the present moment.

You want to be as inclusive and inviting to your class as you possibly can. You could say, "Allowing the eyes to close." Or "Closing your eyes, if that feels right to you."

We also like to include options. For example: "If it feels right in this moment, allowing the eyes to close. If you choose to have your eyes open, softly gazing down on your cheeks." Let the language of your cues always be inviting and supportive of the participant's autonomy and internal locus of control. The language directs them to work at their own practice. But allow yourself the flexibility to vary your language to keep things fresh.

Use of the Possessive Pronoun

We invite you to experiment with the different feeling tones of, for example, "Feeling *your* breath moving" and "Feeling *the* breath moving." As introduced in the beginning of the chapter, you want to invite your students to move more often from the personal ("I, me, mine") to what is common for all, to the "not taking everything so personal"—including the breath. Moving more from "this is what my breath feels like" to "this is what breathing feels like." It can be helpful to feel "the thighs," for example, as compared to "my thighs—which I hate so much and which look horrible in jeans…"

However, there is no need to abandon the possessive pronoun altogether. Just be aware of the different effect it has, and mix it up as it feels appropriate. You can also use pronouns as a skillful means depending on the group you are teaching. If you have, for example (we are using a cliché here), a group of lawyers who are potentially very disconnected from their bodies, it can be helpful to use "feeling into *your* feet" and "feeling *your* body" often, compared to a group of yoga teachers who might possess a tendency to overidentify with their bodies. In the latter instance, focusing on "*the* legs" and "*the* body" might be beneficial.

And last, the absence of the possessive pronoun connects the person leading the practice and the people being guided. There is just breath being experienced: just breathing and the knowing of it.

Inclusivity of Experience

In your instructions and cueing, be as inclusive as possible. Avoid assumptions about your participant's experience:

- *Avoid adjectives that value an experience.* For example, "Breathing in the next yummy breath" or "Noticing how nice and solid the ground feels under your feet." Not everybody experiences the breath as yummy or the ground under their feet as positive. The same is true for the opposite. For example, "Becoming aware how much you hate the noise of the traffic outside." Even if the noise is bad, there might be people in the class who are not bothered by it.

- *Avoid ability bias.* Refrain from suggesting that students do something that may not be possible for everybody. This is true for physical movements, like sitting on the floor or doing a particular stretch, as well as for summoning up a particular mental state in meditation, for example "Feeling appreciation for being alive" or "Accepting the moment as it is." A lot of people can't do these things, and they will be left feeling inferior or like a failure. If you want to introduce the idea of acceptance or appreciation in your guidance, we recommend rephrasing it into something like, "As you feel into your legs, there might be a feeling of appreciation. Or there might not." Or "Inviting a sense of acceptance into the present moment" or "Opening to a sense of acceptance, if that is available to you right now." Or exchange the word "acceptance" for "acknowledging." We can't will acceptance into being. But we can intentionally acknowledge something even if we don't like it (and if we don't accept it).

"We" or "You"?

In general, we recommend that you lead a meditation in the "you" form, not "we." While you might feel that you are more connected to your group when you say, "Now bringing the attention to *our* body," not everybody in the group feels supported by that. It's *their* body. Not general property. An exception is when you want to guide the attention to something that might be challenging, like lower-back pain. Here it can be supportive and inclusive to use a phrase like, "Now feeling into the lower back. This is an area of the body where many of us feel tension." You'll get a knack for the wording with practice.

Voice

Lead practices with your normal speaking voice. Please avoid a special "meditation voice." Sometimes when listening to guided meditations the voices might be very soft, even hypnotic or singsong. Practicing mindfulness meditation is not magical; it doesn't need a special voice. Speak with your normal tone of voice and volume so people can hear you across the room. Make sure your voice has a normal intonation and doesn't become monotonous.

Be aware that your voice might get softer when leading a class through a meditation. You want to find a balance between ensuring all group members can hear you without ever yelling. But if the volume and tone become too low, you will lose the class.

You can also use your voice to help regulate the energy in the room. For example, if you notice that people start falling asleep (you see a lot of head bobbing when you look around, or you hear the sounds of sleep), you might increase your volume and intonation—that might be enough. Or you might say, "If you notice being sleepy, you might want to sit up straight, maybe open your eyes for a moment."

Giving Instructions

When you are guiding a meditation, you are typically either *giving instructions* or *providing cues and space*. Giving instruction is the how-to part of the meditation. A typical meditation frontloads some instruction (and then moves between cues and silent pauses of varying lengths). Keep in mind that when you give instructions, you ask your students to listen, not to practice.

Be clear with instructions. But avoid overexplaining, as you want the meditation itself, not necessarily your directions, to inform the practice experience.

Instructions tell the participants what you want them to focus on in the meditation. For example: "Feeling the sensations of your breath" or "If you notice the attention is not on the breath, gently guiding it back." In general, avoid giving instructions that lead the attention outside the meditation. For instance, you wouldn't want to say, "And this is how you would also bring the mind back *during the day*," since it references a time outside the present moment.

Cueing and Space

Cueing is reminding participants to bring back their attention, and *space* is the silent time given to put into practice what you ask participants to do. Here are three examples:

"Where is the mind now?"

"If the mind wanders, just noticing it and gently bringing it back to the breath." (This is an example of an instruction that is also a very common cue.)

"This moment is like this… And *this* moment is like *this*."

The facilitator titrates the cues and space to match the needs of the particular group and practice. You can adjust both the rate of cueing to impact the spaciousness of the practice and the contents of the cues themselves. For new practitioners, facilitators may want to provide a bit more support with more frequent cues, ensuring the content includes normalizing the wandering mind and any judgments that might arise. It is an important conceptual point that every practice should have enough spaciousness for the meditator to notice that the mind has wandered but not so much that she feels unsupported, lost, and overwhelmed by the task at hand. The more the class advances, the fewer cues are necessary and the more space or silence we want to allow for.

Beginning facilitators have a tendency to talk too much throughout a practice. This might come from a sense of nervousness (which changes the sense of time: a pause might feel a lot longer than it actually is—check your timer if in doubt!) and the feeling of needing "to do something" as the leader, which is typically expressed in talking. Silence can feel awkward to a new facilitator, especially one with little background in a personal practice. It can be hard to trust in the beginning that by holding the space for the group we provide what is needed.

Teaching Tip: Vary pause lengths during the practice from two breaths to eight or more (counting them helps!). If in doubt, talk less.

On the other hand, those who come to teaching from the practitioner path have a tendency to cue too little or to stop cueing altogether, which can leave beginners feeling abandoned. As a general rule, be sure you leave regular silent spaces throughout the practice.

Offer a Range of Experiences and Examples

If you want participants to explore a particular area, it can be helpful to give some examples so they get an idea what could be there to experience. For example, with the Body Scan we give the class many options, including numbness. For example: "Now feeling into your lower legs. What is here to notice? Pressure? Temperature? Position? Maybe nothing at all? There is no need to evoke a sensation. We are just showing up for whatever is already here. Or what is not here." If you ask them during a practice to focus on, let's say, emotional states, list a few. For example, "Now bringing your [or "the"] attention to any emotional flavors that might be present right now." That can be enough, or you can add something like, "There might be some anxiety or restlessness. Or maybe sadness. Or joy. Whatever it is."

Offer Cues from the Middle of Your Own Practice

When you guide your class through a meditation, you have to do the practice yourself. You can't just talk (and please, please don't just read a script—ever). Your example actually helps the participants to get into their own practice. In fact, you and your students will cocreate the experience of kind awareness in the room. While you are attending to your own personal experience, doing it together is a shared event that helps stabilize everyone's practice.

On one end of the spectrum are facilitators who just read the script, do not participate in the class meditation, and do not have a personal meditation practice. On the other end are facilitators who plunge so deeply into their own practice while leading the meditation that they become completely oblivious of the participants, barely present for what goes on outside themselves, and hardly audible; the participants can feel abandoned and will often get fidgety as a result. These two extremes contribute to vastly different class ambiences.

Newer teachers with less personal practice experience tend to believe that in order to "get it right" they have to use the exact words from the meditation transcript. This is particularly true among well-trained clinicians who have a strong sense of adherence to a technique from other forms of interventions. But it isn't about the words. It's about the authentic moment-by-moment unfolding. When you lead from your own experience, everyone can sense this.

Leading a practice is different than doing your own practice. While facilitating, you have to balance your own practice with contact with the class so as not to lose anyone, especially beginners. It's important to never lose track of where the group is, what cues they might need, and how much spaciousness to allow.

Teaching Tip: Imagine there's an immersion scale that can chart how deeply you engage in the meditation while leading it. A 0 equates reading a script and just focusing on the words, while a 10 means getting fully caught up in the meditation to the class's detriment. Aim for a 5.

"Cueing from the middle" is a technique all facilitators need to practice and is a skill related to but separate from practicing itself. In the pauses between your sentences or cues, really connect with your body, your breath. Feel it. Then say the next sentence. Then feel back into your body, your own present-moment experience. Practice this back and forth until it feels natural and not like a back and forth anymore.

Practice Tip: Leading practices in class does not count as your own daily meditation practice! After all, your main focus is on the class, so you can't attend to your own experience the way you do when you just meditate.

Dealing with Distractions

We incorporate whatever comes up in our shared experience. This includes unexpected distractions, like a cell phone suddenly going off. You would address this with something like, "Noticing how the attention gets pulled away by an unexpected sound. And maybe there is also some judgment. See how you can redirect the attention back to the breath." Addressing what's going on in the room will also help the students to feel supported. For example if a latecomer enters the room, you might say, "Being aware that the attention might go to the sounds of a class member entering the room." You would say this once during a session or as it feels appropriate.

Example. We were leading a compassionate breathing practice (see Session +2) to a group of veterans in a substance-abuse treatment program when a new member of the program entered the room. He was clearly surprised to see a large group sitting peacefully with their eyes closed, so he stood in the middle of the room and laughed. He was invited to sit down and join the group, but instead he laughed and snorted derisively, shaking his head in apparent contempt. Every eye in the room popped open, and the group was angry. The man refused to join the group, so he was politely asked to leave and join the group another time. He left the room saying, "Whatever, asshole." The class was incensed. We invited the class to close their eyes once more and just settle into this new moment, noticing whatever was present. And then we invited the class to send this person, who was clearly suffering, compassion and kindness. In moments, the class softened. The kindness was palpable. We were unaware that the veteran was disruptive in an earlier group and had talked about just coming off of a methamphetamine run. The discussion after the practice was well summed up by a veteran who shared with the group with moist eyes, "I was so pissed at him at first, I wanted to kill him. And then you asked us all to send him compassion after he insulted you. It made me realize that he's caught in his addiction just like me. And we can all use more compassion. That was powerful."

Cultural Factors

The mindfulness program offered here is non-Buddhist in nature and intended to be accessible for people from all walks of life. Facilitators are encouraged to promote access for all participants. Issues of specific language and cultural sensitivity impact the quality, utilization, and effectiveness of care. Facilitators actively promote the understanding of culturally and ethnically diverse populations related to gender, race/ethnicity, sexual orientation, religious affiliation, physical ability, gender identity, age, and other factors.

One recent, small qualitative assessment of the cultural relevance of mindfulness for African Americans suggests that inadvertent comments from a facilitator mentioning "Buddha" or "support from the universe" can be perceived as culturally and religiously incongruent and result in a rejection of the practice (Woods-Giscombé & Gaylord, 2014). We encourage facilitators to use inclusive, non-Buddhist language with the utmost of care toward cultural factors.

Facilitator Tools

When leading a group, it's helpful to have a bag with some essential teaching aids: a bell or chime, a timer, a whiteboard and markers, handouts, sign-in sheets, and anything else related to the session's theme. We have listed what you need for each of the sessions.

Scripts

We provide scripts for all of the meditations in this book. However, this teaching tool is best used *at home* while you are familiarizing yourself with the meditation and understanding how to teach it. We do not recommend you read the script in class! As we have stated previously, guiding a meditation asks you to do the practice along with your students and to guide them with *your* own moment-to-moment awareness as appropriate while including the possibilities of *their* own moment-to-moment awareness. A guided meditation script is a transcription of somebody else's moment-to-moment awareness in the past! While that person might be a very experienced teacher, and a lot of the meditation might be what she says pretty much every time, it's still her experience and her resonance *in the moment of the recording.*

Please appreciate that there is no magic in the words of the script itself. The facilitator uses his or her own sensations and kind awareness of each moment as a guide. Students easily sense the difference between mechanically reading a script and when the leader is in his or her own practice, serving as a model for how to be with each moment. Your cues provide the framework that allows each participant to be with his or her present experience without directing any specific result or "right" outcome.

Poems and Stories

Reading poems and stories is a wonderful addition to any mindfulness class. In the session outline we give some examples of poems and stories we like for that specific class theme. Poems in particular are a great bridge between verbal and nonverbal experiences and concepts. Poems are particularly good to read at the end of a meditation, when people are more receptive to really listening (with their head *and* their heart).

Teaching Tip: Start a collection of printed poems and stories that you bring to each class in a binder (or use an app on your smartphone). Choose a poem for that particular meditation before you start the class session (or, once you have more experience, before the start of the meditation) from your collection. You can transition from guidance to the poem by saying something like: "As we are coming to the end of our meditation, I want to read you a poem by…"

We love poems by Rumi, Mary Oliver, David Whyte, Hafez, and John O'Donohoe, to name just a few. In class we try to use poems and stories from different traditions and include a wide diversity of authors.

When it comes to poems, try to step it up: Learn to recite your favorite ones by heart. Practice until they live inside you.

We use stories more to emphasize a teaching point made during the didactic section of the class or to deepen the general topic of that particular class. It also can be very helpful to use a brief story as a clarifying tool when a student is struggling with something. As we point out in "Disclosure by the Facilitator," later in this chapter, a story can be one from your own personal experience.

Facilitator Steps for Working with a New Meditation

Now that we've given an overview of the basics for leading a practice, you might be wondering how to actually learn the meditation you wish to guide, especially if it is new to you. Here are rough guidelines for how to familiarize yourself with the meditation so you can guide it with confidence in the session.

1. Listen to the guided audio (available, for all formal practices, at http://www .sharingmindfulness.com) while doing the practice yourself a few times.

2. Read the script as many times as needed to become familiar with the language and rhythm. Guide yourself through the practice. Allow space. Leave at least one breath length between the sentences. Where it says "Pause," allow for a pause of 2 to 3 breaths, or about 15 seconds. If it says "Long pause," refrain from speaking for 30 seconds, or 4 to 6 breaths or more.

3. Practice with an imagined audience using the script, reading less and less of the script each time, using more and more of your own words (which, of course, can be the same words as in the script but imbued with your presence) from your own experience.

4. Practice with a willing volunteer; ask for feedback. Or record yourself (on your smartphone, for example) and be your own critic.

5. Teach your class (using the script just as a cheat sheet, maybe with some highlighted words).

Exploring Students' Experiences

Facilitators help students to explore their experience in different ways.

Small Group Check-In

Unless a class is very small, we invite students to break into groups of two to three individuals to share about their experience. The topic is usually how either the personal practice during the week went or how the just-finished group guided practice went. We announce how much time the small group has altogether or roughly per person (generally two to three minutes). It is helpful to give a two-minute warning with the bell before the time is up to make sure every participant has had his or her turn.

The small group allows each person a chance to share and to be heard, which is not always possible in the big group. Nor do all participants like to talk about their personal experience in front of the larger group. Sometimes people might express in a small group what they don't want the teacher to hear, like that they didn't practice or that they have doubts about the whole concept. This in turn can encourage other individuals to also be more "real"—which fosters the overall feeling of connection in an intimate setting.

The small group is also a place to practice mindful listening and speaking (for more, see Session 2), which is another very important mindfulness and compassion practice that can easily be translated into everyday life.

Group Process

The large-group format is used to invite a few individuals to share with everyone their experiences or what they learned. Facilitators should endeavor to be open, curious, and nonjudgmental while gathering different experiences. Don't underestimate what participants will learn from just witnessing each other share in a group format. Trained psychotherapists are cautioned not to interpret a student's experience or use this to reveal cognitive distortions.

While a discussion is happening, as facilitators we do a number of different things: We listen to the common thread in all stories from the bigger perspective of the *Three Marks of Existence*. We *reassure and normalize*, which includes sharing our own experience when it supports the learning of the class. We make sure that the *whole range of experience* is included, even its ever-changing nature. And we also use *skillful inquiry* to help participants to deepen their understanding by exploring their own experience.

Dharma Teacher Perspective: On the Three Marks of Existence

As a facilitator in a mindfulness class, you can train yourself to listen for the so-called Three Marks of Existence in the sharing of students. From a Buddhist tradition, the three marks can be summarized in the catchy phrase: "Shit happens. Everything changes. Don't take it personally." Listen for examples of:

1. *Shit happens.* Also characterized as the inherent unsatisfactoriness of life (see also Session +2). No matter how hard we try or how lucky we might be, there will always be something or somebody that causes us stress and suffering.

2. *Everything changes.* Impermanence is a fact of life. Change is the only constant.

3. *Don't take it personally.* A lot of suffering stems from our taking what happens personally. We can see it more as part of the human experience instead.

When you hear this experience coming up in class, gently and skillfully point more to the universal meaning of the story. That will also help other participants, as they can extrapolate more easily to their own experience. The more that students (and that includes us) understand the Three Marks of Existence, the less suffering there will be.

Reassure and Normalize

As people start with any new skill, but particularly something novel like meditation, they need reassurance. They want reassurance that they are going about it the correct way. Some people may be surprised to learn how undisciplined and chaotic their attention and thought content actually are; they may be surprised at the ease with which they can aim their attention on a target but shocked, even stunned, by how readily the mind flits off in another direction. Participants will ask many questions that boil down to some iteration of "Is this typical?" "Am I doing it right?" Your goal as the facilitator is to reassure and normalize.

Whole Range of Experience

Being on the lookout for a wide range of felt experiences will help all participants to feel safe and included with whatever they are experiencing. For instance, when participants share a positive experience about the practice, ask whether any participants experienced something challenging, and vice versa.

This tactic will also help to preempt cases of *good-student syndrome*. Get a sense of the student who wants to do it perfectly—the one who brings in the interesting article, tells you how his life is transformed, and insists every practice is bliss. What he may be lacking is the acknowledgment of other participants' experiences. A good facilitator will validate all experiences in the room and gently guide the enthusiastic participant to observe what his classmates are feeling. This can also aid the overeager participant to relax a little and to perhaps see what he does without the teacher having to point it out.

As a facilitator, it's important to discern between the overachieving student who needs to be encouraged to relax and fall into receptivity and the student who is hesitant and dragging her feet. The hesitant participant needs to be lovingly pushed toward her growth edge. This can be achieved by encouraging participants to ask themselves if they are trying too hard or if they are trying too little in any given moment. This is a good opportunity to introduce the concept of "wise discernment."

Teaching Tip: For wise discernment, it helps to give the classic example of tuning a lute (or any string instrument): If the strings are either too tight or too loose there will be no sound. Only if the strings are balanced just right will the lute sound beautifully.

Intellectual Questions and What's Behind Them

In class sessions we have to be very aware of intellectual questions. This can be even more challenging if you happen to know the answer. We might, with kindness, remind a participant asking an intellectualized question that we come to our own answers as our practice unfolds. We can gently deflect the answer and even check in with a participant after class to avoid chasing intellectual questions down the proverbial rabbit hole. Another strategy is to ask for more information: "I wonder what makes you ask this?" Often a question from a participant that is posed in an intellectual way, like "What's the role of rebirth in this teaching?" comes from a deeper, personal, and more emotional question. Perhaps a loved one recently died or is terminally ill. The question in this case then is not about rebirth but about grappling with loss and grief. This is very specific and can be explored deeper with curious, kind attention.

Trust Emergence

The concept of "trusting emergence" is a big topic in mindfulness circles. In the true sense, it means that a mindfulness class is "cocreated" by the teacher and students alike. This makes it hard at times to stick to your very mapped-out curriculum and timetable. Participants might share insights and challenges that are not about what you had in mind to teach that day. Your job is to discern between true, heartfelt questions that are to be expected when starting to practice and intellectual discursions. It is easy for the class to become mired in the details of a participant's story; a skilled facilitator keeps her eye on the universal theme to ensure that the experience is relatable for everyone. This is a challenge for every beginning teacher, and in particular for psychotherapists trained in the group process who are less familiar with the lens of mindfulness teachings.

Example. DaRa is sharing about her sick dog. She knows he is old and will die soon. She is agonizing over her worries when to make the decision to put him down. She knows he is suffering—and so is she. This comes up for her in every meditation, and she doesn't want to meditate any more because it's so painful.

How can you approach this? Initially you would empathize with DaRa. "Yes, that is painful." All the dog and pet lovers in the class will relate. Then from a mindfulness teacher perspective you would also see at least two other bigger-perspective topics, or *marks of existence* (see "Dharma Teacher Perspective" earlier in this chapter) at work. First: the fact that life comes with pain and unsatisfactoriness, and second: the truth of impermanence. Things change, pets or people we love will get sick and eventually die. This is painful. Of course! But neither of these truths is personal. And while we wish it wouldn't happen, it still does—and will to everybody. With mindfulness practice we learn to relate to this with more spaciousness (compared to the tightening down on our individual story) and also with more compassion: "Oh, I'm not alone in this, and this is to be expected by living a human life."

The Practice of Inquiry

Inquiry is the practice of midwifing a student's learning and deepening the understanding of the underlying principles of mindfulness. It is a specific skill of the mindfulness facilitator and used during the group process after a formal meditation practice. Inquiry done well (which takes some practice!) extends the learning of the practice for the entire group. For this the facilitator draws on his own embodiment of the practice, which is expressed through the foundational attitudes (see chapter 1) and his attunement with the individual student and the entire class.

The most basic step of inquiry is to ask (mostly after a practice or in regard to the home practice): "Who would like to share? What was that like?" The facilitator asks for a direct description of the present-moment experience. He then invites a number of different answers, allowing and encouraging the whole range of experience. It is important to not let the participants get lost in the narrative. The focus is not on "what happened" but "how did you relate to it, in regard to your mindfulness practice." Usually no other answer than a warm "Thank you" or "Thanks for sharing" is necessary. All experience is held in nonjudgmental compassion and is met with genuine curiosity. The participants learn that a) they can intentionally direct their attention to the perception of an experience, b) the full range of experience can be expected, c) somebody else might have the same or a different experience than they do, d) there is no right way to feel, and e) all of experience can be met without judgment.

This form of inquiry is predominant through the early sessions of the program. As the class progresses, the inquiry might deepen into making a connection with (unhelpful) patterns in their lives. The facilitator might often experience an internal "tug of curiosity" upon hearing the student share, which can result in the response: "That is interesting. Would you be okay to say more about this?"

This invites the student, after she has given her consent, to explore more, to feel deeper, to make new connections between points. The facilitator stays close to his own felt experience of arising sensations in the body, thoughts, and emotions as he listens (not just with his ears but with his whole body), using these sensations as guideposts for the next question.

At some point, to assess the typical reaction to the experience, the question might be: "Is this something that is familiar to you in your life?" Or if the participant reports a new response to an experience, "How is this different to how you normally react to a similar situation?"

This gentle questioning is pointing to the way the mind works in general in one's life and how suffering is created mostly in the mind, through our response to a situation. We also model for all the students in the class how they can do inquiry for themselves, without the help of a leader. Coming from a place of friendly curiosity and not knowing (and without a desired outcome) encourages the participant to explore unknown areas of his or her relationship to an experience and the effect this has on his or her health and well-being.

What Inquiry Is Not

While connecting to the class in a meaningful way is important in inquiry, it is not simply through the use of rapport-building skills such as making reflections and an inviting body posture. Inquiry is not psychotherapy, in that we are not reframing an experience, pointing out distorted thinking or cognitive distortions, offering psychoeducation, or attempting to fix something that is broken or needs healing. Inquiry is also not hierarchical from a teacher that is in the all-knowing position to a student who doesn't know. Sometimes the facilitator has a hunch, sometimes there is just the "tug of curiosity." Inquiry is inviting exploration that might—or might not—reveal something previously hidden.

Clinical Psychologist Perspective: On Inquiry

Understanding the purpose of and developing the skills to lead inquiry is one of the most challenging tasks for the mindfulness facilitator who is trained as a mental health clinician. There simply isn't a direct analog for this skill in our development as clinicians who assess, diagnose, and treat mental and behavioral health issues. Perhaps the closest example is a group relations study group. In this type of group, participants study their own behavior in real time as it relates to a group dynamic; this can produce deep revelations and aha moments about how we are in the world. This is similar to inquiry as it relates to the study of our experience in the present moment. Yet it differs in that inquiry seeks to expand our learning in the present moment as revealed through our mindfulness practice, as opposed to the study of our behavior in a group context. Through inquiry, a skilled mindfulness facilitator models a kind, open curiosity to exploring the present moment through the lens of the Three Marks of Existence (see the "Dharma Perspective" earlier in this chapter) and the foundational attitudes of the practice. Given that inquiry must happen through this lens, a facilitator must be well grounded in a personal practice and understanding of the framework to begin to learn this skill. One of the best ways to learn this, then, is to continue with your personal practice and observe a senior teacher in a sitting group who is skilled with inquiry. Be patient! This skill can take years to develop.

Dealing with Backdraft

"Backdraft" is a term borrowed from the firefighting world, first used in the mindfulness context by psychologist and mindfulness teacher Christopher Germer (2009). In an enclosed space, fire can consume much of the available oxygen. A firefighter knows to be cautious and check each door before she opens it, since adding oxygen can create an explosion very different than what is intended. Our practice at times can be just like that. An attempt to find attentional stability and calm can result in the backdraft of restlessness and confusion; trying to extend loving-kindness to yourself can produce feelings quite different than kindness; and trying to warm up your practice with compassion can sometimes result in its opposites, indifference and contempt.

When a participant mentions a difficult experience or practice that is not what was intended, provide reassurance and normalize. This is common. In our practice we can try to send attention and particular feelings into some closed, hardened places. And just as the fire flares up with fresh oxygen, our emotions can flare up with the fresh attention. Advise participants to stay with the emotion unless it feels too overwhelming—in which case they can back off and return later. We like the image of "dipping your toe in." And then maybe the whole foot next time. Throughout, participants can reconnect to their intentions, and let these emotions or thoughts be just as they are as they continue the practice.

When Practice Feels Like It's Getting Worse

In the beginning, for some participants, meditation can feel like it's getting worse before it gets better. Why is that? (This is a good question to ask your group.) It is because you start paying attention to your inner process, and because of this "stuff might come up." These are issues that have been in the background but may not have been fully acknowledged or processed, or may have been suppressed.

> **Example.** Jack, whose wife had died two years earlier, shared with us that a "warning" helped him to keep going with the class. The quiet time with himself in meditation brought up strong waves of grief, which he hadn't really experienced before: "I thought I had grieved her, but now I realize that I only worked through her death intellectually. I hadn't expected those heartbreaking emotions to come up while I took the class. I took up your recommendation to also work with a therapist while taking the class, and I just kept showing up moment after moment for what was there. The waves have calmed down some now, and I'm very happy to report that I now even experience moments of joy again. I realized before I was just numb."

A metaphor we sometimes use to describe this experience of things perhaps getting worse before they get better is the silt in a lake. In the beginning, you don't see anything at all, as the waters of the lake are opaque. As you move into the beginning phase of your practice, the silt begins to settle. This can be exciting, but you can also start to see what lies under the surface. Perhaps you see things down in the lake that you didn't expect, like a few old tires and an old wrecked car. Of course those things were there all along. Our practice is just like this: as things start to settle we can begin to see what has really been there all along.

Disclosure by the Facilitator

Self-disclosure is the act of revealing more about oneself to another. It can be a conscious or unconscious process. An intentional, clinically targeted therapist disclosure can be both therapeutic and deepen rapport. However, as we have said, a mindfulness group is not psychotherapy. Psychotherapists trained to monitor their disclosures may need an adjustment when leading a class. Effective mindfulness facilitators fully embody the practice and serve as a model, showing how one can turn toward that which is difficult in their own lives with clarity and compassion.

What you disclose as a facilitator to a mindfulness group is of much importance. Foremost, it should facilitate the teaching process. If you feel the need to disclose, it should exemplify the universality of the human experience. Disclosures may demonstrate how you can turn toward each experience in your life, or how an open, kind, and curious attitude will often shift the way you perceive the moment or event in your life. Such personal disclosures demonstrate that you are just as human as everybody else in class.

As an example, in response to a participant's expression of incapacitating worry, a facilitator might intentionally disclose: "Knowing our own habit of mind and how to work with it is a central lesson of our practice. For myself, I have the habit of slipping into 'planning mind.' I start rehearsing the future and chewing on what appointments I have next, what I'm doing after work, what food is in the fridge or whether I have to shop, what I will do on the weekend, where my kids will go to college, and so on. It's an endless proliferation of plans that doesn't actually help me prepare for anything. But what do I miss? Being fully in my life and connecting with this moment; the only moment in which I am actually living. We can spend so much time planning that we forget about actually living! But just like our formal practice, I have learned to come back to this moment. Back to my life. To be fully here with the richness of living. And I've learned I don't want to miss it."

As with all disclosure, it is important to use material that the participants in the class can relate to. For instance, don't use an example from living in a college dorm if most individuals in your class don't have a college education. Disclosures should be intentional, universally relatable, and delivered not with harsh judgment but kindness and humor.

Participants are also very interested in and inspired by before-and-after stories. Like, "I used to get so angry and worked up in traffic, but after several years I actually learned to see how each driver is lost in his own story, his own autopilot. I now can even wish him well—a possibility I would have scoffed at before."

Disclosure on the facilitator's part often helps to diminish inaccurate projections on the facilitator and to keep the feeling in the class more real.

Disclosure can also be used to make a teaching point, just like telling a story. For example, we have a teacher colleague who recently shared with her class how she used mindful awareness in her own life. Her dearest friend received a difficult cancer diagnosis and asked her to come to chemotherapy with her. The teacher noticed she was filled with concern and fear for her friend, and dread about how grim and terrible the chemo might be. Yet as she kept herself open to the actual experiences of the moment, she quickly noticed how truly wonderful the community of patients receiving chemo in the clinic actually was. There was so much hope, goodwill, and a deep sense of compassion in the room—a palpable sense of healing. There was a felt sense of *we are in this together*. Our friend's willingness to meet each moment with spaciousness and kindness allowed her to hold all of it—a fear of loss and a sense of hope—with grace. This is a vibrant, real example of embodying the practice and being with life just as it is, and also a good reminder that, if we are open to suspending our expectations, we might be pleasantly surprised by the outcome.

Teaching Tip: You don't want the group to have a sense of burden from your disclosure, or a need to care for you to help you through. You are there for them—not the other way around. If something is too fresh or raw and not yet metabolized, keep it under wraps if that is possible, and if necessary get help outside the group.

FAQs from New Participants

We hope beginning students feel that the group is safe and spacious enough to ask lots of questions. Here's a list of the questions we hear most frequently and how we answer them.

How can I practice when there's too much noise in my apartment...when my dog barks constantly...when my neighbor is too loud? Rule of thumb: If you can easily change it, by all means do. There is no need to make it extra challenging for you. But if you can't: Practice with it. Where do we get the idea that the setting has to be ideal for us to practice? There will be many moments in life when you can't get it the way you want. And how does your mind respond to it? A noisy environment can be a very fruitful place to practice. We can hear sound as noise or the same sound as sound. Same sound, very different experience. Which one provides a sense of freedom?

My mind is all over the place. It bounces around so much. How can I meditate? Is there an expectation here? Or striving? Some days our minds bounce around more than others. That is the mind's nature. Fall into receptivity and see how it is in each moment. If we want our practice to be a particular way or expect a particular outcome, such as a calm mind, we will usually end up disappointed. Expectations keep us from actually seeing what is really here in this moment. Meditation teacher Joseph Goldstein calls it the "in-order-to mind." Paradoxically the mind will often calm down once we have truly accepted how restless or bouncy it is.

I fall asleep all the time. Is that normal? Could it be that you're tired? When we start a mindfulness practice, we frequently notice how tired we are. Many of us in this modern world live in constant sleep debt. So when we get off the treadmill of life for a moment, when we stop trying so hard for a moment, we fall asleep. The obvious answer is to get more sleep! But this isn't always possible. But there are some tips we can use to help us to *fall awake* to the richness of this moment. When you are aware that you're sleepy, try keeping your eyes open just a bit to allow a sliver of light in. Consider increasing the lighting in the room. If you are lying down, try your practice sitting up. If you are sitting and still feel sleepy, try a standing meditation. Or slide forward a bit in the chair to pull your back away from the backrest. Consider a brief break; walk around and stretch a bit before trying again. If you are a regular coffee or tea drinker, maybe you won't be able to practice until you've had your first cup.

The moment I start practicing all I notice is my pain. Why would I want to do that? This is a common experience not only for chronic pain patients but for others as well. As the distractions fall away the volume is turned up on all internal experience. In mindfulness our approach to pain is different. The practice invites us to look more closely, to be more discerning. What else is there, other than the pain? Which parts of your body are not in pain? How much of your body is in pain? Can you allow the pain to be there—just for this moment? It already is here, and tensing up against it does...what...to your experience of the pain? Is the pain really there every single moment? These questions can only be answered when we look with care and kindness at our experience over and over again. (This question needs to be explored more deeply with the student over time as her practice develops. We start with normalizing, reassurance, and developing kindness and curiosity toward our experience.)

I have too much to do! How do I find the time to practice? In the beginning adding a daily mindfulness practice often feels like a chore. Yet another thing to do on your seemingly endless to-do list. *So don't try to fit it in, build it in.* A practice needs commitment, discipline, and an intention to take some time just for ourselves. It can be helpful to commit to practicing for the duration of the program, or six weeks, suspending all expectations as you do. Then assess where you are after six weeks. Growth is not linear, so we often can't see how we change from inside an unfolding process.

Often students will notice that a regular meditation practice actually *saves* time. It's very simple: taking restorative breaks during the day makes us more effective at our daily tasks.

I have been so emotional since I started meditating. What's wrong with me? This is very common. As we slow down in our mindfulness practice and turn toward our experience, strong emotions or even mood swings can occur. This will settle down over time.

I have very vivid dreams since I started meditating. Is that normal? Yes, this is similar to the previous question. This new, friendly attention to our experience can stir up emotions, and that can come out in vivid dreams. Stay with it and see how this unfolds.

I had this cool meditation where everything was bathed in white light...there were flashes of colors...I heard the angels singing. How come it doesn't happen every time now? It sounds like you had a very pleasant meditation. This is great. But it sounds like now your mind probably wants it again. Is this causing disappointment when it doesn't happen? Are you trying to make it happen again? Do you think that this is what meditation should feel like, if "done right"? How does that feel in the body or the mind?

I can't seem to connect with the breath. What's wrong? This happens sometimes, don't worry about it. You can either simply give it some more time or you can use another object for your attention, like sounds or the sensations in your hands. Try different ways and see what works.

I get very spacey when I meditate, almost like I'm drugged. What's that about? This is another common experience for new meditators. As we are new to the practice we can flip-flop between being very tense to being spaced out. It might feel like a drug-induced or hypnagogic state, the transitional stage between wakefulness and sleep. Keep at your practice. As it develops, and as your nervous system steps down into a familiar pattern of parasympathetic activity, this likely won't feel like such a stupor.

I'm not asleep, but I'm not really awake really. I'm kind of floating somewhere. Is that normal? It is very common to have these states in the beginning. They are similar to the hypnagogic states we have right before falling asleep. Don't make anything out of them—they will change.

You say this isn't about relaxation, but is that right? Isn't this just relaxation and the benefits that come with it? Don't confuse one possible *result*, a deep sense of peace and relaxation, with the *purpose* of the practice. The purpose of our practice is to be fully in our lives and to meet each moment with kindness and discernment. When we disengage from rumination and worry, we might find we become relaxed. We can also notice annoyance, confusion, joy, and a near infinite number of other states. And the benefits of mindfulness go beyond the benefits of relaxation alone. In an experiment comparing mindfulness and relaxation, researchers randomly assigned participants to either a one-month mindfulness training, relaxation training, or a control group (Jain et al., 2007). Both the mindfulness group and the relaxation training group increased positive mood states compared to the control group. But the mindfulness group alone showed decreases in distractions and ruminative thoughts, suggesting that this is a unique mechanism for how mindfulness reduces distress.

Summary

We hope that this hands-on chapter on how to guide meditations, including a list of the most commonly asked questions, gives you the confidence and the means to get started to teach. Leading a mindfulness practice can be more complicated than first expected. It might feel a little overwhelming, but with practice your skills as a facilitator will steadily develop.

CHAPTER 5

Launching a Mindfulness Program

I am not afraid of storms, for I am learning to sail my ship.
—Louisa May Alcott

We now turn toward some of the nuts-and-bolts issues in starting a mindfulness program. This chapter includes capturing referrals and describing mindfulness to provider colleagues, establishing the group setting, deciding on an open or closed enrollment format, setting safety and emergency procedures for diverse populations, and how to maximize on the specific clinical skills of the facilitator by integrating mindfulness into particular population settings. We close the chapter by addressing some of the common pitfalls psychotherapists face when they teach mindfulness. We also include a caution for facilitators who are not trained clinicians.

Recruiting Participants

The benefits of mindfulness are literally everywhere lately, and this can make recruitment and referrals much easier. Some of your potential referral sources may already be interested or, better yet, may already be mindfulness practitioners themselves. So how do you find out? Ask around your particular setting. But first do just a bit of homework by identifying the type of setting and then finding relevant literature for that population. Examples of clinical settings include outpatient mental health clinics, residential settings such as substance abuse treatment programs, and oncology centers, among many. Nonclinical settings include education venues, business organizations, and community centers. We have provided a partial list of useful research in chapter 2. It is always helpful to have some of the research handy when starting a new program. You might not need it, but an article about the benefits of mindfulness in your particular setting can help to win over someone who might be uncertain about sending you referrals.

The next step is to assess knowledge and interest. Perhaps, in your particular setting, your colleagues are already excited and interested for the group to begin and might already have a list of potential participants. If this is the case, you may want to skip the next few sections and proceed immediately to the "Class Setting" section. If you discover limited knowledge of and interest in mindfulness, don't despair! This is a great opportunity for an in-service training.

In-Service Trainings for Staff

A great way to recruit participants is to hold an in-service training among your peers or the clinicians or administration of the population you wish to serve. There are a variety of staff-training approaches to introduce providers to mindfulness in order to develop or initiate a mindfulness program. These trainings can range from extensive skill development for continuing education at national conferences to something as simple as joining a small treatment team for five minutes at a daily huddle. Most important, the training you offer should be appropriate for your level of skill and experience. We have been involved with the dissemination of mindfulness at VA hospitals and clinics, university hospital settings, and community and business settings, and we have used many approaches: brief team huddles, department-level meetings, grand rounds, the annual medical staff meeting, and national conferences. In community settings, wider implementation may be preceded by an in-service training to the organization's leadership.

No matter the format, as a general rule mindfulness is best explained through *experiential learning* rather than only through a cognitive process. We want providers to have not only an intellectual understanding but also a *felt sense* of the practice. A typical twenty- to thirty-minute staff in-service training might include a number of elements such as a brief definition of mindfulness, a short introductory practice, a brief review of relevant research, an immediately usable self-care practice, and some questions and answers. We have included a typical clinical staff in-service outline on the website associated with this book (http://www.sharingmindfulness.com).

An in-service training is also an opportunity to share with clinical colleagues the impact mindfulness can have in their own lives. These benefits relate to both care delivery and burnout prevention and job satisfaction. In one recent study, primary care providers with high levels of mindfulness scored higher on patient-centered communication, used a more positive emotional tone with patients, and received higher overall patient satisfaction scores (Beach et al., 2013). In another study, physicians who were taught a modified mindfulness program of only eighteen hours showed reductions in burnout, depression, anxiety, and stress as well as an increase in their sense of personal accomplishment. These changes persisted at nine months post-intervention (Fortney, Lucherhand, Zakletskaia, Zaierska, & Rakel, 2013). So an in-service training is an opportunity to share mindfulness with clinicians, and this can not only impact patient care directly through referrals but can positively impact the provider's experience as well.

Self-Referrals

Another strategy to building a mindfulness program is through direct requests from potential clients. Many of the participants in our classes are self-referred. Sometimes they are seeking a mindfulness class or any mind-body intervention, and sometimes they just happen upon a flyer we have out in the waiting room.

Direct engagement with potential clients in health care settings is not only an effective approach to marketing and populating the class, it can also provide consumer-driven feedback for clinicians who might not typically consider referrals to a mindfulness program.

Finding a Classroom

When looking for a suitable room in which to teach, consider the following questions:

Do you need an area for walking meditation?

Do you plan to do mindful movement?

Do you need equipment other than chairs?

Is the room easily accessible for your group (consider parking, stairs, wheelchair accessibility, etc.)?

Deciding on Open or Closed Groups

Many of the well-known mindfulness-based approaches such as MBSR, MBCT, and MSC are designed around a closed-group model. In this model, all the participants join the group at the first session and complete the entire course together. There are many benefits to this approach. Each class can build upon the previous teachings and, as the practice capacity of each person increases, adjustments can be made to deepen the instruction. For example, the teacher can titrate the cues to create more support or more spaciousness as needed. By the end of the class, there is a real sense of group accomplishment and the creation of a regular meditation practice. In these closed groups, participants have an opportunity to see one another grow and may even develop a sense of support and belonging in the class.

The closed-group format can be deeply rewarding for the facilitator and the participants. Yet this type of class is sometimes problematic for participants for two reasons. First, some clients are not yet ready for the level of commitment required of these programs. Most are eight weeks in length, two to two-and-a-half hours each session, and require at-home practice of thirty to forty-five minutes each day.

The second reason is that the closed format may not work for your setting. An introductory-level mindfulness class has the potential to benefit many people. We work in settings such as inpatient hospital wards, intensive outpatient programs, nursing homes, homeless programs, and other settings that have a constant flow of patients who are admitted and discharged each day. It is simply impossible to bring intensive-level, closed-format classes such as MBSR into some of these environments.

We have designed the Introduction to Mindfulness sequence presented in this book to be offered in a closed-group format. Yet we encourage facilitators to adapt the program as needed in specific settings to an open- or rolling-enrollment format. For conceptual clarity, presenting the information in a closed-group format is more straightforward.

If you adapt our program to an open format, you will need to adjust the times to include a brief introduction to the overall concepts of mindfulness and an introduction to the group for any newcomers at each session. This may sound a bit complicated, but don't lose heart. For about a decade, we have been teaching an open-group version of the Introduction to Mindfulness program at the VA with patients from all phases of substance use disorder treatment. It's just a matter of making the teachings at each session flexible and accommodating a newcomer while also providing something new to returning patients.

Teaching Tip: To scale our program to an open-group format, consider spending more time on introductions and basic definitions each week, though this may result in having time to lead only one formal practice.

Selecting and Excluding Participants

The task of client selection, and matching appropriate selection and exclusion criteria for a particular setting, is an essential one for a mindfulness teacher. Rather than trying to list all those to be included, it is perhaps easier to determine which clients are to be *excluded* from the group and accept all others. For traditional group psychotherapy, there is considerable consensus that certain clients are poor candidates, including those who are acutely psychotic, brain damaged, paranoid, sociopathic, or actively addicted to drugs or alcohol (Yalom, 2005).

But there is not yet consensus on mindfulness group exclusion criteria because so many different populations have been shown to benefit. With appropriate modifications, we have also taught mindfulness to homogeneous groups of those with serious mental illness including active psychosis and paranoia, individuals with histories of incarceration and an antisocial personality disorder diagnosis, and those with mild to moderate traumatic brain injury. Perhaps the first step in determining exclusion criteria is determining the location of the group and what types of diagnostic presentations are appropriate for that setting. A stand-alone mindfulness group for those actively using drugs of abuse is likely problematic. The approach simply doesn't fit the treatment need. But a mindfulness group embedded within a substance abuse disorder treatment program offering harm-reduction treatment and motivational enhancement can be a useful adjunct to care.

One potential exclusion criterion is any specific pathology that would make group participation either too disruptive or dangerous for other participants. Another factor to consider is the seriousness of the disorder or impairment. A certain level of "matching" can be helpful in building the group dynamic while still creating a heterogeneous group. For example, a group of highly functioning professionals with reports of stress and no more than moderate levels of mood symptoms may fit very well together in an outpatient clinic or private-practice setting. The same can be said for a group whose members all have histories of suicide attempt and self-injurious behaviors treated together in an intensive outpatient or residential setting.

Teaching Tip: The mindfulness teacher is well served by carefully considering the treatment setting, her own individual skills and experience, and the range or scope of disorders before establishing a group's particular exclusion criteria.

Safety and Emergency Procedures

Procedures should be established in advance to ensure both clinician and patient safety during any mindfulness class. These include preestablished procedures for both mental health and medical emergencies. In nonclinical settings, such as education and work environments, having access to a cell phone to call for support is likely sufficient. Leading groups in clinical settings with medically and psychiatrically compromised participants will require more thoughtful procedures. In the following section, we will review some of the specific populations that might benefit from mindfulness taught in a clinical setting. Many of these patients would be excluded as not appropriate for a community-based mindfulness group. Given that the population of a clinic-sponsored group is sometimes very different from that of a community group, this can alter the risk profile.

As a safety issue, consider the available support when starting a group. We frequently teach these classes alone with no other facilitators present. This is possible in a clinical setting only when there is backup clinical support immediately adjacent to the group. Any after-hours group in outpatient settings should only be taught with a co-facilitator when working with clinical populations.

In each specific clinical setting, review the procedures for mental health and medical emergencies as well as security issues. Mindfulness groups are generally well tolerated and low risk but, like groups organized around any clinical activity, are not risk free. Patients with histories of trauma, high levels of anxiety, reactivity, poor frustration tolerance, and a history of abreaction or dissociation may need some modifications such as instructions to keep their eyes open a bit during a practice. These are also some of the patients who might benefit the most from learning to bring kind awareness to the present moment. Clinicians are well served using their clinical judgment to scale the class and practice length into a tolerable format for specific populations. For example, a group in an inpatient unit might be just thirty minutes long and include one practice of ten minutes in length.

Nonclinicians, or clinicians who are not trained in mental health, will want to limit their mindfulness groups to psychiatrically stable populations.

Clinic-Based Mindfulness Groups

Mindfulness has been taught quite literally for millenia in a religious context and only very recently as a nonreligious practice. It's now rapidly expanding into clinical settings. This presents an opportunity to bring mindfulness to populations who might be excluded from a community-based group. With the appropriate skills and clinical resources, mindfulness groups in a clinic or hospital context may include those with a wide variety of disorders and clinical presentations. This is an opportunity for clinicians, who have specific skills with target populations, to capitalize on these skills. In a sense, by combining clinical skills and the teachings available from mindfulness we can offer the best of both worlds. This can be an opportunity to offer healing from human suffering that might not otherwise be accessible.

Specific Populations

We turn now to a brief list of specific populations that can be effectively taught mindfulness in a clinic but are considered inappropriate for teaching in a community-based setting. It is assumed that each clinical setting has the needed resources to effectively manage and treat these populations. Some smaller clinical settings will not have the resources or experience with some populations and should refer as appropriate. Those not trained to treat mental disorders should not be teaching mindfulness to clinical populations. We expect clinicians will have all the specific skills and experience needed to work with populations that would be excluded from participation in a community-based mindfulness group.

Suicidality and Self-Injurious Behavior. Mindfulness is one of the core skills in dialectical behavior therapy (Linehan, 1993). The Introduction to Mindfulness format presented in the following chapters is far more extensive than the basic description included in the dialectical behavior therapy (DBT) workbook. Clinicians with the skills to manage the parasuicidal behaviors and intense affective dysregulation can easily incorporate a mindfulness group into care. In most research studies of mindfulness, suicidal ideation is an exclusion criterion. Yet in our clinical setting, we take nearly all comers, and as a result, about a quarter of our patients endorse active suicidal ideation. A mindfulness intervention is effective at significantly reducing suicidal ideation (Serpa et al., 2014).

Severe Depression. Many clinical settings provide care for patients with a moderate to severe level of depression. This care can include medication management, cognitive behavioral therapy in either individual or group format, and case management. It can be challenging to engage the most severely, acutely depressed patients. But we have found that the behavioral activation needed to attend the class is itself a powerful intervention as part of an overall treatment approach.

Inpatient Psychiatric Hospitalization. Mindfulness training is an evidenced-based practice for affective disorders. Yet with the typical length of stay on an inpatient unit measured in days, a more intensive approach such as MBCT is not possible. The introductory sequence described here can be further simplified to include the first three sessions that can be repeated in a daily group. Introducing mindfulness in these settings can facilitate psychiatric stabilization. We well remember the surprise from the inpatient nursing staff when a patient, nonverbal for more than a week, started speaking after just one brief thirty-minute introductory class. We taught the concept of bringing kind awareness to the "noise in our heads." After class he said, "All this noise, I can let it be."

Aggression and Assaultive Behavior. Learning the critical skill of creating a bit of spaciousness between stimulus and response can be life-changing for patients. We have used mindfulness with great success as an optional (and voluntary) supplement in a court-mandated program for perpetrators of domestic violence. Clients have found this to be very empowering, as this opens up the possibility of other behavioral options to aggression.

Thought Disorder Spectrum Illness. Psychosis has long been an exclusion criterion for mindfulness groups not only in the community but in the clinical setting as well. But research (Abba, Chadwick, & Stevenson, 2008) suggests mindfulness training is effective at managing negative symptoms by teaching the skill of allowing things to be as they are and by reclaiming power through acceptance of the self. A recent review of seven random controlled studies (Khoury, Lecomte, Gaudiano, & Paquin, 2013) found significant reductions in negative symptoms (flat affect, lack of pleasure, and limited speech) and hospital readmissions.

Active Drug or Alcohol Abuse and Detoxification. Those seeking recovery have used mindfulness approaches, including mindfulness-based relapse prevention, or MBRP, widely. Individuals doing Twelve Step work may refer to mindfulness as Step 11 work: "We sought through prayer and meditation to improve our conscious contact with God as we understand him." Ours is a nonreligious approach, but it has space for inquiry into the mysteries of life and death. One's gentle, kind awareness to the present moment can help diminish the fervent desire to use through compassionate "surfing of urges" as they wax and wane. In our experience, mindfulness is not limited to only the maintenance or relapse-prevention phase of care but across the treatment spectrum. Consider using mindfulness as part of an engagement strategy for those in the contemplative stage of change, in a harm-reduction program, or in a motivational enhancement group. By modifying the Introduction to Mindfulness sequence to include shorter practices and only the introductory classes, it can also be effective with patients in active alcohol or opiate medical detoxification programs.

Traumatic Stress Disorder. Mindfulness may be helpful for the mood compo-
nent of PTSD as well as the avoidance and hyperarousal symptoms (VA National
Center for PTSD, 2013). Ongoing research continues to examine the role of mindfulness in the treatment of PTSD as well as the integration mindfulness training with
exposure treatments. In a recent randomized study, a mindfulness intervention was
found to decrease PTSD symptom scores as well as normalize the neuroendocrine
markers that distinguish PTSD from other mental disorders (Kim et al., 2013).
Clinical trials for treating PTSD with mindfulness as well as combining mindfulness
with exposure modalities are currently under way.

Community-Based Groups

Clinicians and nonclinicians alike can typically assume a certain amount of medical
and psychiatric stability in the participants who are joining a community-based
group. Someone who is enrolled in an academic program, or participating regularly in
a spiritual community or anywhere else a community group is held, hopefully has
sufficient internal resources to tolerate listening closely to his or her internal experience. Mindfulness groups are low risk, and there are likely to be few problems for
those who meaningfully engage in the community and work settings. There are, of
course, exceptions and surprises—so be prepared. On rare occasions, it may be necessary for the facilitator to request that a participant withdraw from a community-
based group.

Common Psychotherapist Pitfalls

While certainly not a requirement, many who are drawn to become mindfulness
facilitators are trained psychotherapists. And many of the skills of psychotherapy,
such as managing the group dynamic and building rapport, are assuredly useful in
facilitating a mindfulness group. But a number of specific skills of psychotherapy can
cause *interference* with skillful mindfulness group facilitation—where old learning, in
this case psychotherapy skills, interferes with the acquisition of new learning. We
review here a few of the common pitfalls for mindfulness facilitators who are also
psychotherapists.

Lack of embodiment. A skilled mindfulness facilitator will embody kindness, acceptance, and courage to face whatever the present moment brings, drawing from her
own ongoing mindfulness practice (see also chapter 3).

Confusion around appropriate disclosure. Sometimes a therapist has too-rigid
boundaries or a policy of minimal personal disclosure (see "Disclosure by the
Facilitator" in chapter 4). In some psychotherapeutic approaches, clinicians may carefully attend to disclosure and boundary issues to maximize the opportunity to observe

any projection or transference phenomena. Some psychotherapists have been trained to have a more neutral stance in their work—to observe their own internal phenomena as part of the work of psychotherapy. A mindfulness facilitator, on the other hand, models full engagement with his or her own life. Each experience is met in the moment with kindness, and this is all embodied for the class to see.

Hierarchical framework. Another common pitfall for psychotherapists is the perception of a hierarchy when facilitating a mindfulness group. In many psychotherapy models, the therapist holds the expertise or specific knowledge that creates a gradient in the relationship. (Admittedly, in many psychotherapy models, this is specifically not the case.) A mindfulness facilitator is as human as everyone else. We work with our own painful physical sensations and difficult emotions just like everyone else. We teach from a stance of owning our humanity fully—particularly our challenging parts—and modeling how to do this with kindness. The saying in mindfulness is to be a "guide on the side, not a sage on the stage."

Confusing group practice with group process. Psychotherapists starting as mindfulness facilitators can inadvertently turn a mindfulness practice group into a group process. It is understandable that you are drawn to facilitating a mindfulness group since you are passionate about the practice yourself. When group members become passionate about it as well, it is easy for the group to veer into sharing experiences about the practice and how it is changing their lives. Some group process is helpful to normalize the experiences of learning mindfulness. But a skilled mindfulness facilitator allows the practice to be the teacher and doesn't allow the group to be hijacked by excessive process, however interesting.

Interpreting a participant's experience. Another related pitfall for psychotherapists is interpreting or commenting on each experience a student shares. The goal here is not to "make that which is unconscious, conscious," nor is it to elucidate and explain every experience. It is always a good habit to allow the learning to unfold and, again, let the practice be the teacher. Many comments from students don't need to be reframed or expanded upon. Provide support and understanding. That's enough.

Being too "shallow" while leading a formal practice. Another pitfall is leading a practice from a script rather than from within your own present-moment experience. This is what we call being too "shallow" in your practice and not deep enough in your own experience. The words alone are insufficient to lead a practice. It is the facilitator's felt sense of the practice that is conveyed from the "middle" of his or her practice. See "Offer Cues from the Middle of Your Own Practice" in chapter 4.

These psychotherapist pitfalls may seem daunting for the beginning mindfulness facilitator, but keep in mind that a psychotherapist also has many skills that will serve him or her well. Clinicians who provide both psychotherapy and mindfulness facilitation in the beginning might need to consciously shift from the therapist role to that of the mindfulness facilitator as appropriate.

Summary

Launching a mindfulness program takes a bit of planning. Exploring potential referral sources, developing an appropriate setting in terms of space needs, and deciding upon the specific population and any exclusion criteria can help smooth the way in advance. If you are a psychotherapist, be on the lookout for the common pitfalls psychotherapists face when beginning to teach mindfulness. Most of all, trust your instinct when leading a group.

PART III

Introduction to Mindfulness: The Core Program

In this section we move into the core program of the six-week-long Introduction to Mindfulness class. It's helpful to keep the *what*, *why*, and *how* for each class in mind: *what* we are introducing each week, *why* it is relevant for our participants, and *how* they do it.

Each session will include:

- Learning objectives

- A complete class outline

- A list of all needed materials

- Didactic teaching tools such as stories or poems

- Scripts for the introduced meditation (for your initial training)

- Common questions and responses

- Specific perspectives from the Dharma teacher and the clinical psychologist (where applicable)

- Suggested handouts and worksheets and audio links

How to Use This Part of the Book

We recommend that you start by reading through all six sessions ahead of time and then go back to the material week by week. This way you have a sense of where it is all leading; you also can familiarize yourself with the areas that are new to you.

Each class is ninety minutes long. We give you the curriculum week by week, broken down for a ninety-minute class. These estimates are very helpful for the new teacher. We suggest that you place a clock with the time clearly visible on the floor in front of you, along with your bell or chimes, and maybe this book opened to the page with the session outline.

This entire sequence is designed for a closed-enrollment group. If you are facilitating an open- or revolving-enrollment group, you will need to adjust the times accordingly, as introductions and a brief orientation to the class will be needed whenever there are new participants starting the class.

Bells or chimes. If you use a bell, explain its use to the class before the first guided meditation: "At the end of each exercise or meditation I will strike this bell. So when you hear it that means that our meditation is over. It also is a signal to again be in a new moment when a formal practice has ended."

Teaching Tip: Practice ringing the bell before you use it in class.

Scripts. Please work with a new meditation according to the guidelines described in "Facilitator Steps for Working with a New Meditation" in chapter 4. Remember to allow sufficient space (pauses) during the meditation. Leave at least 1 breath length between the sentences. Where it says "Pause," allow for a pause of 2 to 3 breaths, or about 15 seconds. If it says "Long Pause," refrain from speaking for 30 seconds, or 4 to 6 breaths or more. These are just rough guidelines; you will find your own rhythm soon.

Teaching Tip: Make sure you have practiced the guided meditations yourself and have practiced leading them a number of times *without* a script (see chapter 4 on this). It is okay to use a "cheat sheet" with notes or clues, but it's crucial that you lead the practice from your own experience. Don't actually read the scripts in the group session.

Handouts. Depending on your participant population and setting, you may want to provide written summaries of the individual sessions. These can be distributed as hard-copy handouts, posted on a website, or sent via e-mail.

Poem. At the end of the class, we like to read or recite a poem that has to do with the theme of the class. Your students are in a more open and receptive place at the close of the session and are more likely to receive the poem not just intellectually. Note that the poems provided are just suggestions, a starting point.

Story. Telling a story is a suggestion to reinforce the session's topic or theme. This can be done in different places throughout the class. It can open the didactic portion for example, or close the class at the end, like a take-home message.

E-mail communications. Again, depending on your participants and their access to the Internet, it can be very helpful to ask for e-mail addresses at the first session as part of the sign-in process. After each class, you can send a reminder to practice at home. For more vulnerable populations, it may not be clinically appropriate to communicate via e-mail. Facilitators should consider the setting and any specific procedures for handling expressions of suicidal ideation and acute distress.

SESSION 1

Introduction to Mindfulness

In the first session, we make introductions and establish group rules to create safety in the group. We define mindfulness (*what*) and give the class a firsthand experience of different mindfulness practices (*how*). We tie it into how this is relevant to their everyday life (*why*). We emphasize the importance of daily practice between classes.

OBJECTIVES OF SESSION 1

- Set ground rules and create a safe space for the class.

- Define "mindfulness" and it's relationship to kindness and compassion.

- Introduce three mindfulness practices: Grounding, Mindful Eating, and Body Scan.

- Give class participants a first experience of mindfulness in action and the power of being in the present moment.

- Define "formal" and "informal" practices.

Session 1 Outline

Time (in minutes)	Cumulative Time	Activity
5	5	Welcome
5	10	**Grounding Meditation**
10	20	Class Overview: Logistics, rules for the group, and expectations or reassurance
10	30	Participant Introductions
10	40	Theme: What Is Mindfulness?
5	45	**Mindful Eating: Raisin Exercise**
10	55	Processing the Mindful Eating Exercise
5	60	Introduction to Body Scan
15	75	**Body Scan**
5	80	Group Process
10	90	Wrap-Up and Homework: (5-minute Grounding Meditation or 15-minute Body Scan)

Materials. Roster, sign-in sheet, bell or chimes, raisins (in individual small boxes or 2 to 3 small bowls with a spoon), yoga mats if people can lie down for the Body Scan, and handouts if you have planned something to share

Poem. "The Journey" by Mary Oliver or "Your history is here inside your body" by Martha Elliot

Story. "Upstream, Downstream," a classic public health tale that applies to mindfulness

Once there was a village at the banks of a big, strong river. One day a villager saw a person crying for help being carried down the river. The villager, who was a strong swimmer, jumped in and pulled the drowning person ashore. Briefly afterward, another person was carried downstream, and then another, and another. The villager called his friends for help and they all came and helped. They got really busy and exhausted by more and more people in high distress in the river, and then fighting for their lives to save others in the currents day after day. So the villagers invented a net that was cast across the river so it would catch people. They built shelters and clinics for the people whose lives they had saved...

You might want to stop the story at this point to get the class involved. Ask, "What is it the villagers are missing?... They miss finding out why people are falling into the river upstream in the first place!... How does that relate to what we are doing here?... We have tried to fix our own 'downstream' long enough. Now we are willing to start the journey to find out what's happening upstream of our own lives."

Welcome (5 MINUTES)

As we welcome people into our class we congratulate them on taking this step. Depending on the circumstances of your group, participants might have hesitated for a long time, not sure if it's the right thing. We commend them for wanting to make the time to take better care of themselves and for committing to look at the stressors in their lives through a different lens. We congratulate them on deciding to do something that nobody else can do for them: become an active participant on the path of their own growth and healing.

Most participants will have tried "what is out there" to get a grip on the reasons that bring them to class. This might include all kinds of different therapies and medical procedures for chronic pain or diseases, or take the less skillful form of too much alcohol, prescription medication, work, food, or sex. Many will have achieved respite for a little while and are now hoping for something longer lasting, something that better aligns with their own inner capacity for wholeness and well-being.

Grounding Meditation (5 MINUTES)

After a brief welcome, it's important to get the class settled by leading them through a brief and simple grounding exercise. This helps the participants to arrive at the present moment. "Let's jump right in and actually do a short guided mindfulness exercise to get us out of our heads and into the body." If you use a bell, consider explaining its use ahead of time.

GROUNDING SCRIPT

Let's start with a short mindfulness practice that helps us to bring us here, into our body, in this moment. We call it a Grounding Meditation.

This won't be long, just about 5 minutes.

Finding a comfortable posture, with both feet on the floor.

Allowing the eyes to close gently if that feels okay, or just lowering your gaze.

Now bringing attention into the areas of contact that your feet are having with the floor. Feeling into your feet.

Noticing the solidity of the ground under your feet.

Maybe feeling where your shoes are in contact with your feet.

[Pause]

Now moving on to the thighs and buttocks and noticing where they have contact with the chair.

Just allowing the ground and the chair to hold and support your body without you needing to do anything.

[Pause]

Now moving the attention to your back. Where does your back touch the back of the chair?

Can you feel the difference between where there is contact and where there is none?

[Pause]

Now moving the attention to your hands. Feeling into your hands.

Maybe noticing the position of your hands.

Maybe noticing what they are touching.

Perhaps the chair, your thighs, or maybe the other hand.

[Pause]

You can ask yourself, "How do I know I have hands without looking?"

You just know, right? We can feel the hands from within.

[Pause]

Now opening the awareness. Feeling your entire body sitting here, in this moment, on this chair.

[Pause]

And now, for the last minute or so of our short meditation, bringing the attention to the breath. If you like you can make the next couple of breaths a little bit deeper, so you can *really* feel the breath.

Ask yourself where you feel it the most, or where the sensations are the most pleasant.

At the nostrils, where the air comes in?

At the back of your throat?

In your chest?

Or maybe in your belly?

[Pause]

Using that place as the anchor for your attention. This is where you come back to over and over, whenever the mind wanders off.

Now letting the breath just breathe itself. No need to make it any other way than it wants to be.

[Pause]

And when you notice your attention is somewhere else, gently bring it back to the breath.

[Pause]

In a moment I will ring the bell, and that will end our short mindfulness practice. [You can omit this sentence if you already explained the function of the bell to your students or have used it for a practice with them before.]

[Ring bell]

Class Overview (10 MINUTES)

The grounding meditation doesn't need processing, so you can move right on to cover what the particants should expect.

Logistics

Take a minute or two to indicate the locations of restrooms and drinking water. Point out any other relevant concerns with the space you're in.

Ground Rules

Take the time to go over the ground rules with everyone:

- **Keep it confidential.** It might help to remind participants that learning from each other is a big part of why the class is so effective. But in order for people to feel like they can honestly share what's going on, participants need to feel safe and that nothing will leak outside the group. The process of normalization from others, hearing others' struggles and successes and being heard, is very important. Ask the class to agree to hold what others say in confidence, but let them know that they are always welcome to share their own personal experience with those outside the group.

- **No cross-talk and no advice giving.** In mindfulness we take the stand that nobody needs to be fixed and that we all have the inner capacity and wisdom for growth and healing. We don't assume we have answers for others. This is about the participant's own experience and being able to express that.

- **Be accountable.** How you phrase this depends on your class context and how much you can expect. In a closed-enrollment group we ask people to let us know when they have to miss a class (usually via e-mail). In a nonclinical setting and where it feels appropriate you can put people into small "buddy" groups (a group of four works well). Have them share their e-mails and phone numbers (with permission), and then ask them to check in with each other (by e-mail or text message) once a day (or every other day) after they finish their at-home practice. We like to quote writer Anne Lamott to explain why this is helpful: "My mind is like a bad neighborhood—I'd rather not go there alone." An accountability structure such as this can support the creation of connections among class members. You would avoid this in most clinical settings, especially in mental health, where you wouldn't ask participants to share e-mails (due to privacy and the need to protect personal information).

- **Make a commitment.** You want to insist that participants' commitment to do the home practice, to show up in class, and to be real about what is going on not only helps them but everybody else in the class as well. "We are all in this together." It also really helps if you make it clear that you, too, do the practice every day and are right there with them.

- **Practice at home.** Without regular practice, mindfulness won't be transformational (see next section and also chapter 4). Any change happens not through intellectual understanding but through the mechanisms of regular practice.

Expectations

It can also be helpful to briefly review some expectations for the class. It can be reassuring for participants to understand some of the specifics; it is likely they haven't been in this type of class before.

- **Not psychotherapy.** It's of particular importance for the therapist teaching the class to understand that the sessions outlined in this core program are not a place for psychotherapy (see also chapter 5). For example, when somebody launches into a longer story, gently interupt and ask, "How does this make you feel now?" And then maybe gently inquire how the particpant can use her mindfulness skills to be with it—in this moment. We want to encourage participants to share the insights they gained either during the week or in class—as long as the focus is on the practice. It is often helpful to mention that while this is not group psychotherapy, this work can surely be therapeutic and healing.

Teaching Tip: There is no requirement that participants share their life story or hardest struggles. That is actually often contraindicated. We want to encourage participants to stay with the present-moment experience and keep their comments focused on the practice.

- **Not a Buddhist class.** It may be useful to emphasize that this is not a Buddhist class. It is a modern approach to ancient teachings that is useful to people from all walks of life regardless of their religious background.

- **It takes time.** Let participants know that seeing results takes time. Reassure them that in the beginning it can feel like it's getting worse before it gets better. "Why is that?... It's because you start paying attention to your inner process, and when this happens, issues that have been in the background but may not have been fully acknowledged or processed, or may have been suppressed, rise to the surface." Tell the class to trust in the process, that it is the beginning of healing.

Participant Introductions (10 MINUTES)

The participant introductions can easily be a time hog, so be careful with how you set it up. You only have 10 minutes for this activity. So for groups of five participants there is time for more spacious introductions; but if you have ten participants or more, you need to move quickly. Invite them to share their first name and briefly why they are in the class. Encourage them to be specific if that feels safe to them, instead of just saying, "I have a lot of stress in my life." A key skill for a facilitator is to keep the group on track, so learn to be comfortable gently interrupting participants if they go on too long.

Allow people to pass. Speaking and sharing in front of a group is a heart-pounding experience for some people. Let everyone know that they always have an option to just say their name and pass if that feels right to them. Encourage participants to take care of themselves by adding that the first person who does pass makes doing so safe for everybody else.

Theme: What Is Mindfulness? (10 MINUTES)

We like to use Jon Kabat-Zinn's definition of mindfulness. It is brief and to the point: "Mindfulness is the awareness that arises from paying attention in a particular way: on purpose, moment-by-moment, and non-judgmentally." Please revisit chapter 1 for more on this.

It pays to unpack some of the details for the class. The first section is "paying attention in a particular way." "So how do we pay attention? What way?... In a non-judgmental way with kindness, if possible. Life can be hard at times. For all of us. It can also be wonderful and miraculous. But a key element of our practice is to cultivate a curious, kind attention on all of our experience."

There are a few other threads of mindfulness that typically resonate with a beginning class: "The mind is hardly ever in the present moment but is instead either rehashing the past or rehearsing the future. In being in this state, we miss the present moment, the only moment we ever have to be alive, to make decisions, to grow, to heal, to be there for the people we love. We live most of our lives on *autopilot*, lost in thoughts. We realize that we have not really been there for important times in our lives and might feel the pain of that loss acutely." Participants are often painfully aware that they spend too much time worrying about the future or ruminating over past events.

"Often it feels like this moment, the one we are in right now, isn't really worth paying attention to. We'd rather plan the wonderful future, plan the great times ahead, the times when it's totally worth being present. But when you do get to have these future amazing moments, be honest, are you fully present for them? Chances are you are not, because your mind is untrained to stay in the present moment and will just do what it always does—look to the future or the past.

"Have you ever been on a fabulous trip or vacation that you had been looking forward to for months, only then to be thinking about the past or the future—maybe already planning the next trip? The trained mind will not only be more pliable, it will more easily be with what you want it to be with, whether that's vacation or reflecting on an uncomfortable realization."

Foundational Attitudes of Mindfulness

Please familiarize yourself with the foundational attitudes covered in chapter 1. The class is too brief to cover the attitudes at length with participants, but it is important for you, as the facilitator, to know about them, to practice them yourself, and to be able to weave them in and to keep mentioning them during the entire class series when appropriate.

What Mindfulness Meditation Is Not

It's not a relaxation exercise. "Meditation might be deeply relaxing, and you will experience states of calm and ease, but that is not the goal. Sometimes when we practice we are just not relaxed (and we can't force ourselves to be relaxed). The goal is to be present with what is already here in this moment and, if possible, to hold it with kindness. Strictly speaking, the goal is to let go of a goal!"

It's not a quick fix. "While we sometimes can feel deeply at peace and at home right away when starting to meditate, we will have many meditations during which we are bored or restless or anxious. The practice is a process and unfolds over time."

It's not a technique. "It becomes a way of life, a particular lens through which we choose to see what is happening."

It's not a religion. "While the practices and the philosophy are derived from the Buddhist tradition, they are not a religion. Mindfulness can be a spiritual path if you choose to practice that way. Many people report that it enriches and supports their own spiritual life as they become more familiar with the practices of steady kind attention, loving-kindness, compassion, gratitude, and so forth."

Formal vs. Informal Mindfulness

End the introduction with the explanation of the differences between a formal and informal mindfulness practice (see the Introduction for more).

Mindful Eating: Raisin Exercise (5 MINUTES)

Be sure to have small individual boxes for each participant (recommended in medical and clinical settings) or two bowls filled with raisins ahead of time, plus a spoon, ready to use. We like to have them close by, the bowls covered with a towel.

Invite the participants to share out loud what they experience. It helps to build community through sharing, which engages people and makes this a fun, pleasant experience.

We go through the senses one by one: sight, touch, smell, sound, and taste. Leave about a minute for each of the five senses. Invite people to share when prompted.

MINDFUL EATING SCRIPT

Now I'm going to show you that mindfulness is nothing special but something that we all already know how to do.

We will practice this with something that we all do multiple times a day and usually don't give a lot of thought to.

We will practice Mindful Eating.

Please each take a box and take one of the little objects out that are inside. Please don't eat it yet.

[Pause]

Something that comes in very handy in this practice is something that we call *beginner's mind*. Beginner's mind is the attitude of doing something or experiencing something as if for the first time. When we have done something many times we lose beginner's mind, and we start doing it on autopilot.

So, stay with me here and pretend that you have never seen something like this in your entire life.

We will examine this yet-to-be-named thing one sense at a time.

Let's start with seeing. Tell me what you see.

[Long pause]

Now let's touch it. Tell me what you feel.

[Long pause]

Now let's smell it.

[Long pause]

Now let's listen to the object.

[Pause]

You need to roll it—or it won't talk to you.

[Pause]

Now let's just hold the object for a moment between thumb and index finger, but don't move it. Perhaps just imagine putting the object in your mouth. What do you notice?

[Long pause]

Now I invite you to bring the object to your lips and feel it with your lips.

What's that like?

Is that the same or different than feeling it with your fingers?

If it's different, in what way?

[Long pause]

Now put it on your tongue, but don't bite down yet.

Feel it with your tongue.

Again, is that the same or a different sensation than with your fingers or your lips?

[Long pause]

Now bite down once. What happens? What do you notice?

[Long pause]

Now slowly begin to chew the object. Perhaps you notice an urge to swallow, but don't. It's just an urge. You don't have to give in to every urge you feel.

[Long pause]

Continue chewing until there's nothing left of the object. Pay attention to how your tongue and cheeks expertly position the bits remaining so they are between your teeth.

[Pause]

When you are ready, when you decide, go ahead and swallow. Noticing you are exactly one raisin heavier.

[Pause]

So, what was that like? What did you learn, if anything?

Variation: Urge Surfing and the Mindful Raisin

If you work with people with addiction issues, it can be very insightful to introduce working with urges at this point. You can model how to "urge surf" with the impulse to eat the raisin. Urge surfing becomes a central skill in relapse prevention. To adapt the raisin exercise for this population, we recommend stretching out the time a bit and include specific cues as follows:

URGE SURFING AND
THE MINDFUL RAISIN SCRIPT

Taking one and only one bite of the object. What do you notice?

[Pause]

Perhaps you notice an urge to chew and swallow. It's only an urge. You don't have to give in to every urge you feel.

[Pause]

Slowly begin to chew the object. Noticing the buildup of saliva and the urge to swallow. But don't. It's only an urge!

[Pause]

Continuing to chew whatever little bits remain. Noticing how much attention it takes to not give in to an old habit. Just noticing if the urge to swallow is growing or diminishing. Just surfing the urge.

[Pause]

And now when you're ready, when you decide, go ahead and swallow the raisin.

The goal is to push the experience from simply pleasant eating to one of building frustration tolerance. In just about every group, someone will report that he or she couldn't wait and swallowed the raisin. You might respond by saying, "Changing behaviors of course is hard; if it takes so much energy and attention to override how we eat one raisin, how much attention will it take to surf the urge to drink or use?"

For more guidance on urge surfing, see our website at http://www.sharingmind fulness.com.

Processing the Mindful Eating Exercise
(10 MINUTES)

Allow as many people to share without giving much input other than "Isn't that interesting?" or "Right!" or "Yes" and so forth. We want to have as many different experiences in the room as possible. If you get only positive comments ask, "Did anybody have a different experience? Did anybody not like this exercise?"

There are two teaching points in particular about this exercise that we like to make sure are mentioned. Most of the time you will get them right from the students, but if not, they are worth mentioning.

1. **"How is this different from how you normally eat?"** People will likely report that they usually eat fast, often while standing or driving, and almost always with their main focus on something else: Internet, texting, TV, another person.

    Teaching Tip: Depending on where you teach, different scenarios than those listed here regarding food may pop up. Be open to different eating patterns and to those with a different relationship to food.

    You might say, "Most people tend to eat their meals on autopilot. Autopilot is going through life without a human operator being at the controls! We all know the feeling of discovering the empty bag of chips on the couch next to us while we watch TV. On some level we know we have eaten the chips, but we barely remember it. The opposite of being mindful is being on autopilot.

    "What changes when you eat that way?" The gist of the answers will usually reveal that slowing down and paying attention with all senses is pleasurable. That eating itself is pleasurable. Often somebody in class will admit, "This was the best raisin I have ever had in my life."

2. **"Where was your attention when we did the exercise?"** Most people will say that it was either completely on the raisin or, when it did wander off, that they were able to quickly bring it back. You can then ask, a little jokingly, "What happened to your problems and worries while we did this?" You'll probably get laughter and something like "Gone" or "Not here." As you explore this a little more, make sure that this teaching point sinks in: "When we are fully engaged in something in the present moment with our senses, the worrying mind—the ruminating mind—recedes or is gone for that moment completely. What a relief!"

To skillfully elicit these points from your group can have a deep and lasting effect on the remainder of the class. Participants now not only know intellectually that there can be moments of joy and ease with being in the moment—they have *experienced it firsthand*.

Introduction to Body Scan (5 MINUTES)

You might begin by saying, "In this practice, which sometimes is called 'journey through the body,' we pay attention to all the different areas of the body one by one. In this short (15-minute) version we start with both feet, move up the legs, through the torso up to the shoulders, then to both hands and up the arms, then to the neck and head. We finish by opening the awareness to the entire body."

Why a Body Scan?

By way of introducing what a Body Scan is to the class, consider sharing these rationales for teaching the Body Scan as a first formal practice:

1. **Constant change of focus.** It is a great first (longer) practice for beginners, as it changes the focus of attention frequently and is likely to grasp the attention of the meditator more easily than if the focus were one continuous object, like the breath.

2. **Focus away from cognition.** Mindfulness practice is not just an intellectual exercise; it is about deepening the mind-body connection. The Body Scan helps the meditator to get reacquainted with the body and physical sensations as they manifest as sensual or emotional responses. What goes on in the brain has an influence on the body—and vice versa. But many people are so disconnected from what their body feels like that they can't detect emotions or other, more subtle sensations in the body.

3. **Letting go.** Because we move through the body with an even pace, we practice "letting go" and "tolerating" or "accepting." We might want to linger longer in pleasant areas but we move on—or we might not want to feel into an area of tension or pain, but we stay (or repeatedly return to it) until it's time to move on.

Posture

Give people options for the Body Scan. In the clinical setting and with just 15 minutes, it might be most feasible to have people stay in their seats in a comfortable position. Allow people to choose if they want to have their eyes open or to just look down with a soft gaze.

What to Pay Attention to During the Body Scan

We pay attention to the sensations or to the absence of sensations in the different areas of the body, one by one. We pay attention to whatever is already there, not to what we think we should feel.

Common sensations are temperature, proprioception (position in space), pressure, tingling, tension, touch (fabric against skin, for example). There is no need to elicit a sensation if there is none ("You might feel an impulse, like to wiggle your toes, but you can just observe the impulse and not react"). If there are no sensations, we can still pay attention *as if* sensations were present, just as one can listen for a sound even if there is none.

The Body Scan is a great practice for *nonstriving*. You might say, "We are not asking anything from the body. It is more a receiving of sensations. This might be something completely new to you. Normally we only pay attention to the body if we want it to perform, to do something, or to look good. This can be quite a challenge in the beginning."

Pain

It isn't unusual to have a participant come to class in search of relief from physical pain. When you as the facilitator introduce the Body Scan, you might hear, "But I don't want to pay attention to what's going on in my body since it hurts!" Let participants know that we are learning how to deal with our pain differently. We are bringing each part of our body into our awareness with kindness, even if what we notice is unpleasant. But if the pain in a particular area is simply too overwhelming, participants are encouraged to skillfully take their attention to another part of the body, or to the breath for a short time. By also focusing on body areas that are not in pain, we also retrain the nervous system to not focus solely on the area of pain in the body.

Avoiding Sleepiness

Your students might not fall asleep during the first Body Scan they do in class, but this topic will certainly come up after one week of home practice. You might say, "We are tired, and as soon as we start to unwind we may fall asleep. That is normal, and it's actually healthy that the body claims what it needs. But if you fall asleep every time you start to meditate, even though you will feel more rested, you will miss out on other benefits of the practice."

Variation: Feeling Your Hands Exercise

If you are working with a group that is very disembodied, it might be helpful to do a short demonstration with them before launching into the full Body Scan.

FEELING YOUR HANDS SCRIPT
(2 TO 3 MINUTES)

With one hand, tap against the other hand.

[Pause]

Now please close your eyes for a moment and feel into the hand you tapped.

[Pause]

Can you feel the hand?

[Pause]

You can probably feel tingling or something, right? What you are doing now is paying attention to your hand. This is what we do with each area of the body in the Body Scan. And we can do that even if we don't have any sensations in that area. We feel into it *as if* there was something to feel.

We like to say that numbness counts as a sensation in this practice. Make it clear that nobody is able to feel every part of the body. And that it will get easier over time.

Body Scan (15 MINUTES)

Once you have sufficiently introduced the practice and the class is ready, you should begin the formal Body Scan exercise. Please be sure to reread the section on leading practices (and especially use of language) in chapter 5 *before* class begins. It's important to have these practical guidelines fresh in your mind.

BODY SCAN SCRIPT

The next practice is a mindfulness practice whereby we go through the entire body one area at a time. We start with the feet and make our way up to the head.

[If you will keep your students in their chairs, no further setup is needed. If you invite them to lie down, do so now.]

If you like, you can also lie down for the Body Scan. We will be practicing this for about 15 minutes. Please take a mat to lie on. If you decide to lie down, it can be nice to put your legs up on the seat of your chair.

It's up to you if you want to close your eyes or just lower your gaze.

[Continue to talk as people lie down. Allow the time for everyone to settle. Add cues if needed.]

Finding a comfortable posture.

[Pause]

Now feeling into your body lying [or sitting] here.

[Pause]

Feeling into the areas of contact in this moment.

Where the feet are touching the ground [or the chair].

The legs…your back…the arms…the head…

Maybe also noticing your breath, entering and leaving your body.

[Provide some instruction about the practice. This can also be done before starting the practice but these instructions can be a nice transition into a formal practice.]

The intention of the Body Scan is to be present with our body without wanting anything at all. Not even relaxation. Of course, it's nice to relax and it's great if it happens, but that is not the goal of the Body Scan. The goal is to be checking in with each area of the body in a nonjudgmental way. We simply feel what is there to feel. No need to stir up sensations by moving the body.

[If you have a group with a high likelihood of past trauma, invite them to move a little or wiggle about as you go through the body and ask them to see if that changes the way they feel. In people who we suspect have been immobilized through a trauma, having permission to make small movements often makes it possible for them to actually stay with the Body Scan.]

And you will notice that there are a number of areas in the body that you might not be able to feel at all. And that is normal and okay. Just check into those areas *as if* you could feel something.

Starting with the feet.

Feeling into both feet right now.

[Pause]

Feeling into the areas where your feet are touching the ground [or the chair].

Maybe feeling your toes—or not.

Maybe feeling tingling—or temperature.

[Pause]

Now moving the attention to your ankles and lower legs. What is here to feel—if anything at all?

Pressure of your calves against the mat?

Perhaps the fabric against the skin?

And if you notice that your attention is suddenly somewhere else, just gently and without judging returning it to your legs. It's not a problem at all. The mind likes to wander.

[Pause]

If you find it helpful you can imagine that you are breathing into your lower legs. As if your attention could ride on the breath.

Or as if your attention would light up the area like it was a flashlight.

[Pause]

Now letting go of the lower legs and moving the attention to your knees and thighs.

What is here to feel?

Again, maybe pressure, temperature, the position of your legs—or nothing at all. Numbness counts as a sensation in this practice.

Noticing that *thinking about* an area or *picturing* it in your mind's eye is different from actually *feeling* it.

[Pause]

Now letting go of the thighs and moving the attention to the lower trunk. The pelvis and the belly up to the belly button.

Noticing any sensation in this area.

Maybe feeling the breath in the lower belly? Or not.

[Pause]

Then letting go and now feeling into the upper trunk…the stomach area…the chest, feeling the sensations of the breath here…with each inhalation…and each exhalation…

[Pause]

Feeling the spine against the floor [or the back of the chair]. Noticing any sensations that are here—or the absence of sensations.

[Pause]

From here now moving the attention into your hands. Feeling your hands.

You might notice how well you can feel your hands without having to see them.

[Pause]

Feeling the individual fingers.

Feeling the position of your hands.

[Pause]

When you are ready, moving the attention to the wrists and forearms now.

What is here to feel?

Touch? Pressure? Warmth?

[Pause]

Now moving the attention to your elbows and upper arms.

Noticing any sensations here.

And if your mind wanders off, just bringing it back to wherever we are. Just starting again.

[Pause]

From here, moving the attention to your shoulders…the back of your neck…and then to your head.

[Pause]

Feeling into your jaw.

Feeling into your face.

What does your face feel like?

Mouth…nose…cheeks…eyes…forehead…your entire face.

[Pause]

And now opening the awareness to include the entire body again. Lying [or sitting here].

Being alive. Breathing.

If you like, imagining to be breathing from the crown of your head all the way down into your toes—and up and out again.

[Pause]

Noticing all the sensations of the body and allowing them to be just as they are in this moment.

[Long pause]

[Ring bell]

Allowing some movement back into the body, like wiggling your fingers and toes.

Stretching the body in any way it wants, if that feels good.

And when you are ready, in your own time, opening your eyes [and coming back into a seated position]. And taking a moment to reflect on your experience in this new moment.

On occasion, participants may be so eager to ask questions or share their experiences that they will immediately begin to talk. Gently and warmly, encourage these eager individuals to appreciate the moments after a formal practice without launching into the next task. "Just take a few moments to notice what sensations are present in your body right now, observe the thoughts going through your mind, and check in with the emotions of this moment."

Group Process (5 MINUTES)

After the Body Scan, invite participants to share with the class what the experience was like for them. Make sure they understand what they were supposed to be doing. You might want to ask explicitly: "Was it clear for everybody that we were *feeling the sensations* of the body, not *thinking about* the body?"

Be sure to familiarize yourself with the section "FAQs from New Participants" in chapter 4 in preparation for this part of class. Here are some additional participant comments and questions, along with suggested facilitator responses.

Participant:	"I could feel some of my feet, but the lower legs and knees: zero. It was kind of creepy, actually."
Facilitator:	"Yes, that is normal. *[Speaking to the group:]* Can I have a show of hands who else couldn't feel their lower legs? *[Speaking to the participant:]* So you couldn't feel your lower legs. What happened or what did you do?"
Participant:	"I noticed that my attention was drifting off much more easily in the areas I couldn't feel. I felt like I couldn't do it or I didn't get it."
Facilitator:	"Of course, that makes sense. It's hard to pay attention to what we can't even feel. But I want to point out that you did it just right: because you noticed all of this. So mindfulness was right at work."

Wrap-Up and Homework (10 MINUTES)

It pays to take some time to cover the importance of regular practice ("homework") in the first class. You want to revisit this briefly every class.

Commit to a practice. Make it clear that "It only works if you work it." Find an analogy that works well for your population. Exercise is one that many can identify with: "If you want to be fit and healthy, you need to put in time for exercise on a very regular basis. You can't just listen to lectures or read books on the topic; that won't make you fit." Emphasize that the same is true with meditation.

Make it daily. For the first week, ask the class to do a formal practice once a day for 5 to 15 minutes (Grounding Meditation or Body Scan). Because life gets in the way of our best intentions, we found it helpful to make flexible commitments for the daily practice: Ask your class what would be realistic for them to do during the week. "How many days? Which days? How long? What time of day?" As the class goes on and their practice gets longer it might be helpful to have them think in terms of "regular day" and "minimum day" practices.

> *Teaching Tip:* To help participants stay on track with their at-home practice, consider sharing Web links to download guided meditations and daily practice log sheets—or provide them via e-mail or as printed worksheets.

Find inspiration. Ask participants if there is anything helpful they can bring to mind when they are debating if they will do the meditation that day or skip. "What would inspire you? Peace of mind? Health? Sanity? Calm? Ease?" To build and maintain a regular practice, participants might want to write down an inspirational message and post it somewhere where they will see it regularly.

Be accountable. It helps with accountability if you have your group members share with each other what they commit to doing and what helps them to be inspired. For example, each participant can turn to his or her neighbor and share how many times a week and for how long he or she will practice the Body Scan.

Validation. It can be reassuring for participants to let them know "we're all in this together," which can be done not only by sharing your own human experience as the facilitator but by letting them know you will be doing the home practice right along with them. Some points to emphasize:

- "It's not always fun to do it. Sometimes it's boring, sometimes even outright unpleasant. That is normal and to be expected. You'll get the benefits nevertheless."

- "When you practice at the same time of day, in the same posture, you will create a type of muscle memory that will make it easier to find your practice."

- "Just as with exercise, as you meditate more regularly, you may begin to see positive benefits that generalize to other parts of your life. This can help motivate more regular practice."

If you have handouts, like the daily practice log, hand them out at the end of the class. Be sure to remind participants when the class meets again.

SESSION 2

Be Right Where You Are

In Session 2, we introduce the core concept of staying with your present-moment experience. We discuss how we rehash the past and rehearse the future in a constant stream of mental activity (*what*). We repeat the Body Scan practice from last week and introduce the Mindfulness of Breathing practice as well as mindful speaking and listening (*how*). By noticing the mind's tendency to be lost in the future or the past, we create an opportunity to come fully into our lives in the present. And the present is the only moment in which we can experience joy, grow, or change (*why*).

OBJECTIVES OF SESSION 2

- Provide support for an ongoing formal practice and reassurance about common barriers.

- Introduce the formal practice: Mindfulness of Breathing.

- Introduce the techniques "2 Feet, 1 Breath" and "3Ps: Pause—Present—Proceed."

- Describe the importance of returning to the present moment.

Session 2 Outline

Time (in minutes)	Cumulative Time	Activity
5	5	Welcome and Check-In
20	25	**Body Scan**
5	30	Introduction to Small Group Check-Ins (mindful listening/talking; share 2 minutes each)
10	40	Group Process (Q & A; follow-up from last week)
20	60	Theme: Be Right Where You Are Techniques: 2 Feet, 1 Breath *and* 3Ps
5	65	Introduction to Mindfulness of Breathing
10	75	**Mindfulness of Breathing**
10	85	Group Process
5	90	Wrap-Up and Homework (15-minute Body Scan, informal practice)

Materials. Bell, watch or timer, Session 2 Outline, whiteboard and markers, handouts if you use them

Poem. "Enough" by David Whyte or "Wild Geese" by Mary Oliver

Story. "The Man Who Always Waited to Be Happy," abridged version (or see the longer version available on http://www.sharingmindfulness.com)

There once was a boy who always worried about what he would do with his life and how he would make a living. There simply wasn't time in his life to be happy. All he had time to do was plan for the future. He would tell himself, "I'll be happy once I get a career and start making money. Then I will be happy." He worked very hard indeed until he established himself in a good career where he was respected by many. But he wasn't happy. He was too busy thinking about all the things he didn't have. So he told himself, "I'll be happy once I have a family." And so it went on: He got married. He had kids. He had enough money to put them through school. He had grandkids…and so on. But there was always something. And in the end, he died having had a wonderful life—yet he never took the time to appreciate it.

Discuss the moral of the story with the group: "Don't wait to be happy. Life shows up for all of us. But don't be so worried about the potential difficult moments of life that you forget to actually live. The man in the story seems a bit ridiculous, but don't we all have some magical thoughts about life being somehow 'better' once a current hardship is successfully over or once some pesky symptom we don't like is fully resolved? There is only one right time to be happy: This moment. Right here and right now."

Welcome and Check-In (5 MINUTES)

Begin the class by inviting participants to briefly reintroduce themselves by name and offer one brief sentence of how their practice is going or how they are doing in this moment. The goal is to build a sense of community in the group and also normalize the range of possible experiences in starting a meditation practice. Move quickly, with warmth, through the introductions. It's very easy to get pulled into legitimate questions in the second week. Remember, learning mindfulness is an experiential rather than a cognitive process. Inform curious participants that there will be time to discuss experiences later.

Body Scan (20 MINUTES)

Trust the practice to be the best teacher. It is essential to maintain the time frame for the in-class practices for everyone but particularly for the participants who might not be practicing at home. To begin, refer to the Body Scan instructions in Session 1, but lead the practice from your experience in the present moment. You can extend that 15-minute practice for an additional 5 minutes by adding in more detail and space.

Establish a routine of nonjudgmental, friendly reflection following each formal practice.

Introduction to Small Group Check-Ins (5 MINUTES)

When the class seems ready, introduce the convention of small group discussions. Quickly divide the group into pairs and introduce the practice of *mindful talking* and *mindful listening*. It's fine to have a group of three if you have an odd number of participants in the group.

Mindful Listening and Mindful Talking

The importance of mindful listening as an informal practice can't be emphasized enough. We all thrive on being fully "heard" and "seen." Most people have a keen sense of knowing if the other person is really listening or is lost in her own story or is impatiently waiting for her turn to talk. Many people share with us that the practice of mindful listening does wonders for their relationships, personally and professionally. Foster an atmosphere of curiosity and nonjudging.

Explain that everyone will have a minute or two to share his or her personal experience with the Body Scan with a partner. During this share, the partner who is listening doesn't interrupt or get distracted thinking about what she will say, or if the listener does get distracted she will use the skill from her formal practice to just come back to listening in the moment. The listener simply tries to listen with her whole body: to hear, to see, to take in, to understand what is being said deeply. Explain that this is called *mindful listening*.

The person talking has the opportunity to be fully heard and should be mindful of the words he uses. The talkers can ask themselves: *Am I sharing too much or too little? What is being asked for, and what is appropriate in this situation?* Being aware and thoughtful while conversing is called *mindful talking*.

Inform the group that you will provide a verbal cue for the partners to switch in about 2 minutes so that everyone has a chance to be both the mindful talker and the mindful listener.

Common Questions

The first time this is done in class, particularly when the class members don't know one another yet, there may be some questions or moments of hesitation.

Participant: "I don't understand. What are we supposed to be talking about?"

Facilitator: "You may share about what you noticed during your practice. Or perhaps you would like to share about how your home practice is going. There is no 'right' answer, only your personal experience. Share what you feel comfortable sharing."

Participant: "But I don't know what to say."

Facilitator: "Simply tell each other your names again, decide who will talk first, and answer the question, 'What was the Body Scan practice like for me today? What did I notice?' Now let's begin. I will let you know when 2 minutes have passed and it's time to switch roles."

Why Small Groups?

The importance of these small group discussions cannot be overstated. They provide an opportunity for everyone to share his or her own experience with the practice and hear directly from someone else about what he or she experienced. Beginners just learning to meditate for the first time are often surprised to find just how busy their minds actually are and how challenging it can be to simply notice the sensations in the body. A chance to trade experiences with another beginner helps normalize the process of learning to meditate.

Group Process (10 MINUTES)

Ring the bell at the end of the small group discussion period and invite everyone to reconvene in the large group. Take about 10 minutes to allow the large group to process the small group experience. The skilled facilitator will model nonjudgmental curiosity and openness.

Tasks to accomplish in this section of the class include checking in and reinforcing the use of the daily practice log sheet (if this is being used), normalizing a wide range of experiences with the practice, highlighting common barriers, and answering any questions the participants may have (but being cautious not to fall into the trap of intellectualization instead of the target of direct experience).

If time allows, it may also be useful to explore in the group what it was like to actually talk with someone who was intent on just listening. As always, maintain a sense of warm spaciousness in the class, as this contributes to a shared sense of discovering the practice together. We present one possible narrative to begin this discussion:

Facilitator:	"I would like to invite someone to share with the large group any similarities or differences you might have discovered with your partner in the small group."
Participant 1:	"Well, we talked about how it is a lot harder to do than it sounds. I mean, 'Just notice the sensations in your foot,' sounds easy but actually doing it isn't easy at all."
Facilitator:	"Not easy in what way?"
Participant 1:	"Not easy because in just a few seconds it seems like my mind wanders away and starts thinking about something else. I don't even realize I've drifted off until you say something and it brings me back. I'm just bouncing all over the place."
Participant 2:	"I thought it was just me. My body is still but my mind is doing gymnastics!"
Facilitator:	"So it sounds like you both noticed something similar. And from the nods and smiles around the room it seems this experience is familiar to a few others. Let me ask you, was this sort of restlessness you noticed in your mind or experienced as sensations in your body, or both?"
Participant 1:	"It was in my mind. I just wanted to turn it all off so I could better notice the sensations."
Participant 2:	"For me it was my body. I could hardly sit still! I had to peek out every now and then to see everyone else sitting so quietly, for encouragement."

Facilitator: "Congratulations to you both! You noticed your experience just as it was. There are many common experiences or struggles with our practice that many of us share. In this case it is a sense of restlessness. But we are also all a bit different; maybe it is a restless mind or restless body or both. It is key that we aren't trying to change or control our experience in any way. We are just observing it with kindness. In creating space to notice what is actually happening, we are actually creating a different relationship to our lived experience—an experience of kind observation rather than observing as a harsh critic or feeling as if we're locked in a struggle to change things. We aren't trying to relax, since that would mean striving to reach a particular state. We are allowing things to be just as they are."

The dialogue with a beginning meditator is significantly different than the instructions a facilitator might give to an advanced practitioner. In the example above, the facilitator first created space to explore some common experiences, offered both encouragement and normalization of the comments, and reviewed the principles of nonjudgment and letting things be as they are. This is an appropriate general framework for beginners. If an advanced participant had said, "I just wanted to turn it all off," an appropriate response from a facilitator might be simply, "Ah…a judgment?" The advanced participant would immediately recognize the judgment, the trying to change things, the lack of acceptance of the present moment, and know how wanting things to be different is itself the mind's manifestation of a struggle no doubt reflected in held tension in the body. But for a beginning participant, be cautious about noting every judgment, as this may simply create further ripples of judgment in the thought structure. Simply model a curious, nonjudgmental stance and let the practice do the teaching as it unfolds.

Daily practice. As a facilitator, our interest and attention will clearly communicate the importance of the various elements of the class. At-home practice is an important part of the program and warrants our full attention. In the large group discussion, if everyone is talking about the Body Scan completed in class, ask about how the practice is going at home. Take just a few moments to ask about what everyone learned by using the daily practice log or from practicing every day. Frequently, there is an opportunity to mention how each practice is different and to remind students about the principle of bringing a beginner's mind to each practice.

Normalize experiences when possible. Use the group dynamic and setting to normalize common experiences. Be particularly attentive when there is an expressed common reaction, and create space for alternative experiences. Facilitators want to leave beginning participants with an understanding that all experiences are fine just as they are, even the uncomfortable ones such as restlessness or boredom.

The Five Hindrances. Be aware of the Five Hindrances (see "Dharma Teacher Perspective" at the end of this chapter). It is easy for beginning meditators to feel unique in the struggles of their practice. It can come as an unexpected relief to learn that practitioners have struggled with these same obstacles for more than two thousand years.

Keep your eye on the time. It is easy to get pulled into fascinating discussions about our practice. The class counts on the facilitator to keep things moving.

Theme: Be Right Where You Are (20 MINUTES)

It is helpful for the facilitator to segue into the didactic portion of the class to indicate a shift in the teaching style. Perhaps something like, "Let's move on to the topic for today. We introduce the importance of training ourselves to be right where we are." It can also be helpful to move to a whiteboard and write "Be Right Where You Are." This isn't essential but can help shift the group onto the new topic. We leave it up to the facilitator to decide what style of presenting this section best meets the needs of the class. For a higher-functioning group, we prefer a more Socratic style of exploration about the mind to pique the group's interest. Other types of groups, such as those just entering substance abuse treatment or psychiatric inpatients, may be better suited to a more direct and concrete approach.

Here are some discussion points:

Habits of mind. "When we begin to observe the mind, we start to notice our habits, or what we might call our *habits of mind*. Our minds frequently are rehearsing what's to come or rehashing what has already happened. With all this rehearsing and rehashing, we hardly pay attention to this moment, the moment in which we are actually alive. Start noticing, without judgment and with as much kindness as you can muster, what your mind is doing."

A wandering mind is an unhappy mind. Some people might ask, "What's the big deal if my mind wanders? So what?" You might answer, "A wandering mind is an unhappy mind." In an ingenious bit of research, a Harvard team installed apps on thousands of cell phones that asked three simple questions: What are you doing right now? What is your mind doing? How happy are you? The results demonstrated with science and technology what spiritual teachers have been saying for thousands of years: A ruminative mind is an unhappy mind (Killingsworth & Gilbert, 2010).

Depression and anxiety. "Certain habits of mind are related to certain mood symptoms. If you are in *rehearsing mode*, constantly planning what's to come and worrying about all that might go wrong, you are more likely to experience tension and anxiety symptoms. If you are in *rehashing mode*, replaying how a conversation went south and what you might have said instead, for example, you are more likely to experience depressive symptoms."

Cognitive fusion and letting go. "All of our habits of mind—planning, worrying, fantasizing, rehashing, and so on—can be quite seductive. We do think with our thoughts after all! But we can easily fall into the mind's trap: an overidentification with our thoughts, a *cognitive fusion*, that tricks us into believing our thoughts are actually facts." Someone with depression may have the thought, "I am worthless" while someone in substance abuse treatment might think, "I am going to die if I don't

113

get a hit soon." Explain to the group: "Our mindfulness practice helps us with *letting go of our thoughts*; we see thoughts as simply thoughts in the moment. We can attach to the thought less, believe it less, when we recognize it as just a thought."

Being in the moment helps the body calm down and heal. Training your attention to be right where you are also creates a more healthful state for your physical body. Rumination downregulates immunological function. Being right where you are unleashes the "rest and digest" function in the body related to the activation of the parasympathetic nervous system. A mindfulness practice can lower blood pressure, enhance immunological biomarkers, and even change our brains in meaningful ways (Campbell, Labelle, Bacon, Faris, & Carlson, 2012; Carlson, Speca, Patel, & Goodey, 2004).

Storytelling. Here we like to tell the story of the man who was always ruminating about the life he would have in some happier future once all his problems had been resolved (see "The Man Who Always Waited to Be Happy" at the beginning of this session).

Techniques

These practices can help to create mini-breaks during the day to recalibrate the nervous system. They might be very short but they are very effective if done in combination with a daily meditation.

2 Feet, 1 Breath

The 2 Feet, 1 Breath technique is the shortest mindfulness technique we know of. It simply requires us to first feel one foot, then the other, and then to take one conscious breath. When we do it with kids we let them lift up each foot ("Don't stomp!"), put it down, and then take a big breath. Repeat often during the day as a small reminder that you are actually living in a physical body.

3Ps

This technique is adapted from the University of Wisconsin School of Medicine, Family Medicine Program. The 3Ps are particularly helpful for people who have to open doors a lot during the day, like nurses or doctors walking from patient room to patient room. For this you use the doorknob as the trigger for the 3Ps. As you reach for the knob take 1 second, or the length of one breath, to:

- **Pause.** Take just a moment for yourself. Even just a single breath. Let go of the planning mind and the task orientation of the day and simply notice the moment.

- **Be Present.** Be aware of what is happening in this moment by experiencing the sensations of the body, noticing the thoughts, and feeling the emotions just as they are without trying to change anything.

- **Proceed.** Using mindful speech and skillful means, respond compassionately to whatever needs your attention in this moment.

Introduction to Mindfulness of Breathing
(10 MINUTES)

Briefly introduce the new formal practice, Mindfulness of Breathing. As with all the formal practices, it is preferred to let the practice do the teaching through direct experience rather than through extensive preamble and explanation. We offer a few possible talking points to assist with the introduction. Mention a point or two that works for you and move right into the practice.

Posture. Start with a few words about posture. For a short meditation, posture doesn't matter so much, but it is helpful to point out that the body will start to associate a certain posture with meditation, which in turn will make it easier to transition into the practice. We like to encourage people to get into a posture that evokes a sense of "dignity and ease": sitting upright, but not rigid. If you haven't yet mentioned it, consider reviewing the concept of *stimulus control*. This is just like Pavlov's dogs, but in our case the conditioned stimulus is a specific posture rather than the sound of a bell. After repeatedly pairing posture to meditation practice, the posture alone will bring a sense of ease. (For more on posture, see chapter 4.)

Don't manipulate the breath. "Mindfulness of Breathing is simply attending to the breath with our kind attention moment by moment. We don't have to breathe deeply or in any particular way. We are not manipulating our breath, or any other part of our experience. But we might often find that by just paying attention the breath naturally slows down and becomes deeper, because that is the body's response to calming down"—a.k.a. activating the parasympathetic nervous system. "But there is no need to try to make that happen purposefully. Just notice the breath exactly as it is without judgment." People who have been practicing yoga and yoga breathing often have a particularly hard time "letting the breath breathe itself." It just takes a little more practice to unlearn this habit.

Thinking is not sensing. "We aren't thinking about the process of breathing, how oxygen binds with hemoglobin and travels through the body. That's thinking, not sensing. We are sensing the breath as it moves in and out of the body. We feel the chest moving, the air flowing in and out of the nostrils. This is a direct sensory link to being alive, right here in this moment."

Just two instructions. "With Mindfulness of Breathing we are doing only one of two things: We are being aware of the sensations of breathing right in this moment, or we are noticing that our minds have drifted away and redirecting ourselves back to the breath. It is that simple. Sensing the breath, or noticing our attention is elsewhere and bringing our awareness back without judgment. Breathing, and the knowing of it. Mind wandering, and the knowing of it. You may notice your mind wanders constantly. That's what minds do. Just gently come back to the breath over and over again."

The anchor. "In Mindfulness of Breathing you notice the sensations of the breath in the body. The actual placement of your attention is not as important as using that same place consistently as a sense anchor. You can focus on the place in your body your breath is the easiest to sense or the place your breath feels the most pleasant. For some, this would be noticing the breath in the chest as it rises and falls. Breathing in and out. For others, it might mean noticing the breath in the belly or in the nostrils."

The wandering mind. "The kind attitude you bring to your practice of Mindfulness of Breathing is essential. Our minds will wander. That's what they do. We like to say, 'The brain produces thoughts like the mouth produces saliva.' We train our attention, a bit like training a beloved puppy or an adorable toddler. They wander all over the place but this is their nature. We bring steady, persistent, kind attention to the practice. Each time we notice the mind has wandered away, this is a moment of mindfulness. A moment of doing it 'just right.' And we kindly return our attention to the breath."

Mindfulness of Breathing (10 MINUTES)

Transition into the guided practice. Sometimes a clue like "Okay, let's put this into practice now" and visibly adjusting your own posture can help to move into the meditation.

MINDFULNESS OF BREATHING SCRIPT

Taking a moment to find a dignified and upright posture with both feet flat on the floor. Allowing the eyes to gently close, or soften your gaze down to the floor if that feels right to you. Checking in for just a moment with the sensation of the body, what emotions are present in this moment, and noticing as best you can what your mind is doing. And letting that all be just as it is. Letting yourself be just as you are.

[Pause]

As best you can, taking your awareness into the body to notice the sensations of the breath.

[Pause]

If it's helpful, take two or three breaths that are just a bit deeper than you would normally take, just to help you sense that place in the body where you feel your breath the most. Or maybe that place you feel the breath is most pleasant. It might be the chest or the belly.

[Pause]

Letting go of your control of the breath and not manipulating the breath in any way. Trusting the abundant wisdom in your body to breathe just right. Just observing rather than controlling the breath.

[Pause]

Perhaps you may notice how the breath expands the chest on the inhale and falls away on the exhale. Sensing how the chest lifts and falls away with each breath.

[Pause]

Tracking as best you can the entire cycle of the breath. The inhale and the exhale.

[Pause]

Simply tracking the sensations of each inhale and each exhale. Allow yourself to get as close as you can to the sensation of your breath.

[Pause]

Using the awareness of the breath as your anchor to the present moment. Noticing this breath right here.

[Pause]

Noticing this breath here.

[Pause]

Noticing each breath as it develops. Allowing any tension in the body that isn't needed to be released with each exhale. Yet allowing any tension that remains to be just as it is.

[Long pause]

Where is your attention now? Where does it go during the quiet moments? Each time you notice that your mind has wandered off, you're doing the practice just right. That is a moment of mindfulness. Gently bringing your awareness back to the breath. Sensing how the chest lifts or expands on the inhale. And falls away on the exhale.

[Pause]

This lifting and falling away of the breath is completely familiar. A reliable anchor to the present moment. Right here. Right now. This breath.

[Pause]

Allowing yourself the space to be just as you. Breathing in. And breathing out. Right here in this moment.

[Ring bell]

Group Process (10 MINUTES)

Pause briefly after the practice for a moment of reflection. Invite participants to share their experiences with the group. Again, the main point is to normalize a wide range of experiences, from a deep sense of peacefulness to agitation. Encourage class members to have a beginner's mind with each practice.

Wrap-Up and Homework (5 MINUTES)

Encourage people to keep practicing every day. This week it's a 15-minute guided Body Scan and an informal practice at least once a day.

Dharma Teacher Perspective: On the Five Hindrances

When people start to meditate or to pay attention to their mind states in general, they are often surprised by how often they are caught in restlessness or sleepiness, in wanting something or in aversion against something else. Class participants will share those internal experiences without your asking them. We start the process by inviting all class members to share, to make it clear that everybody has those reactions. But you can bring even more perspective into it by pointing out that these mind states are so common that they have been taught for the last 2,500 years to meditation students everywhere. They are so ubiquitous that they even have a name: The Five Hindrances. Each of them has a very particular flavor, and it is very helpful to be able to identify them all in your own experience and in those of the participants'.

The Five Hindrances are mental states that cloud or obscure our ability to see the mind as it really is.

1. Wanting/desire

2. Not wanting/aversion

3. Restlessness/worry

4. Sleepiness/lethargy

5. Doubt

The traditional analogy is that the mind is like the sky: clear, blue, endless. (Most people have had at least a taste of that mind before.) The hindrances are like clouds that obscure the sky. Sometimes there are so many clouds, or they stay for such extended periods of time, that it feels like the clouds are the true nature of the mind. Interestingly, this is how some people who suffer from depression describe how it feels to be depressed.

Wanting/desire. We are all caught in wanting something. This can be as big as wanting a partner to share your life with or as small as wanting the piece of gum that is in the pocket of your jacket. We often experience wanting as pleasurable and might be seduced to get lost in daydreams about the object of our desire. It may feel unpleasant if we can't have what we want.

Not wanting/aversion. As desire, aversion comes in all shapes and forms. Aversion against a political party or aversion against the length of a particular sitting meditation or against the pain in your shoulder. We usually experience aversion as unpleasant and try to get rid of it.

Restlessness/worry. You could say that restlessness is felt in the body, while worry is restlessness of the mind. Restlessness makes it hard to sit still. For meditation practice, it is helpful to point out that restlessness gets worse if the meditator acts on the impulse to move.

Sleepiness/lethargy. This one needs no explanation. Everybody knows it and can recognize it. It's hard to be mindful of sleepiness, as it's a slippery slope into dozing off. The state of lethargy is similar. It's a sense of moving through molasses.

Doubt. Doubt comes last, as it is the most dangerous one. Why is that? Because the mental hindrance of doubt can get you to stop practicing. Doubt comes in the form of thoughts like, "I can't do this." "I don't think this mindfulness stuff works. Maybe it works for others, but it doesn't do anything for me. Maybe I should try Sufi dancing [or whatever else] instead…"

In a nutshell: When working with the hindrances, keep in mind that they are not a problem if you don't make them into one. You identify them, name them, and don't take them personally. "Oh, that is just aversion doing its thing." "This is what restlessness feels like." If you let them be, they will change. Trying to get rid of them would be falling into another hindrance again—aversion against the hindrance.

SESSION 3

Our Storytelling Minds

In Session 3, our mindfulness practice turns toward the fundamental matter of our storytelling minds. A mindfulness practice helps us to work with our thoughts in two very important ways. First, we become aware of the constant torrent of thoughts cascading through our minds. This is simply what our minds do and is neither good nor bad. But it is essential to be aware of these thoughts, as they are a driving force in our mood, behavior, and, ultimately, our life (*why*). Second, we learn to extricate ourselves from the stories we are constantly creating. We can acknowledge the experience of a story unfolding, and the emotions and body sensations related to the story, without identifying with it or becoming lost in it (*how*). These skills transform one-sided thoughts of certainty into a world of liberating possibilities. Mindfulness of Sounds and Mindful Walking are introduced (*what*).

OBJECTIVES OF SESSION 3

- Describe the body's reaction to stress, and how worries are like Velcro and pleasure is like Teflon.

- Describe how we are not our thoughts. Encourage the practice of noticing thoughts and observing them without reacting to each experience.

- Introduce the formal practices: Mindfulness of Sound, Mindful Walking.

- Introduce the technique: STOP.

- Discuss stress in the body.

- Relay the ocean metaphor.

Session 3 Outline

Time (in minutes)	Cumulative Time	Activity
5	5	Welcome and Check-In
5	10	Introduction to Mindful Walking
10	20	**Mindful Walking Meditation**
10	30	Group Process (Q & A; follow-up from last week)
20	50	Theme: Our Storytelling Minds Technique: STOP
5	55	Introduction to Mindfulness of Sound
15	70	**Mindfulness of Sound** (and introduce labeling)
5	75	Small Group Check-In
10	85	Group Process
5	90	Wrap-Up and Homework (10-minute guided Mindfulness of Breathing or Mindfulness of Sound; continued informal practice)

Materials. Bell, watch or timer, Session 3 outline, handouts, whiteboard, and markers

Poem. Rumi's "The Breeze at Dawn" or David Whyte's "Tilicho Lake"

Story. "Mind Like the Ocean"

Have you ever tried to swim out into the ocean when multiple sets of large waves are breaking onto the beach one right after another? With each bit of progress you make, another wave breaks and pushes you back toward the beach. You can quickly become exhausted fighting all the waves. You might even tell yourself, "Wow, the ocean is really kicking my tail."

But the waves are not the same thing as the ocean.

Caught up in the energy of the waves and our desire to go out for a swim, we can forget that the ocean is spacious and vast. It can be helpful to "duck under the waves" when they come. In this way, we can make progress on our swim without getting caught up in the sway of each individual wave. Never forget that, even during a hurricane, the ocean is miles out and miles deep. And underneath the power of what is happening on the surface, there can be stillness and calm.

So when your own life seems to be filled with storm, when the big waves of thought are coming in one right after another, remember that you are the ocean and not the waves. Your awareness is spacious and vast—and under the surface you can find stillness.

Welcome and Check-In (5 MINUTES)

Begin the class by inviting everyone to once again introduce him- or herself and encourage participants to share how their practice is going. As a more welcoming alternative, and if you know everyone by name, greet each group member and ask him or her to describe how his or her practice is going or what she or he is noticing in a sentence or two.

Introduction to Mindful Walking (5 MINUTES)

Let participants know that mindfulness practice is traditionally taught in four body postures: sitting, lying down, standing up, and walking. While we do most of the formal practice in the seated posture, it's important to keep in mind that mindfulness is not dependent on a particular posture but can (and should) be practiced in any position.

Mindful walking is the most commonly taught moving practice and requires no equipment or skills from the participant other than the ability to walk. (If you happen to have somebody in a wheelchair in your class or somebody on crutches, he or she can still explore movement, in whatever way he or she is able to move—be creative here!)

Begin along these lines: "Walking meditation sounds deceptively easy. We all know how to walk after all, right? But usually we only walk to get somewhere. In walking meditation, we simply bring our attention to the experience and sensation of walking. This may sound easy to beginners but it doesn't take much of a practice history to realize there's a catch. When we are walking, we are also taking the ruminative mind along for the ride! So we aren't just walking—we are planning dinner, worrying about work, fantasizing about the weekend, or very often just thinking about what we are going to do when we get to wherever it is we are walking to. We hardly notice the sensations of walking, as we take it for granted.

"In walking meditation, we notice the sensations of the soles of our feet pressing into the earth or, in a variation of the practice, we break down each step into three parts: lifting—moving—placing. We silently name each part of the sequence as we walk. This can be helpful to keep the mind more engaged. Your mind inevitably wanders. And as in the Mindfulness of Breathing meditation, you simply notice it—and return to this new step." Many people find it hard at first to connect with the walking practice; for others it is a welcome respite from sitting still in meditation.

Mindful Walking Meditation (10 MINUTES)

Let participants know where they can go for the Walking Meditation. Choose a stretch of 15 to 20 feet and walk it back and forth. If your room is big enough, it can be there. It's nice to walk outside, but that's not always possible. Hallways work well, too.

Have everybody stand up while you demonstrate and they explore the first part of the practice. Then instruct them to begin walking on their own.

MINDFUL WALKING MEDITATION SCRIPT

Stand with your weight evenly distributed between both feet, with the knees slightly bent and soft, and the upper body straight yet relaxed. The gaze is soft and directed toward the ground about 5 or 8 feet in front of you. You don't have to stare at your feet with a bent neck—keep the neck in a normal position. Bring your awareness to the soles of the feet and notice the weight of your body in the heels, the balls of the feet, and the toes. Even before you start walking you may notice a mind full of thoughts and stories, distracting sensations throughout the body, and a variety of emotions. Simply notice each distraction with kind curiosity as much as possible, and gently return your awareness to the weight in the feet. Continue on with the lifting-moving-placing sequence step by step as you move forward along your walking path. At the end of your path, come to a stop, pausing briefly to feel the weight evenly on both feet. Turn around to face the other direction, and walk back the way you came. Continue walking back and forth along your walking path, noticing the lifting-moving-placing-shift sequence of each step.

You may want to experiment with changing your walking speed. Notice how the experience changes when you slow down even further, but don't walk so slow that you lose your balance. If you find balancing a challenge in general, make sure you walk close to a wall so you can support yourself with one hand. If you are feeling restless or very sleepy, you can walk at full speed or even faster than a normal walking pace during your practice.

[Facilitators walk in silence with the participants. After 10 minutes, pause in place for a breath or two and ring the bell. Transition back to your seat in silence.]

Variation: Mindful Movement

If your group is not able to do walking practice (for example, too old, too obese, too sick) you can do a Mindful Movement meditation instead. Please go to http://www.sharingmindfulness.com to download instructions for Mindful Movement and a simple series of poses for chair yoga.

Group Process (10 MINUTES)

Following the Walking Meditation or Mindful Movement practice, gather in the large group for about 10 minutes to create space to process the experience. Foster a sense of warmth and curiosity for a wide variety of experiences. Many group members will report a sense of peacefulness or calm. But some may notice restlessness or agitation. Again, remind the group that all of these states are in fact accessible to all of us. This is not a relaxation practice but a practice to become aware of what is happening in your life just as you are.

Theme: Our Storytelling Minds (20 MINUTES)

Stories are powerful elements in our lives. Master teacher Jack Kornfield is himself a wonderful storyteller. Yet he also says, "We must understand the power of the stories we tell and differentiate them from the direct experience of life. In this way, we can use thoughts without being trapped in them." You've probably heard of the saying that the mind is a wonderful servant but a horrible master.

"Imagine you have a constant companion who is with you every moment you are awake. Now, this companion may be well intentioned and quite decent but he has this habit of whispering a constant monologue in your ear. This monologue contains a variety of random observations, worries about the future, rehashing of past events, and an assortment of malicious judgments about you and the world around you. So imagine this companion whispering the following into your ear, 'This is boring. You want to do something more fun? Hey, look at the shoes that woman is wearing—who would pay for such ugly shoes? You need a vacation, but you better concentrate on paying your credit card bills instead. Why did your boss put you down in front of everyone yesterday? Maybe you're going to be fired…you never fit in there anyway. And stop eating so much—you're fat.' This monologue never ends. Would you tolerate such a companion? Would you find this speech particularly compelling? You would probably do everything you could to get away from it. And it is easy to see how hearing this constant stream of commentary could drive negative mood states and tension in the body. But we not only tolerate the constant chatter in our minds, we are seduced and mesmerized by it. We somehow come to believe that these ruminations, judgments, and worries are an accurate representation of how our lives and the world 'really are.'

"Our mindfulness practice lets us see into this stream of thoughts. We soon learn to identify thoughts as simply that—thoughts. Our thoughts are not reality, not the way things 'really are,' and, more important, our thoughts aren't even who we are. We get pulled deeply into the constant chattering of the mind. The *story* we tell ourselves seduces us. It pulls us into a narrative, which might not even be all that accurate, and pulls us away from the sensory experience of the present moment. Our thoughts can pull us away from the felt experience of being fully in our miraculous lives. For example, if you have a history of lower-back pain, you have a story about your back.

Even if you *don't* have a history of lower-back pain you likely have a story about 'how your back is.' This story is not always aligned with the sensory experience of your back right this moment.

"Our mindfulness practice allows us to look deeply at our thoughts in a kind and nonjudgmental way. We learn that thoughts and stories are always present but not always true."

Here are some additional talking points to assist you in teaching a class how to identify and work with thoughts without becoming lost in them:

Our minds are always on. "Even when you lie down on the couch to rest for a minute, your mind isn't in *neutral mode* but is filled with thoughts, even if they are just below the level of awareness. And the nature of these thoughts shape and drive our lived experience, so we want to understand them. We bring our kind awareness to these thoughts to see the mind's patterns. This is a fundamental skill of a mindfulness practice: observing the mind with kind awareness without getting lost in any particular story."

You can't turn off the thoughts. "The goal of our mindfulness practice is not to 'empty the mind' or turn off the thoughts. This isn't possible. As we said before: The brain secretes thoughts like the mouth secretes saliva. It's just what the mind does. Be cautious of falling into the trap of expecting to 'control' the thoughts or the wandering mind. Thought structure has a tendency to proliferate; we start thinking about one thing and this branches out and out again until we are thinking about something seemingly unrelated and don't know how we got there."

Just because you can think it doesn't mean that it's true. "We all have wonderfully creative minds. Just imagine riding through the sky on the back of a dragon. Feel the wind in your face and taste the scorched, sulfurous air of your pet dragon's fiery breath. We can think about all this but that certainly doesn't make it true. But that one is easier to see as fantastical than other thoughts we might have that are made up by our creative minds and have just as little to do with reality as riding a dragon. For instance, what if, after some of your friends got together and didn't invite you, you thought, 'I must have done something to make them mad at me.' After thinking this thought for a few hours, we convince ourselves it must be true. Mindfulness-based cognitive therapy or MBCT uses the expression; 'Thoughts are not facts—even the ones that tell you they are.'"

Don't distinguish between good and bad thoughts. "We don't have to 'work' with our thoughts in any particular way." Clinicians trained in cognitive behavioral therapy teach patients explicit skills to identify negative thoughts (or hot thoughts), examine the evidence of their truth, and seek alternative or more balanced interpretations of events. Mindfulness is different. "From a mindfulness approach, we don't have to work with each thought; we just learn to relate to *all* thoughts differently." This is a very important point, as we don't have to deal with the thoughts on a content level.

Waterfall. The waterfall metaphor is useful for some practitioners who feel overwhelmed by the unending torrent of negative thoughts. "Sometimes it can feel hopeless and bleak to sit with a stream of difficult thoughts, like standing at the bottom of a giant waterfall. Tons of water come pouring down directly on your head, much like being constantly bombarded by negative thoughts. The instinct might be to try to turn off the waterfall. But this is a hopeless and impossible task. It takes skill to realize you don't have to stand right in the spot where tons of water falls. Simply take a few steps back, or move behind the waterfall. You can find refuge beneath an overhang where you can observe the powerful cascading water without being consumed by it. Learn to lean back from your experience and observe it without getting lost in it."

Two-step process on how to work with thoughts. Jack Kornfield suggests two steps to relate to our thoughts in useful and healthy ways. "The first is simply to come into contact with, or bring into our awareness, the contents of our own thoughts. This is our internal soundtrack. We need to notice our habits of mind and how repetitive our thinking is. Second, we must develop the skills to disentangle ourselves from all of our thoughts. We discover with great relief that our stories do not fully define us. Much of our mental suffering comes from desperately holding on to our thinking and beliefs. The insubstantial, endlessly repetitive nature of thinking is revealed from within the stillness of our mindfulness practice. And we can rest in the spacious embrace of the loving heart instea d of getting lost in the labyrinth of thought."

Stress in Our Lives and in Our Bodies

It is helpful to briefly review stress in an Introduction to Mindfulness program. The challenge, of course, is what to select from a large and ever-growing body of scientific evidence on stress and the benefits of mindfulness, and how to condense the essence of this work into an accessible, 5-minute presentation that fits into our theme of the storytelling mind.

An essential and highly readable reference is Stanford primatologist Robert Sapolsky's book, *Why Zebras Don't Get Ulcers*. We repeatedly refer to this book when teaching about the impact of stress on the body.

For our introductory class, we have distilled a number of key points into an accessible overview. Understandably, such a brief overview includes a risk of oversimplifying the many complex processes involved. Nevertheless, here are some key talking points to summarize stress in the body and link the topic to this session's theme:

Define stress. "We all understand personally what stress is, but it can be a challenge to define. One definition is the emotional or physiological tension or strain from adverse circumstances. There are a number of sources of stress. These include both external sources—like traffic, financial issues, work demands, or social and family struggles—and internal sources—like our thoughts, such as a negative interpretation of a situation that triggers a stress response."

Stress is very subjective. What one person finds enjoyable (for example, knitting or motorcycle racing) might be stressful for the next. Be sure to normalize this fact in your discussions.

Interpretation and perception matter. An individual's stress level is directly related to his or her cognitive appraisal of the event that triggers the stress. An innocent garter snake may cause fear and a great deal of stress in one person and a playful sense of working in the garden for another.

No one can avoid stressful experiences. "Our lives are brimming with them. The goal is to manage stress skillfully. A key element is to be aware of internal ruminations and worry. Our thoughts and stories can contribute to our stress."

Not all stress is bad. A low to medium level of temporary stress can lead to optimal performance. Chronic stress that is unremitting not only makes us miserable but also downregulates the immune system and plays a roll in cellular aging (Simon et al., 2006).

Chronic stress negatively impacts health. Life expectancy in the year 1900 was about forty-four years, with the leading causes of death all linked to infectious agents including pneumonia, tuberculosis, and diarrhea or enteritis. Now, more than one hundred years later, life expectancy is about seventy-nine years. Modern medicine (and modern plumbing) has nearly doubled the average life span. The leading causes of death are now heart disease, cancer, and respiratory illness (CDC, 2014). These are chronic rather than acute illnesses, and we increasingly understand how stress plays a major role in immune dysregulation and disease (Glaser & Kiecolt-Glaser, 2005).

The fight-or-flight response. "It is essential to understand that our activating systems, the *sympathetic nervous system* and its fight-or-flight response, are designed to protect us and to keep us safe. Our ancestors needed this burst of energy and racing heart to get away from those saber-toothed cats. And the ancient people who were always relaxed and mellow? We aren't related to those people—they became some predator's lunch! The problem then isn't that we have this activation mechanism in the body; the issue is it gets triggered not only in life-threatening situations but throughout the day. This can happen when we are stuck in traffic or a coworker gives us an unpleasant look." In our modern life, we spend too much time in the sympathetic nervous system, or arousal (including in adrenaline rushes we actively seek), and not enough time in the *parasympathetic system* of restoration and healing.

A natural negativity bias. "We are hardwired to notice threats and bad situations immediately and strongly. This negativity bias is meant to keep us safe. Neuropsychologist and meditation teacher Rick Hanson sums this up with the phrase, 'Your brain is like Velcro for negative experiences and Teflon for positive ones.' Our mindfulness practice allows us not just to focus on the negative experiences but to also savor and soak up the benefits of positive experiences and promote a nervous system shift to a more healing state."

Mindfulness and locus of control. Mindfulness helps us to become less reactive to stressors by providing some space between what happens and our reaction. As Viktor Frankl says: "Between the stimulus and the response there is a space. This is where our freedom lies." Through this practice we move the locus of control from being outside of us back to ourselves: *I can't control this happening to me, but I can control how I respond to it.* As we open up to the present moment and let go of the ruminative mind, we can find more joy and less tension and stress. We are less likely to get "lost in the story."

Technique: STOP

The STOP technique is simple, easy to use, and very helpful. Yet a word of caution is needed about the expectations some participants have with this technique. They may feel it only *works* when they find a sense of calm, feel less reactive, or an urge goes away. Reassure them: The fundamental purpose of the STOP technique is to come fully to this moment and observe what is happening rather than just reacting. Sometimes you may notice that the sensations in the body, your thoughts, or your emotions have changed, and sometimes you might notice that they haven't changed at all. You are still doing it just right. The goal is to notice, not to change your experience.

"Stressors make us vulnerable to reacting in a habitual way. And when we are under stress, we frequently have limited access to our internal resources. This habitual reacting may not be the most skillful means available to us in any moment. So when you want to *respond* skillfully, instead of *react* mindlessly, try the STOP technique. It is easy to remember—STOP—even in a stressful situation. The goal isn't necessarily to change how you feel but to come out of automatic pilot and notice things just as they are."

S–**Stop** for just a moment. Don't react. Give yourself the gift of brief reflection.

T–**Take a breath.** Breathe in and out. Track your breath. Sense the chest rising and falling.

O–**Observe your experience.** Notice the sensations in the body. Observe the thoughts or the story going through your mind, and appreciate that thoughts are not facts. Explore your emotions and get a sense of where you are in this moment.

P–**Proceed.** Move forward in a way that feels right to you and is consistent with your values.

Example. Jack, a combat vet with PTSD, came back to class the week after he learned this technique very happy to share his experience. "The STOP practice is just what I needed. I've been using it at least ten times a day. I used to react to everything, like a puppet bouncing on the end of someone else's string. Now that I use STOP, I don't have to fly off the handle. I have more choices."

Introduction to Mindfulness of Sound
(5 MINUTES)

Just as sensation in the body is used as the anchor to the present moment in the Body Scan exercise, so too is the sensory experience of sound used as an anchor to the present moment in Mindfulness of Sound.

It is important to note that using sound as the primary object of mindfulness works better than the breath for some people. The breath is the traditional object for many good reasons, but it isn't always a comfortable choice for certain individuals. For example people with asthma, COPD (chronic obstructive pulmonary disease), or a near-drowning experience might never be comfortable and at ease with focusing on the breath. The same is often true for people who suffer from GAD (generalized anxiety disorder), who might be hyperfocused on sensations in the chest, like their rate of breath or the beating of the heart.

For these people, we recommend sound as their main mindfulness object. Alternatively, they can focus on the sensations in their feet or hands—whatever helps them more to stay present.

When introducing Mindfulness of Sound, describe how this mindfulness practice uses another sense, the sense of sound, to come fully to this moment with kind acceptance. The task is simply to notice the soundscape of the present moment. You don't have to interpret the sound or identify what might be making the sound. You also don't have to extend your sense of hearing to seek out sound. You can allow the sounds of the moment to simply come to you. Mindfulness of sound is also a good practice to teach the skill of falling into receptivity versus striving and seeking. Become receptive to the soundscape. It might even be helpful to shift the weight back a bit into the chair, the opposite of sitting on the edge of one's seat, to provide a postural reminder of being in receptivity.

It is useful to start the practice with what is familiar and then transition into Mindfulness of Sound. So the sequence might go as follows: An invitation to close the eyes, beginning with 5 to 10 minutes of Mindfulness of Breathing, transitioning to 5 to 10 minutes of Mindfulness of Sound, and coming back to the breath before closing the practice. This also provides an opportunity to reinforce the Mindfulness of Breathing practice introduced last week. Again, allow the practice itself to be the teacher.

Labeling Practice

Once you have established the focus of attention, and people have had some time to try out the new practice for a couple of minutes, introduce the labeling practice. Labeling is softly naming to yourself where the attention went to, like "Planning, planning," "itching, itching," and so forth. Then instruct participants to bring the attention back to sound (or whatever object of attention is the focus). This helps to disengage with the content of the thought or the meaning of the sensation. A 2007 study out of UCLA showed that people who named the facial expression in a picture (for example, as "angry" or "fearful") had less reactivity in the "alarm center" of the brain, the amygdala (Creswell, Way, Eisenberger, & Lieberman, 2007). Name it to tame it.

Mindfulness of Sound (15 MINUTES)

Like Mindfulness of Breathing and the Body Scan, Mindfulness of Sound is an attentional practice. We are using the sensations of sounds as the anchor to the present moment.

MINDFULNESS OF SOUND SCRIPT

Taking a moment to sit in an upright and dignified posture with both feet flat on the floor. Maybe having a sense that your body is supported yet at ease. Allowing the eyes to close, or simply softening the gaze. Noticing what is here for you right now in your experience. And letting yourself be just as you are.

[Pause]

As best you can, taking your attention to your breath. Noticing each breath and sensing how the chest rises on the inhale and falls away on the exhale.

[Pause]

Observing this breath right here.

[Pause]

Using your breath as your anchor to the present moment. And each time your mind wanders away from the breath, simply noticing it, and, without judgment, bringing your kind attention back to the breath.

[Pause]

Breathing in. Breathing out. Observing the rhythm and quality of the breath just as it is.

[Pause]

There's no need to control or manipulate the breath in any way. Simply allowing the breath to breathe with its own natural rhythm.

[Pause]

And now, as best you can, change the anchor of your practice from the breath to notice the sounds all around you. Directing the attention to the soundscape around you. To the sensation of sound.

[Pause]

Sound is the perfect object of mindfulness, as we hear only the sounds of this moment. We don't hear the sounds of the past or the future.

[Pause]

What is being heard in this moment?

[Pause]

There's no need to identify the sound or try to figure it out in any way; just notice the quality of the sound. Observing the sounds of each moment.

[Long pause]

Noticing where your mind is right now. Has it bounced into the future? Into planning what is yet to come? Or are you rehashing the past? Just noticing where your attention goes in the silent moments and gently, with kindness, bringing your attention back to the soundscape that's all around you.

[Pause]

There's no need to reach out and search for sounds. Fall into receptivity. Perhaps, without really moving, having the intention to lean back just the slightest bit. You can imagine placing the attention right at the opening of your ears and let the sounds come to you.

[Pause]

Each time the mind wanders away, kindly bringing the attention back to the sounds of this moment. The sounds around you are the sounds of this very moment. Notice them.

[Long pause]

Perhaps you might also notice an automatic sense of liking some sounds more than others. Birdsong might register as more pleasant than the rumble of a garbage truck. Just notice this. Everything is actually just the sound of the moment. It's only a wave of sound. First, there is only the sound itself, and then the liking or the disliking of it. You as the one who is hearing adds the interpretation and judgment, if any. Letting it be just as it is.

[Pause]

You may notice some sounds are quite close to you. Other sounds are off in the distance and may be very far away. And if you pay very close attention, you may notice there are even sounds inside your own body.

[Pause]

Using the soundscape as an anchor to this moment of your life. Right here. Right now.

[Pause]

Perhaps you are repeatedly distracted by another sensation, emotion, or thought. If it seems particularly sticky, you can try labeling the experience. Such as, "Ah, this is itching…. Itching." Or "This is the planning mind." Simply labeling whatever your experience is in the moment. And then, without judgment, returning your attention as best you can to sound.

[Pause]

What are the sounds of *this* moment?

[Long pause]

And now shifting again, moving the attention away from sounds and back to the breath. Breathing in and out. Resting in the observation of the breath and your own good company.

[Pause]

Each time the mind wanders away, coming back to the breath. This breath right here. Breathing in. Breathing out. Right here in this moment.

[Pause]

[Ring bell]

Small Group Check-In (5 MINUTES)

It is always helpful to break up the class into small groups of two or three. Ask the participants to discuss what the practice was like for them and what they learned. This form of sharing is particularly important when introducing any new practice. Small group discussions allow everyone to comment on their experience.

Group Process (10 MINUTES)

The large group format allows for the normalization of the full range of experiences among participants. We like to close the class with a final metaphor that simultaneously addresses the disengagement with the stream of cognition and a sense of spaciousness. It only takes a minute or two yet nicely summarizes the content of today's session. See the ocean metaphor in the "Story" section of this chapter.

Wrap-Up and Homework (5 MINUTES)

For Session 3, the homework is as follows: Practice the 10-minute guided Mindfulness of Breathing and Mindfulness of Sound meditations daily. Continue to cultivate an informal practice of mindfulness with everyday activities such as brushing your teeth and taking a shower. Practice the STOP technique at moments when you're prone to reactivity in order to create space to respond in more skillful means.

SESSION 4

Cultivating Kindness

In session 4 we introduce loving-kindness as a concept (*what*) and as a practice (*how*). It not only matters that we pay attention but also *how* we do that. Attention sometimes can have a cold or harsh quality to it. Loving-kindness starts with our intention to cultivate a more open and friendly stance toward ourselves and others. Ultimately, the difference between a joyful, happy life and misery has as much to do with the frame through which we see our experience as it does the events we experience (*why*). It is developed through the formal practice of Loving-Kindness.

OBJECTIVES OF SESSION 4

- Introduce the Loving-Kindness practice for other and self.
- Describe how loving-kindness changes experience and supports growth and healing.
- Introduce the technique: Anchor Phrase or RAIN (working with challenging emotions).
- Provide support for ongoing formal and informal practice.

Session 4 Outline

Time (in minutes)	Cumulative Time	Activity
5	5	Welcome and Check-In
10	15	Introduction to Loving-Kindness
25	40	**Loving-Kindness for Other and Self** and **Mindfulness of Breathing**
10	50	Group Process (Q&A; follow-up from last week)
15	65	Techniques: RAIN (how to work with challenging emotions) or Anchor Phrase
10	75	Small Group Check-In
10	85	Group Process
5	90	Wrap-Up and Homework (10-minute guided Loving-Kindness or 5 to 10 minutes of Mindfulness of Breathing or Mindfulness of Sound starting with short Loving-Kindness for Self; continued informal practice, Anchor Phrase or RAIN)

Materials. Roster, watch or timer, sign-in sheet, bell, Session 4 outline, handouts

Poem. "Saint Francis and the Sow" by Galway Kinnell, lines 1–11

Story. "Story of the Golden Buddha" inspired by Jack Kornfield's telling, loosely based on the true story of how the world's largest solid gold statue was discovered

There was a thriving monastery in the north of Thailand in the mid-1950s. Among its many Buddha statues there was one very big one that was made out of clay. It wasn't particularly pretty, but the monks favored it because it had been part of the monastery for centuries and they loved it for its longevity. After an especially strong rainy season followed by a hot spell, the monks noticed that the statue had gotten some cracks. One curious monk took a flashlight and shone it into the biggest crack. He was very surprised to see something shiny reflecting the light. He called the other monks, and they carefully opened the crack a little more. What they found was a solid gold statue beneath twelve inches of clay.

The statue is now in a temple in Bangkok and visited and revered by millions of visitors every year. In turned out that in the thirteenth and fourteenth centuries, the monks had covered the statue in thick clay to protect it from marauding clans. Generations later, the knowledge of the Buddha's gold core had been lost to time. Everyone thought it was an unassuming mud statue.

We, of course, are just like this. We cover ourselves up with layers of protection. Our goal is to protect ourselves from harm, but over time we forget our true golden nature. It is a nature of friendliness and kindness.

Never forget your own nature. Be the gold, not the mud.

Welcome and Check-In (5 MINUTES)

Welcome everybody to Session 4. Invite participants to share a short, one-sentence check-in describing how their personal practice went during the past week.

Introduction to Loving-Kindness (10 MINUTES)

The theme of "cultivating kindness" is woven throughout the entire class, starting here with the introduction of loving-kindness. From working with many hundreds of people over the years and from our own personal practices, we know that those who have the strongest Loving-Kindness practice working for them get through life's ups and downs much better than the rest. We see this in groups, through working with individuals, and in supporting people on retreat. This is what we also hear from other experienced mindfulness teachers. It is not only important that you pay attention to the present moment, but also *how* you pay attention.

Loving-Kindness is a traditional meditation practice that is as old and established as Mindfulness of Breathing. It aims to increase feelings of caring and warmth for the self and for other people.

Until recent years, the common belief among scientists was that every person has a *mood set point* that doesn't change much over a life span. That explains why people who win the lottery or become paraplegic in an accident will (after some transitional time in elation or depression) return to their mood set point. There is also a relationship between mood set point and which side of an individual's prefrontal cortex is dominant. When the right prefrontal cortex is more active, there are higher rates of depression. When the left prefrontal cortex is more active, an individual's overall mood is happier.

Neuroscientist Richard Davidson from the University of Wisconsin–Madison discovered that Tibetan monks, who have decades of training in meditation and compassion, have the highest left prefrontal cortex activation out of hundreds of people tested. The research question was obvious: Was this due to meditation practice, or some other difference such as lifestyle? To explore this, the team studied before-and-after brain images on participants who volunteered for an eight-week MBSR class. Davidson and colleagues demonstrated that meditation for forty-five minutes every day for eight weeks is sufficient to increase the left prefrontal cortex and that these changes corresponded to mood improvements (Davidson et al., 2003). Our mood set points *can* be altered.

This is something that mindfulness teachers can attest to. People who practice Loving-Kindness or compassion as a regular practice become happier over time.

Tell your class, "Loving-Kindness helps us to set the intention to be better friends to ourselves and to others, by realizing that we all want to be happy and free of suffering. It counteracts the loneliness and sense of separation that comes from not feeling connected to other people. It is a powerful practice that can change how we respond to difficult situations over time. We can learn to turn down the volume on the internal, snide monologue of self-judgment and be kinder to ourselves. After all, if we aren't going to be kind to ourselves, who will?"

Barriers to the Practice

Many beginners to the Loving-Kindness practice struggle with the idea of loving-kindness as phony or contrived. Or they might think that it's a sign of weakness. Meditation teacher Sharon Salzberg says, "I think kindness in many ways is an overlooked force. Culturally it might be considered a secondary virtue, as though to say, 'Well, if you can't be brilliant and you can't be wonderful, be kind. At least it is something.' Yet the reality in our lives is that kindness is a powerful transformative tool" (Goldstein, 2014).

You can say, "We can be very clear and strong—and even say no to things that are not right—coming from a place of kindness instead of anger or resentment.

"So even if we 'don't feel it,' the practice will work anyway. If you keep doing it, staying with the intention and just repeating the phrases and making a connection with yourself, it will inevitably work."

The Practice of Loving-Kindness

So, what's the practice like? Loving-Kindness, like all of the meditation practices we offer here, is primarily a body practice. "We first connect with our body, our felt sense of the moment. Ask yourself, 'How do I feel right now?' Feeling the body as it's sitting or lying down, feeling into the areas of contact as usual, and checking what else is there. Is there tension in the shoulders? A sense of dread about the work we have to get done later? What's our inner dialogue like today?

"Then we check into the area of the heart. For most people, love and connection (if felt in a physical way) is felt in the area of our physical heart. We don't talk of heartache or a tug at the heart strings for nothing." Some people feel love in their belly, in the area of the solar plexus—mention this in your guidance to give people an option. "As we place the attention there, we might feel something—or nothing." Many people will understand if you ask them if their heart feels open or closed, but not everybody.

"We bring to mind a loved one and we send him or her friendly wishes by silently repeating four different phrases." Traditionally, the phrases come from each of the following four categories:

- Safe and protected

- Physically healthy

- Mentally happy
- Ease of well-being

"As we say the phrases, we aim to connect with the felt sense of the words we wish for, like 'peaceful' for example. But we are aware that the goal is not to feel 'all warm and fuzzy'—rather, it's to stick with our intention to develop a friendlier stance in life toward ourselves and others. You can adapt the phrases so that they feel more meaningful to you or are easier for you to connect with." As a facilitator, pick the phrases that work best for you, wishes that are personal and enduring. You can also give class participants permission to alter the phrases a bit so they fit better with their own personal wishes for health and happiness.

Here are some suggestions for loving-kindness phrases:

"May you be safe and protected, free from inner and outer harm."

"May you be healthy and strong."

"May you be physically healthy and free from pain."

"May you be truly happy and deeply peaceful."

"May you live your life with ease."

"May you be peaceful and free from worry."

"May you accept yourself completely—just the way you are."

"May you accept yourself completely the way you are—for *this* moment."

Often the people in our class who have a life active in prayer will tell us that the Loving-Kindness practice feels like praying to them.

Loving-Kindness Phrases Are Not Positive Affirmations

We can't emphasize this point enough. Many people have heard or even used positive affirmation and, judging by the number of self-help books on the topic, they work great for many people. But because of this, many of your class participants will have interference with what they have learned previously. It's not uncommon for us to hear at the end of class, when we ask what people found most helpful, someone characterizing the loving-kindness phrases as "the positive affirmations."

A *positive affirmation* is a technique used to effect change by repeating (or meditating on) a key phrase with a desired outcome in the present tense to bring about this outcome. For example, a positive affirmation would be "I am healthy." In contrast, a loving-kindness phrase is a *wish* for something that is universally desirable for all beings, one that starts with the words "May you..." or "May I..." The loving-kindness phrase in this example would be "May I be healthy." In our experience, a positive affirmation can clash, sometimes cruelly so, with reality. A loving-kindness phrase can feel unreachable, but as it is a wish, we can connect with it on a different level. It might be something that we still can connect with even when we feel very far from what we wish or what is wished for us. We can open our hearts toward the intention and possibility that it carries.

In this six-week class series we only focus on loving-kindness for a friend and for ourselves, as this is sufficient for an introductory-level class.

Loving-Kindness for a Friend

For a beginner to the practice of Loving-Kindness, we start by calling up the image of a friend, a loved one, a teacher, a spiritual being, or even a beloved pet. "Don't get hung up on who to choose. You might also realize that some relationships are not so easy: You might love your best friend, but she might have really talked out of line at the last party... What to do? Choose her anyway. We suppose that you can still wish her well and to be happy."

Recommend that participants work with the same person over a period of time. "This will help you to see the changes in your relationship more clearly on your end. Some days you may feel more connected, some less. Why? Because *things change*." See also chapter 4 on "impermanence" for other ways to approach this subject. "But this shouldn't keep you from doing a round of Loving-Kindness at times when you include all of your friends and loved ones.

"Once you have established the image or connection, start repeating the phrases silently for a number of times before moving on to the next. It is helpful to see if you can get a sense of the meaning of words—for example, a sense of 'safe' or 'peaceful.' It doesn't mean that you need to feel safe yourself, but most people have a sense of what 'safe' or 'peaceful' feels like."

Loving-Kindness for Oneself

Once participants have practiced Loving-Kindness for a friend for about 5 minutes, give the class two options: "You can shift the attention to yourself and start sending the wishes to yourself; you can do this for the adult you are today, or you can go back in your own history and see if there was a time when making a connection with the younger you, as a child or even an infant—maybe you remember a photograph from that time?—seems easier. Or if loving-kindness feels way too steep at the beginning, you can imagine that now your friend, loved one, teacher, or pet sends you the very same wishes; you start practicing by just receiving the loving-kindness wishes. It can be helpful to consciously recall that your friend indeed loves you and wishes you well. It is probably very easy for that person!

"Repeat each phrase a number of times before moving on to the next. Just as before, feel into the meaning of each phrase."

Receiving Loving-Kindness

How does one practice receiving loving-kindness? We mentioned at the beginning of the chapter that Loving-Kindness is a body practice. We use the body as a kind of sounding board. We sometimes tell our students "listen not with your head, but with your entire body." If this doesn't make any sense it can be helpful to check into the area of the heart, as well as the entire chest and the face. Do those areas feel more relaxed, warm, maybe tingly? These areas are just suggestions; it might be different for you or for your students.

Hands-On Loving-Kindness

You might want to offer your students the lovely technique of hands-on Loving-Kindness. This is done by putting a hand over one's heart when practicing Loving-Kindness for oneself (see also Session +1 for the supportive touch practice). The physical contact and warmth of a hand, even one's own, can help with making a felt connection with the practice.

Loving-Kindness in Action

How do we know that Loving-Kindness works? Interestingly enough, we often hear that in the beginning people don't feel much change themselves. However, those close to them might mention a difference. Like Mona, who shared in class: "I wasn't sure that this loving-kindness stuff works, but the other day my boyfriend said that he had noticed that I don't get so down on myself anymore when I make a mistake."

Loving-Kindness Practice (25 MINUTES)

You will guide your class through 10 minutes of Loving-Kindness for other and self, then transition into 15 minutes of Mindfulness of Breathing. You might want to give participants the option to stay with Loving-Kindness longer if they wish.

Adapting this script to the needs of your group is of particular importance. Loving-Kindness can easily come across as too soft, weak, or sugary. It is not. It grows strength, courage, and a sense of connection. You need to find a language that participants can hear and relate to. Do that with the loving-kindness phrases as well. Let yourself be guided by the question "What wishes for themselves will allow my group to feel safer, more at ease, more connected?" The phrases need to be concrete and relevant to their life circumstances.

Finally, because this is a lengthier meditation, reinforce the extra support participants can experience from a dignified posture. See "Meditation Postures" in chapter 4. Be sure to offer options for those who need them.

LOVING-KINDNESS FOR OTHER
AND SELF SCRIPT

Finding a comfortable posture. Relaxing, if that is possible. Relaxing the body and also the mind. We are not trying to make anything happen.

For Loving-Kindness practice, a comfortable position is of particular importance.

Sitting up straight, with your feet on the floor.

[Pause]

Starting by bringing attention to your chest, to your physical heart, or to wherever you feel kindness and connection in the body, if you do feel it. For most people that is the actual heart, but for some it can also be the belly, or perhaps some other place.

[Pause]

Notice if your heart feels open or closed today.

Or anything in between.

Checking in, not in order to change anything, but in order to know.

[Pause]

Remember that in this practice we work with intention.

The intention to cultivate an open heart and a friendlier stance toward others and ourselves.

It may feel fake or contrived as you start out, and that is okay.

[Pause]

Now bringing to mind one person you feel a connection with.

[Give three to four options appropriate for your group, from the following list. When choosing, ask yourself, "Who might my students feel connected to?"]

a loved one

a friend

a family member

a comrade

a teacher

somebody who was kind to you

a spiritual being

a pet

Don't get hung up on who to choose. Whoever you choose, imagining the person being here with you, maybe sitting across from you and looking at you, if that imagery works for you. The more detail you use to recall his or her image or presence, the more likely you will feel a connection.

Maybe feeling your gratitude for this person being in your life. Maybe recalling something that you like about this person or something kind that he or she has done.

[Pause]

Now, starting to send this person friendly wishes, or loving-kindness.

I will be saying some phrases that you can repeat silently to yourself. It is helpful if you can get a sense of the meaning of the words, even if you yourself don't feel this way in this present moment.

Feel free to adapt the words so they resonate with you.

[Choose one of the two phrases below]

"May you be safe and protected from internal and external harm."

[Or]

"May you be safe and protected, free from internal demons and external threats."

[Repeat the phrase after 2–3 breaths]

[Choose one of the two phrases below]

"May you be truly happy and deeply peaceful."

[Or]

"May you experience moments of peace and happiness."

[Repeat the phrase after 2–3 breaths]

"May you live your life with ease."

[Repeat the phrase after 2–3 breaths]

"May you be healthy and strong—and if that is not possible, may you accept your limitations with grace."

[Pause]

Now moving the attention from your friend to yourself.

You can send loving-kindness to yourself as the adult that you are today. Or perhaps it might be easier to imagine sending loving-kindness to a younger version of yourself. You can also connect with what you like about yourself or a good deed you have done. And if nothing comes to mind, just connect with your genuine wish to be happy. A wish that you share with everyone.

And if even that feels too challenging, you can also have the person you just sent loving-kindness to send you those very same wishes. Which would be so easy for him or her.

So choose what works for you. And then use the phrases in a way that makes sense.

[Pause]

[Choose one of the two phrases below]

"May I be safe and protected from internal and external harm."

[Or]

"May I be safe and protected, free from internal demons and external threats."

[Repeat the phrase after 2–3 breaths]

[Pause]

[Choose one of the two phrases below]

"May I be truly happy and deeply peaceful."

[Or]

"May I experience moments of peace and happiness."

[Repeat the phrase after 2–3 breaths]

[Pause]

"May I live my life with ease."

[Repeat the phrase after 2–3 breaths]

[Pause]

"May I be healthy and strong—and if that is not possible, may I accept my limitations with grace."

[Pause]

Finding your breath. Gathering up these wishes for yourself. For safety and protection, health, happiness, and ease. And allowing yourself to savor these kind wishes. Getting a sense for how this feels in the body.

[Long pause]

Coming to an end with loving-kindness for yourself in your own time and transition to the breath. But feel free to just keep doing loving-kindness for the rest of the session if it feels right.

[Begin Mindfulness of Breathing practice; see script in Session 2]

[Ring bell]

Group Process (10 MINUTES)

Give your group some moments to transition back into talking mode. Then invite questions about the Loving-Kindness practice.

You usually will get a mix of people who like it and can see how doing this on a regular basis will help them be kinder with themselves over time, and others who initially have a really hard time with the practice and will go through the motions for quite a while. It's important to validate and normalize both experiences and make it very clear to the reluctant participants that the practice will support their change anyway. It might be helpful to share the following story with them:

> **Example.** In her book *Lovingkindness: The Revolutionary Art of Happiness*, Sharon Salzberg tells her own story of struggling mightily with the practice. She was so sure that her self-loathing was too strong to be penetrated by anything. But determined to give it her full try she started a longer silent retreat where she did nothing but Loving-Kindness day in and day out. After a couple of days, an emergency at home called her out of the retreat. As she packed her things, annoyed about having to leave early, she dropped a glass, which shattered on the floor. Her first, immediate response to this was, as usual, her inner critic saying, "You are such a klutz!" Normally her inner dialogue would go immediately into ugly berating, but now a new voice came up and added, "And I love you anyway." She was shocked. And she realized that the practice did work after all.

Make sure that you also inquire about the past week: "How was the formal practice? Informal practice? Any other mindful or mindless moments anyone would like to share?"

Techniques: RAIN or Anchor Phrase (15 MINUTES)

At this point, you as the class facilitator have a choice. If you are teaching in a mental health setting, you might skip the RAIN technique on how to work with challenging emotions and introduce the Anchor Phrase technique instead. In most other settings, RAIN can be a very helpful practice tool.

RAIN

This acronym is a step-by-step technique that helps us to work with both physically and emotionally challenging experiences. From working with thoughts in the previous week we now turn the attention to another "sticky" area: our emotions. We introduce RAIN in this session in combination with Loving-Kindness, since it is much easier to infuse our approach of working with an intense or challenging emotion with kindness. As with other techniques, we strongly recommend that you as the facilitator get very accustomed to practicing this tool successfully yourself before you start teaching it.

It is helpful to use a whiteboard to write down the acronym and its meaning as you explain it.

R–Recognize. The moment of recognition is the moment when awareness kicks in (like the S in STOP), and we suddenly realize that we are in the grip of a strong emotion. It is recognizing the truth of this particular moment.

A–Acknowledge or **Allow.** We acknowledge that what we're experiencing is in fact so. This doesn't mean that we need to like it or accept it—we simply acknowledge that, yes, this is what's happening right now. It is turning toward our experience instead of turning away, which is what we typically and habitually do with something intense or unpleasant.

I–Interest or **Investigate.** In this step we become curious about what this moment, this emotion, actually feels like. It's very important that we don't confuse this opportunity with trying to find out why we are feeling this way. This step of RAIN is about exploring how this particular emotion manifests in the body *right now*. We investigate with curiosity and kindness (here is the tie-in to the topic of the week).

N–Non-identify. Often the physical manifestation of the emotion isn't the problem, it's the meaning we give it or the identification with the emotion that is. For example, "I'm anxious, therefore I'm an anxious person." If we use the analogy of weather (it's RAIN, after all!) we can loosen our grip on the emotion. If we see the emotion like weather passing through, we don't have to take it personally. We don't have to like the storm or to identify with it—we trust that it will pass. It can be very helpful to have your participants do a short experiment here. Ask them to repeat a few times silently to themselves the sentence: "I'm very angry" or "I'm very anxious" (or whatever challenging emotion they choose for themselves). Ask them how that feels in their body. Then ask them to change their sentence to "Wow, there is a lot of anger here" or "There is so much anxiety here right now" or "This is what anxiety feels like." How does that feel in comparison? Most people will feel a clear difference and will describe the latter option as open, more spacious, less threatening, not who they are, and the like.

If you have time and it feels appropriate, you can walk the class through all the steps of RAIN with one recent challenging emotion (make sure they choose something that is not too upsetting or overwhelming).

Anchor Phrase

This technique can be considered a shorthand version of the Loving-Kindness practice. It can be used anytime throughout the day when participants encounter a challenging moment. It introduces the capacity to provide a kind response in the face of struggle.

Encourage them to "Choose a word or a phrase that helps you to stay connected to your intention or to help you through a challenging moment.

"Gently say the phrase to yourself in that moment. If you are by yourself, try placing one hand over your heart for added support." Here are just a few example phrases:

"It's okay."

"This, too, shall pass."

"Yes, this hurts. May I stay open."

"Yes, this hurts. May I be kind to myself."

"Yes, this hurts. May I meet this moment with an open heart."

Give this example: "You notice the stress rising during the day. Your to-do list feels endless and you feel disheartened. Becoming aware of this, you can turn internally toward this stress and tension and keep saying, or whispering, 'It's okay. One moment at a time.'"

If you have the time with your group you can ask them to take a moment to reflect on what might be a supportive phrase for them.

Small Group Check-In (10 MINUTES)

Have participants turn to a neighbor. Ask them to share, in whatever way feels comfortable, what came up for them around the topic of loving-kindness or the anchor phrase. If you are teaching RAIN, you could also use this time to walk them through RAIN (if you haven't already) with an example and maybe have them briefly share with a neighbor.

Group Process (10 MINUTES)

Invite the group to share depending on what they did: talk about experiencing the RAIN practice, or discuss the common themes that came up in the small groups about loving-kindness and anchor phrases.

Wrap-Up and Homework (5 MINUTES)

This week's daily practice: 10 minutes of guided Loving-Kindness practice *or* 5 to 10 minutes of Mindfulness of Breathing (or Mindfulness of Sound) starting or ending with a short Loving-Kindness for self, along with continued informal practice.

Maybe end the class by telling them the story of the golden Buddha.

Clinical Psychologist Perspective: On Working with Emotions

If you are a mental health clinician, chances are you spend a good part of your professional life "working with emotions." You may be helping patients through medication management or by using any number of psychotherapy approaches or orientations. It is likely that much of this is very helpful, even lifesaving, to those you treat. The "working with emotions" framework used in mindfulness can be initially confusing for trained mental health clinicians, since it is simultaneously quite similar to other approaches while also being completely different!

How is it similar? Like many psychotherapy approaches, a core tenet of mindfulness is to eliminate the *avoidance* of an unpleasant stimulus, such as a difficult emotion like anger. We encourage participants to get as close to the emotion as possible! So if you are really mad at a coworker, instead of ruminating about the particular event that made you angry (this is *thinking*), delve deeply into the body to directly experience and sense the emotion (*feeling*). Many psychotherapy approaches similarly target the elimination of avoidance behaviors.

But how is mindfulness completely different? We aren't trying to work with our emotions or trying to change them in any way. We simply let them be as they are, observing them as they morph in our moment-by-moment awareness. Anger becomes confusion and shifts to hurt before it returns to anger. And we hold these emotions in kind, loving awareness. It is the *lens* through which we observe our experience that we hope to infuse with kindness. And the practice of Loving-Kindness really does make it easier to be with everything, even unpleasant or challenging emotions.

Dharma Teacher Perspective: On Loving-Kindness

Traditional Loving-Kindness practice. Traditionally, the full Loving-Kindness practice has five steps, or five categories: loving-kindness for oneself, for a friend or benefactor, for a neutral person, for a challenging person, and for all beings everywhere.

Practice Tip: While we work at calling up a felt sense of love and connection in the body for the different people we wish loving-kindness to, it doesn't really matter if we actually feel it during the practice. Remember that this, too, gets easier with regular practice.

147

As we do the practice with the same wishes through the different categories, we realize that indeed there are common human wishes: for safety, health, peacefulness, joy, strength, acceptance, and so forth. It will become another strong teaching on our shared humanness, our being together in this instead of the struggle in isolation.

Loving-kindness for oneself really comes first? In the traditional instructions, you start with yourself as the center of your experiences and spread out from there. Where else would you start? You can only start changing yourself and then expand the ripples of that change to others. This seems to be a very hard concept for most people in the West. We grow up in a culture where we have the paradox of widespread narcissistic behavior on the one hand, and on the other, the idea of being kind to ourselves being considered selfish, especially for women, or a weakness, as is often the case for men. (This concept of compassion as weakness can even extend to the compassion men might have for others, not just themselves.)

During the last few years, many leading teachers have put a special emphasis on loving-kindness for one's self and changed two things in the instructions: First, they switched the first and second category. We now start with a friend and then move on to self, which many people report is an easier entryway into the practice. If we can generate a felt sense of connection and friendship toward a friend, it might feel easier to then shift to the self and sustain the feeling of loving-kindness. The second change was to start with an emphasis on the first two categories, instead of practicing all five from the beginning.

The Four Immeasurables. Loving-kindness, compassion, sympathetic joy, and equanimity are called the "four heavenly abodes" or the "four immeasurables."

Loving-kindness, or *metta* in Pali, is the friendly, caring attitude toward all beings, including ourselves. You could see this as the baseline feeling. When loving-kindness encounters suffering it turns into *compassion*. Self-compassion arises when the person suffering is oneself. When loving-kindness encounters happiness, joy, and success, it transforms into *sympathetic* or *empathetic joy*. Being happy for and with the other person. Or being happy for ourselves. Rejoicing in the happy circumstances of the other—or oneself.

And because there is so much suffering at all times in the world—but also so much joy and happiness, we need to cultivate the fourth of the immeasurables in order to hold it all: *equanimity*. Equanimity is the ability to stand firm, but not rigid, like a tree in the midst of the always changing winds of life, swaying at times but not blown around helplessly like a sapling.

SESSION 5

Willingness to Be with Things as They Are

In Session 5 the focus is on our resistance against what we see as unpleasant (*what*). We learn that our experience of something—be it pleasant, unpleasant, or neutral—is simply another layer in the richness of the moment. This layer, traditionally called a *feeling tone*, is always present. Think of it as a lens through which we experience life. Our ability to observe this layer, without getting swept away by it, helps support equanimity (*why*). The willingness to be with things as they are *for this moment* can radically change the way we relate to the stress and pain in our life (*how*).

OBJECTIVES OF SESSION 5

- Introduce Loving-Kindness into walking or movement; deepen understanding of loving-kindness as a practice.

- Introduce the technique: exploration of unpleasant, neutral, pleasant.

- Describe how the willingness to be with something unpleasant will lower resistance and therefore the suffering. Introduce Suffering = Pain x Resistance.

- Provide support for ongoing formal practice and reassurance.

Session 5 Outline

Time (in minutes)	Cumulative Time	Activity
5	5	Welcome and Check-In
30	35	**Walking Meditation with Loving-Kindness** (10 minutes), **Loving-Kindness for Other** (5 minutes), **Loving-Kindness for Self** (5 minutes), and **Mindfulness of Breathing** (10 minutes)
10	45	Group Process (Q&A; follow-up from last week)
10	55	Technique: Explore Unpleasant–Neutral–Pleasant
5	60	Group Process
15	75	Theme: Willingness to Be with Things as They Are
10	85	Small Group Check-In
5	90	Wrap-Up and Homework (continue with the Anchor Phrase practice from Session 4, and to be aware of more moments during the day as informal practice; practice 10 to 20 minutes daily of guided meditations of your choice)

Materials. Roster, sign-in sheet, watch or timer, bell, Session 5 outline, handouts, whiteboard, dry-erase markers

Poem. "The Guest House" by Rumi

Story. "The Farmer Whose Horse Ran Away"

Once there was a farmer whose horse ran away. His neighbor came over to tell him he felt sorry for him, only to be told in return, "Who knows what is good or bad?"

It was true. The next day the horse returned, bringing with it eleven wild horses it had met during its adventurous escape. The neighbor came over again, this time to congratulate the farmer on his good fortune. Only to be told once again, "Who knows what is good or bad?"

True this time too. The next day the farmer's son tried to tame one of the wild horses and fell off, breaking his leg. His neighbor came back again one more time to express how bad he felt. But for the third time all the farmer had to say was, "Who knows what is good or bad?"

And once again the farmer was correct, for this time the king of that land had started a war, and the following day soldiers came by to draft young men into the army. But because of his injury, the son was not taken.

Welcome and Check-In (5 MINUTES)

Welcome everybody to Session 5. Go around and ask participants to share their name and a brief snapshot of how they feel in this moment.

Walking Meditation with Loving-Kindness (30 MINUTES)

Start with a short recap of the Loving-Kindness practice from last week. Emphasize the following points:

- It's the intention that makes the practice work, not the way it feels during this meditation.

- It's okay if it feels contrived or you don't feel like you "get it."

- The phrases are wishes, not positive affirmations.

This session we will practice 10 minutes of Walking Meditation with Loving-Kindness (Session 3), followed by 10 minutes of Loving-Kindness for Other and Self (Session 4). We will end with 10 minutes of Mindfulness of Breathing (Session 2).

If your group can't do walking meditation, choose 10 minutes of Mindful Movement (Session 3) and stretching.

Transitions

Transitions between exercises can be tricky for the beginner. During transitions, it's prudent for the facilitator to be extra aware of the trap of autopilot. Invite participants to see the entire 30 minutes of practice as *one* meditation period, even though they will be cycling through different meditations. The short time it takes to transition from one meditation focus to the other may be easily perceived as a break where there is no need to be mindful. But we want to encourage the exact opposite. Instead of the bell serving as a signal to move into autopilot, invite the class to perceive the bell as a chance to pay even more attention, to carefully hold on to the present moment as they transition from one activity (such as walking) to another (a seated practice).

Encourage your class not to talk to each other for the entire 30 minutes. Silence helps with remembering to pay attention.

Walking Meditation with Loving-Kindness

Refer to the Mindful Walking section in Session 3. Give a brief recap of a walking meditation:

151

- We just walk for walking's sake, not to get anywhere.

- We use the feet as the object of our attention or the entire moving process of the feet.

- We walk at a pace that allows us to track the different stages of each step.

For loving-kindness walking, we use different words to say with each step. As a start you might want to use: *safe, happy, healthy, at ease.* Use one word with each step. When you put the foot down, you say the word silently to yourself: First step "safe"; second step "happy"; third step "healthy"; fourth step "at ease." Some might find it more comfortable to repeat a word silently on every other step. It helps if you aim to connect with the meaning of the word. For example, ask participants, "What does 'safe' feel like in the body? Happy? Healthy?" And so on.

The facilitator should complete the walking meditation with the group and will also need to keep track of the time. Right before the period ends, continue to practice the Walking Meditation while you make your way to the bell. Ring the bell and model slowly returning to your seat without making eye contact with the participants. Settle into your practice posture. It is fine to make a supportive transition comment such as, "Settling into your seat and finding your seated practice posture. Gently closing your eyes whenever you are ready, and simply following the breath while we wait for everyone to settle in."

Loving-Kindness for Other and Self

Guide participants through roughly 5 minutes of Loving-Kindness for a friend, followed by 5 minutes of Loving-Kindness for oneself. See the scripts from Session 4.

Mindfulness of Breathing Practice

Lead participants through 10 minutes of Mindfulness of Breathing. See the script from Session 2.

Group Process (10 MINUTES)

It's good to start with the question: "What was this like?" Have a number of people share. Acknowledge and validate more than interpreting or saying much. Get a sense of how 30 minutes of practice felt to them. Some questions you could explore if the sharing is reluctant: "Did you feel like you could do it? Did it feel long? Too long? Short? What were the transition periods like? Was it helpful to have two transitions? Or would you have liked one long practice better? Did anyone notice different mind states during the half hour? Or was it pretty even? What mind states?"

Then invite questions about the homework or anything practice related.

Technique: Explore Unpleasant–Neutral–Pleasant (10 MINUTES)

The following practice gives students a firsthand experience that all three *feeling tones* (see "Dharma Teacher Perspective" at the end of this chapter) are usually present at the same time.

Please allow yourself roughly 1 minute for setup and 2 minutes for each of the three feeling tones. Time yourself to stay on track.

EXPLORE UNPLEASANT–NEUTRAL–PLEASANT SCRIPT

We will be doing a short guided exploration now where we will focus on different aspects of our experience. We will move from something unpleasant to something neutral to something pleasant. Please make sure that you don't overwhelm yourself with focusing completely on a big pain.

[Pause]

Assuming a comfortable position and allowing the eyes to gently close if that feels okay to you.

[Long pause]

I now want to invite you to check your experience for an unpleasant sensation in the body. This shouldn't be something big, more something like a discomfort or tension, maybe in the shoulders, maybe a dull pain that is more in the background…

Maybe check your shoulders…your back…any other area that might call your attention.

[Pause]

Perhaps there are no unpleasant sensations in your experience in this moment. That's okay. Just noticing if there are any sensations in the body related to tiredness or achiness. If you can't feel something unpleasant, find an area that feels neutral.

See if you can feel the sensation and silently note to yourself: "unpleasant, unpleasant."

[Pause]

You might want to ask yourself, "Which piece of my experience is it that makes this unpleasant?"

[Pause]

Is it the sense of tightness? Burning? Pressure?

[Pause]

Breathing now into this sensation. What happens to it?

[Pause]

What is your attitude? Is it kind or maybe tight and harsh? Neutral?

Is it hard or easy to stay with it?

[Pause]

Can you feel resistance?

Is it the same or something different than the actual sensation?

[Pause]

Now letting go of the unpleasant sensation and moving to something that feels neither unpleasant nor pleasant.

[Pause]

Scan your body for a neutral feeling.

[Pause]

Now resting the attention there, like we practiced during the Body Scan meditation.

[Pause]

Again, you might want to ask yourself, "Which piece of my experience is it that makes this neutral?" What does "neutral" feel like to you?

[Pause]

What happens to your attention?

Is it hard or easy to stay with it?

[Pause]

What happens as you imagine to breathe into this area?

[Pause]

Now letting go of the neutral feeling and sweeping the body for a pleasant sensation.

[Pause]

This doesn't have to be something big. Maybe a sense of ease or relaxation in an area.

[Pause]

How about your earlobes?

Your eyes?

Your hands?

How about the breath?

[Pause]

Maybe just the fact that you are finally being honest with yourself.

The truth of this moment can feel pleasant, even if the body doesn't feel that way.

[Pause]

Now coming to an end of our short exploration.

Ending with a couple of breaths in silence.

[Long pause, at least 1 minute]

[Ring bell]

Group Process (5 MINUTES)

Take a few minutes to check in with your group about how they experienced this exercise. Often people are very surprised that they were able to find all three feeling tones in those short minutes. "What does that mean? Could that mean that you actually have a choice in what you pay attention to?"

Theme: Willingness to Be with Things as They Are (15 MINUTES)

Introduce this topic by explaining, "The practice of mindfulness invites us to 'see things as they really are.' Not as we imagine them to be or wish them to be. This 'seeing things as they are' asks us to look deeply into all areas of our lives. This is usually a big challenge, especially in the painful areas or the ones we try to avoid at all costs. You can see how the practice of Loving-Kindness, the attitude of friendliness and benevolence, can support this.

"All of our experiences can be categorized in one of three feeling states: *Unpleasant, pleasant,* or neither pleasant nor unpleasant, which we call *neutral.*

"Habitually we try to avoid the unpleasant, try to hold on to the pleasant, and ignore what we see as neutral." In Session 5, we ask participants to be willing to be with something that is unpleasant, as this is the most challenging of the three feeling tones. "Why would you want to be with something unpleasant or painful? It's a great question! Isn't it normal to want to get rid of it? Of course it is!" But let's do a quick reality check here: Why are people in this class? A typical participant will be there because there is some—or a lot of—unpleasant, stressful, and painful things in his or her life that just won't go away. Or if one unpleasant situation does happen to change, it's replaced by the next distressing thing—yet another thing to fight, resist, and get rid of. To that, one of our teachers would often ask, "So, how's that workin' for ya?"

What We Resist Persists

We normally fall so automatically into resistance against what doesn't feel good that we don't see that the experience and the resistance against it are not the same thing. What we learn to see is that it is exactly the resistance against whatever is unpleasant that makes it so hard to be with.

Mindfulness teacher Shinzen Young came up with a very pithy equation for this:

$$Suffering = Pain \times Resistance$$

(We could also phrase it as: Suffering = Pain x Worry)

When we teach this in class there is usually laughter of recognition in the room. It's just common sense that the more we resist something, the worse it feels. Or as the saying goes: What we resist persists. Being with things as they are takes practice and patience.

Teaching Tip: Write the equation "Suffering = Pain x Resistance" on a whiteboard and do some math. Ask, "How much suffering do you have if you have 10 units of pain and your resistance is 10? What happens if you reduce your resistance to only 1? And if you can reduce your resistance to zero?"

"Pain is inevitable in life. It's a constant. If we are not in physical or emotional pain right now then very likely somebody we are close to is. So if the resistance or worry goes up, so does the amount of suffering. If it goes down, we experience that pain in a different way."

We dare people to take the equation to another level: "What happens when there is zero resistance to the pain? What happens to suffering?" The room is usually silent for a second as they take this in; then somebody will burst out: "Then the suffering is zero!"

Examples. Try to elicit examples from your group. If they don't know where you are going, prime them with questions like, "Anybody here have a tattoo? What was it like getting it?" or "Has anyone every done weight lifting?" For a lot of people this idea is completely new, but as we explore this more we get examples like this: "When I had my baby it hurt like hell, but I wasn't suffering. I was so happy that I would have her in my arms soon." "After I have finished a race, my body hurts for days. But I'm so pumped I did it." "I have days when my chronic pain is just a presence, but I'm okay with it being there. Other days, when my resistance is high, the same pain level is hell." "When I finally broke up with my boyfriend, it was so overdue that moving all my stuff out of our apartment felt like a joy and relief, even though it was painful."

Working with Resistance

We ask our students to be willing to explore this relationship of pain, suffering, and stress and their relationship to it. Because: "The good news is that resistance is not a constant. If it were we would be doomed. But resistance is something we can work with and learn to let go of or to at least soften—and a Loving-Kindness practice comes in really handy here.

"How do we do that? By first being able to *recognize resistance*. What does it feel like in your body? Where? What are the thoughts that are common with resistance? Can you see how resistance flavors an experience in a very recognizable way, but that it is separate from what is happening?"

> **Example.** José shared this story: "Recently I was at a camping store with my family. When I had gotten the things I was looking for I just sat down in a comfy folding chair in the display area and waited for my family to get done. I felt relaxed and had fun watching the other shoppers. Then suddenly resistance kicked in. My mind was wondering, 'Why is everyone taking so long—*again?*' My shoulders and jaw tensed up. Externally nothing had changed. Just my interpretation of the situation. And suddenly there I was, upset."

Now describe the second step: "Start *training your tolerance* muscles in small ways to be willing to be with something mildly unpleasant. Like your itching nose in meditation. You will notice how your mind will kick up a storm against why this is so ridiculous not to scratch. But you can just watch your mind railing and let the nose itch. Then you will discover what might be revolutionary to you: the itch will eventually go away by itself.

"Why is this revolutionary? You could say that we live in a scratch-your-itch-society." (We the authors, in particular, living in Los Angeles!) "We have many means to fulfill our whims. As a result we might have lost the knowledge that we are able to just tolerate a craving—and it will go away by itself. What freedom!"

We introduced *urge surfing* in Session 1 for people who may be dealing with urges to misuse harmful substances. Alan Marlatt, the founder of MBRP, used to say it's either the PIG (**P**roblem of **I**nstant **G**ratification) or urge surfing. But the practice of urge surfing can be helpful to everybody, because we all deal with impulses all day long.

Neuroscientist Jill Bolte Taylor, known for her book *My Stroke of Insight*, says that the electric brain circuitry for a thought, an emotion, or an urge lasts only ninety seconds if it's not reinforced but just watched (2007). "You can be with most anything for ninety seconds, don't you think? If you have ever felt like acting like a puppet on a string to an urge, why not put this to the test?"

Working with resistance repeatedly over time will result in a number of things:

1. You become more familiar with resistance and tolerate it much better.

2. You will notice that more often the resistance will lessen significantly or dissipate by just noticing it.

3. Resistance, as an automatic reflex to everything we don't like, will diminish in many situations. Or, as Joey, one student, put it: "I stopped sweating the small stuff so much."

Small Group Check-In (10 MINUTES)

After you have discussed the willingness to be with something unpleasant and introduced the suffering formula—let participants turn to one or two people to share, if they are willing. They can talk about an experience when there was pain but no or little suffering *or* an experience when an impulse or craving went away by itself and what that felt like. Make sure everybody gets a turn.

In the beginning, some people will have a hard time separating the experience itself from the resistance against it. It's helpful to gather some examples from other participants to make it clearer, or give an example yourself.

Wrap-Up and Homework (5 MINUTES)

This week's assignment is to work with resistance: Notice it, become more familiar with it. See if it's helpful to use the image of breathing into the resistance. Ask students to continue with the informal practice of simply being aware of more moments throughout each day. Finally, continue with the Anchor Phrase technique from Session 4 and practice 10 to 20 minutes of guided meditations of your choice daily.

Dharma Teacher Perspective: On Feeling Tones

Feeling tones make up the second foundation of mindfulness (see also chapter 1). They exist as unpleasant, neutral, or pleasant. Feeling tones should not be confused with feeling emotions. While feeling tones co-arise with each experience, they are separate from the experience itself, which is a very useful concept.

Three phenomena come together to start an experience: The *sense* (for example, the eye), *what is seen* (for example, an apple), and *consciousness* (for example, "I'm aware that I see an apple"). Experiencing feeling tones is therefore something that (within limits) is particular to your unique mind-body system: if you like apples, then a pleasant feeling will arise; if not, then a neutral or maybe even an unpleasant one will appear. The feeling tones co-arise with the experience. If the feeling is pleasant then craving or wanting will arise. I want the apple! If it's unpleasant, you most likely will experience aversion or resistance. So far the process is automatic and we can't do anything about it.

But at this point we have a choice: We can simply experience the craving or aversion and observe how it changes over time. Or we can try to act on it.

With practice we learn to see that we can step out of the system of this constant stream of the arising of wanting or aversion. We can learn to just let experience do its thing and enjoy the freedom of deciding what we want to act on instead of feeling dragged around by endless impulses.

Clinical Psychologist Perspective: On Feeling Tones

The concept of feeling tones can be confusing for beginning mindfulness practitioners. It is easy enough to get a sense if something is pleasant, neutral, or unpleasant, but this sometimes leads to comments such as, "But I thought the goal was to be nonjudgmental?" or "Isn't my thinking 'I hate this' just a thought?" The term "feeling tones" isn't easily translated into everyday usage, since we commonly use the word *feeling* to mean *emotion*. (Which does remind me of the time a veteran had a eureka moment and nearly shouted out, "Oh, my god, I get it! We call emotions 'feelings' because we can actually feel them in the body!") "Feeling tones" are simply the felt sense of registering an experience as pleasant, neutral, or unpleasant. They aren't judgments. And they aren't thoughts, although when we analyze them and start thinking about them we are, of course, using our thoughts.

Learning to be with things as they are, to not resist that which is unpleasant, is a crucial skill and appropriate for a beginning-level class. The specifics about "feeling tones" and the "second foundation of mindfulness" are background comments for the facilitator's understanding and not typically a useful topic of discussion in class. It is essential to teach the importance of how to be with things just as they are, whatever they might be. It isn't at all important for beginning students to know the origin of particular foundational concepts.

SESSION 6

Moving Forward

Session 6 is the wrap-up session for this class series. We focus on deepening and reinforcing the practices and concepts learned during the course of the six weeks (*what*). Questions that are still open get answered. We take time to explore "what is next" and "where to go from here" (*how*), so people can move forward and keep their practice going (*why*).

OBJECTIVES OF SESSION 6

- Provide support for ongoing formal and informal practice.

- Deepen participants' understanding of Loving-Kindness and Mindfulness of Breathing practices.

- Offer suggestions and opportunities for continued practice.

- Introduce Mindfulness of Breathing with Spaciousness.

- End the group with a memorable ritual to reinforce learning and a sense of community.

Session 6 Outline

Time (in minutes)	Cumulative Time	Activity
5	5	Welcome and Check-In
25	30	**Walking Meditation with Loving-Kindness** and **Loving-Kindness for Other and Self**
10	40	Group Process (Q&A; follow-up from last week)
15	55	Theme: Moving Forward
5	60	Group Process
5	65	Introduction to Mindfulness of Breathing with Spaciousness
10	75	**Mindfulness of Breathing with Spaciousness**
5	80	Small Group Check-In
5	85	Group Process (comments and final Q&A)
5	90	Wrap-Up and Closing Circle

Materials. Roster, watch or timer, sign-in sheet, bell, Session 5 outline, handouts

Poem. "Love After Love" by Derek Walcott or "Hokusai Says" by Roger Keyes

Story. "Yelling at Empty Boats"

Life can be a bit like drifting down a beautiful river at dusk in a little boat. Everything seems perfect and peaceful. We see another little boat off on the horizon moving slowly in our direction. As the other boat gets closer, we begin to worry. "Will it run into me? Will it sink my boat?" As the boats come quickly together we get more and more energized. We start by waving our arms and yelling, "Hey over there, move your boat away from me!" As the boat gets closer still, we become afraid of a collision that will leave us drowning in the water. We stand up, jump up and down, and shout, "Stop your boat! Turn away!" Then the boat smashes right into your boat. But the boat is empty. There is no damage. It just drifts harmlessly away on the river's current.

Our lives, of course, are just like this. There are many empty boats out there. These empty boats aren't dangerous to us but our reactions to them, the screaming and jumping up and down trying to avoid them, actually puts us at risk of falling into the river. The boat story is a reminder to cultivate a sense of kind spaciousness to our experience, spaciousness in our very awareness.

Our mindfulness practice isn't about being passive. It's not about just sitting calmly and letting every boat hit you. It's about skillful means or wise discernment to determine what events are worth our effort to jump up and down and rock the boat about. There are lots of empty boats out there.

Welcome and Check-In (5 MINUTES)

Briefly welcome your class to its last session. Give a short overview of what will happen in class today, if you have done so in previous sessions. "As a group we will practice Walking Meditation with Loving-Kindness [or gentle movement with loving-kindness words if your space or group doesn't allow for walking] and then seated Loving-Kindness for Other and Self." Then without much ado move into the meditation. Since people in an ongoing class have done both practices before, ease right into it. If you teach the group as a drop-in class, give a short intro. Or give a very quick review as a reminder or for people who might have missed a class. Remind your group that the next 25 minutes are one whole meditation and to stay aware to the present moment during the transition.

Walking Meditation with Loving-Kindness and Loving-Kindness for Other and Self (25 MINUTES)

Allow 10 minutes for Walking Meditation with Loving-Kindness (see description in Session 5). Explain before the practice begins that you will ring the bell to indicate the time to silently transition into the seated practice. Once everyone is seated, immediately begin the next practice. Allow 15 minutes for Loving-Kindness for Other and Loving-Kindness for Self (see Session 4). Consider ending the practice with a poem for reflection before ringing the bell.

Group Process (10 MINUTES)

After the bell rings, ensure space for reflection. Inquire about the practice or any questions that came up during their week of at-home practice. At this point, many people are anxious about the class ending and may ask questions or make related comments. This can provide a transition to the week's theme: moving forward with your practice.

Theme: Moving Forward (15 MINUTES)

Today's theme is simply to offer the reassurance to move ahead with the resources appropriate for your setting and to make a plan for your population. Participants who have been diligent with the practices will have a strong foundation to continue their practice. But it helps to explain what that might look like.

A Plan for Continuing a Personal Practice

Everyone in the class should have a general plan for a continued personal practice (you might want to review "Your Personal Practice: How to Begin" in chapter 3). One way is to select a favorite attentional practice (like Mindfulness of Breathing) and one compassion- or kindness-inspired practice (like Loving-Kindness) and continue to use the recordings provided for this class to establish a near-daily practice. For many class participants, this may be the right approach. Let them know that they are welcome to use the recordings as long as they are helpful. However, encourage them to develop a practice without the use of recordings if that feels right.

Encourage Next Steps

This might mean taking a more intensive course, like MBSR, or finding a sitting group. In your own clinical setting, you might have a drop-in group or might even offer MBSR, MBCT, or mindful self-compassion (MSC). In educational, business, and other settings, there may not be any additional classes on site to deepen the practice, so explore local community resources. Many communities have mindfulness centers or sitting groups. As the facilitator, it can be useful for you to do an Internet search to explore what might be available in your community. Search terms for you to try include: mindfulness, mindfulness meditation, insight meditation, vipassana, vipassana meditation, or MBSR with your local community's name. Ensure it is "mindfulness" or "insight-based meditation," as "meditation" alone is a catch-all term that can include many different approaches.

A typical progression for a beginning student of mindfulness might be an introductory-level class as we have described here, continuing with a personal near-daily practice at home, joining a sitting group to hear from an experienced teacher, attending a nonresidential mindfulness retreat on a weekend, then attending a multiday residential mindfulness retreat. Not everyone will be interested in going through all these discrete stages. But it can be helpful to describe the general path so students who are interested know what might come next.

A sitting group is typically offered at a meditation center on a drop-in basis through donation. Some of these groups are Buddhist teaching groups and some are secular. While not all the same, the group typically follows this format: 30 to 40 minutes of sitting practice (Mindfulness of Breathing or of your choice) with instructions in the beginning and then silence; 10 to 15 minutes of walking practice (optional); a 20-minute talk by the teacher; and questions and answers or sharing of experience.

We also recommend a number of books (for new facilitators and practitioners alike) for additional study. While a book doesn't take the place of a personal meditation practice, it can introduce new topics and concepts. In general, these books are not read from cover to cover as a novel but in small doses to inspire and take the teaching into your own practice. See our online bibliography at http://www.sharing mindfulness.com for recommendations.

After you have answered questions, supported an ongoing practice, helped students select practices for their ongoing at-home use, and explored local resources, it is time to introduce the final practice of the series.

Group Process (5 MINUTES)

Take a few minutes for a group process related to moving forward with the practice after the class ends. Answer any questions that arise.

Introduction to Mindfulness of Breathing with Spaciousness (5 MINUTES)

This is an excellent practice for the last class, as it simply adds a new perspective to a familiar practice. It won't be surprising to hear from your class that some of them have already "discovered" how to create more mental space in their own practice. In these introductory comments, you will explicitly explain the concept of spaciousness, how it can be helpful not just in participants' meditation practice but in their lives. Discuss how to consciously "open up" awareness when feeling constricted around something, such as when "closing down" around the feeling of shame or anger about a particular situation. Some students might not understand this subtle quality of awareness. So introduce the topic and move into the practice without getting bogged down in too many intellectual questions. Allow the experience of the practice to once again be the teacher.

Here are some brief points to make:

- Try sharing this example of why "opening up space" can be useful in everyday life as well as in meditation: When you take a spoonful of salt and mix it into a glass of water, the water will be very salty. If you take the same spoonful and mix it into a bathtub, you will barely taste it. It's not about the amount of salt, but about how big you make your container! This practice allows you to make the container bigger for your distress or pain.

- We use the term "spaciousness" to describe the mental quality of awareness that is open to all experience and feels expansive and vast. This can be a challenging concept to think about, but it can be felt and experienced directly in the body. When we are upset or worried about something, it can feel "tight" or "closed down" in the body. When we obsess about something, this constricted feeling is the opposite of spaciousness.

- A mental stance of spacious awareness allows us to hold our experiences with more ease and less reactivity. A *constricted focus* is linked to the fight-or-flight response, or sympathetic nervous system, while *spacious awareness* is associated with the parasympathetic nervous system, or relaxation response. This is by design; when there is a perceived threat, our attentional system narrowly focuses on the threat.

- With practice, we can learn to focus our attention on a single object, like the breath, and "collect and gather" our attention. Or we can open up our attention into spacious awareness.

- Adding a sense of spaciousness to the Mindfulness of Breathing practice is much easier with stable attention. If the mind is very busy in a particular practice, it might not be the right time to open up into spaciousness.

Mindfulness of Breathing with Spaciousness
(10 MINUTES)

You don't have a lot of time in the session, so you can introduce only a short taste of this practice. If your group is very restless, you might decide to skip this part. Otherwise, stabilize them with about 3 minutes of Mindfulness of Breathing before you give them the option to open up into more spaciousness. The image of the camera lens works really well for this practice. "The Mindfulness of Breathing practice is like a zoom lens: We get very detailed and intimate with the sensations of the breath, to the exclusion of everything else—at least in the moment. In the spaciousness practice, we reverse the zoom into a wide-angle view. The breath is still there, but so is everything else."

MINDFULNESS OF BREATHING WITH
SPACIOUSNESS SCRIPT

Sit in an upright and dignified posture with both feet on the ground and, when you're ready, allowing the eyes to gently close. Or soften the gaze down to the floor if that feels right. As best you can, noticing the sensations of your breath and where you feel the breath in the body.

[Pause]

It might be helpful to take a few breaths that are a little deeper than you might normally take. Breathing all the way in and exhaling completely. In and out, really noticing where you feel the breath in the body.

[Pause]

Now letting go of control of the breath and just allowing the body to breathe on its own. Trusting the wisdom of the body to find its own natural rhythm with the breath.

[Long pause]

When you feel ready, opening up your awareness to include the breath in the whole body. Feeling your whole body, sitting here, breathing. We don't let go of the breath; we just include more, like we would open the lens of a camera to include a broader picture.

[Pause]

You might also become aware of any flavors of emotions that are present, or stories that are running through your mind.

[Pause]

Perhaps this sense of space is enough for you. Or you can open the awareness even more, to include the entire room, with all the people and objects in it.

[Pause]

Or opening up as wide as you like. Even like an immense blue sky. Allowing everything to arise—be here—and change into something else. Noticing whatever is present for you in this moment and just observe it with ease. It's like sitting directly in the center of a giant meadow on a clear summer day. Allowing your awareness to be as expansive and vast as the sky. A sky that stretches from horizon to horizon.

[Long pause]

If at any time the mind starts to get too busy, feel free to return to zooming in on the breath. And then open again, once the mind feels a little more stable.

[Pause]

Breathing in and out. Allowing awareness itself to be spacious and open. Breathing in. Breathing out. Resting in this spaciousness.

[Long pause]

Where is your mind now? Noticing where your mind is without judgment. And gently coming back to your breath and the spacious awareness of this moment. Allowing everything to be just as it is.

[Pause]

Just as clouds can appear in the enormous sky and linger for a while before drifting off over the horizon, we can have thoughts or sensations that drift into our awareness and capture our attention for a time. Each time this happens, gently returning the awareness to the breath. Resting in the spaciousness of awareness itself and letting be.

[Pause]

Some thoughts and experiences come sweeping into our attention like the dark, energetic clouds of a storm front. They can seem to demand our attention. But just as the sky holds every cloud, every storm, with ease, our spacious awareness can hold our experience with ease. Resting in the spacious awareness of experience and allowing it to be just as it is.

[Pause]

Breathing in. Breathing out. Awareness is the spaciousness of the sky itself.

[Pause]

Be the sky, not the clouds. Breathing in. Breathing out. Allowing yourself to be just as you are in the moment.

[Pause]

[Ring bell]

Small Group Check-In (5 MINUTES)

Put people into dyads and let them share with each other how the practice went.

Group Process (5 MINUTES)

Take just a few minutes to bring the group together and answer any last questions about the practice. This might be a good place to tell the "Yelling at Empty Boats" story if you didn't share it during the earlier discussion.

Wrap-Up and Closing Circle (5 MINUTES)

An emotionally resonant ritual is a wonderful way to close the program. This is typically only possible in a closed group where all the members have started together and feel a sense of connection to one another, and it is time to have a procedure to neatly mark the end of the program. This wouldn't work in an open format or for a class that simply repeats again the following week.

A closing circle doesn't need much preamble. Simply state that it is time for the final task in the class. Ask everyone to stand in a circle and hold hands. Explain that each person, starting with the facilitator, will share two words that best summarize what he or she has learned or is taking away from the class. It can be helpful to stall just a bit to give people time to reflect, so we often relay a maple syrup metaphor: "You need to harvest a lot of sap and distill it down to make the sweet syrup. So what is the essence of the class for you? How do you boil it down into just two words to describe it?" Explain that you will begin and then squeeze the hand of the person next to you to signal it is his or her turn. Give everyone a few breaths in silence before you begin so they can reflect and "distill their sap." Begin with your two words ("peaceful and loving" or "grateful and connections" or whatever you feel). Make your way around the circle.

Closing circles are typically memorable and rewarding shared experiences for facilitators and participants alike. Savor the experience. Resonate with everyone's experience. Take it all in. And then thank them for their practice and say good-bye.

SESSION +1 (OPTIONAL)

Finding Compassion Within

The previous six sessions represent the core Introduction to Mindfulness program. If you are a beginning mindfulness facilitator, we recommend developing proficiency with the formal practices in the previously described sessions while strengthening your own daily personal practice. After you have developed competency with the core program, you might begin to introduce the practices described in Sessions +1 and +2 into your own practice before teaching them to others.

As with all other practices in this book, it is critically important for facilitators of self-compassion to embody their practice of self-compassion in their own lives. It is completely normal for you to struggle a bit with new material and concepts; we just don't do things perfectly the first time! But keep at it, continue with your personal practice, and model self-compassion for your students.

In Session +1, we present the first of two optional sessions to identify and nurture the inherent capacity for self-compassion that lies within every person. We define self-compassion (*what*) and introduce the Affectionate Body Scan (*how*). There is an ongoing debate about the optimal path for teaching self-compassion that is referred to as the "caught versus taught" approach. We trust that with extended practice, a student can certainly "catch" self-compassion from a gifted, compassionate teacher. By explicitly introducing these teachings early on, however, we believe students can be taught to nurture and kindle their own internal resource for self-compassion. This reservoir of kindness and compassion from within can help us to tolerate the burdens of living with grace and diminish our suffering (*why*).

OBJECTIVES OF SESSION +1

- Introduce the formal practice of the Affectionate Body Scan.

- Introduce the concept of self-compassion and explore why this is helpful for everyone.

- Define self-compassion and contrast this definition with mindfulness, empathy, and loving-kindness.

- Define the difference between self-compassion and self-pity, as this is a common place where students get stuck.

- Explicitly give permission to use self-compassion and dispel faulty notions that a harsh internal critic is necessary for achievement or motivation.

- Introduce the techniques of Supportive Touch and the Self-Compassion Break.

Session +1 Outline

Time (in minutes)	Cumulative Time	Activity
5	5	Welcome and Check-In
5	10	Introduction to Affectionate Body Scan
15	25	**Affectionate Body Scan**
5	30	Small Group Check-In
5	35	Group Process (Q&A)
20	55	Theme: Finding Compassion Within
5	60	Introduction to Supportive Touch and the Self-Compassion Break
20	80	**Supportive Touch** and the **Self-Compassion Break**
5	85	Group Process
5	90	Wrap-Up and Homework (Affectionate Body Scan; use Self-Compassion Break as needed)

Materials. Bell, watch or timer, Session +1 outline, handouts, whiteboard and markers

Poem. "Myself and My Person" by Anna Swirszczynska or "Allow" by Danna Faulds

Story. "A Story on Kindness," from Jack Kornfield's *The Wise Heart*

    Some years ago I heard the story of a high school history teacher... On a particularly fidgety and distracted afternoon she told her class to stop all their academic work. She let her students rest while she wrote on a blackboard a list of the names of everyone in the class. Then she asked them to copy the list. She instructed them to use the rest of the period to write beside each name one thing they liked or admired about that student. At the end of the class she collected the papers.

Weeks later, on another difficult day just before winter break, the teacher again stopped the class. She handed each student a sheet with his or her name on top. On it she had pasted all twenty-six good things the other students had written about that person. They smiled and gasped in pleasure that so many beautiful qualities were noticed about them.

Three years later this teacher received a call from the mother of one of her former students. Robert had been a cutup, but also one of her favorites. The mother sadly passed on the terrible news that Robert had been killed in the Gulf War. The teacher attended the funeral, where many of Robert's friends and former high school classmates spoke. Just as the service was ending, Robert's mother approached her. She took out a worn piece of paper, obviously folded and refolded many times, and said, "This was one of the few things in Robert's pocket when the military retrieved his body." It was the paper on which the teacher had so carefully pasted the twenty-six things his classmates had admired.

Seeing this, Robert's teacher's eyes filled with tears. As she dried her wet cheeks, another former student standing nearby opened her purse, pulled out her own carefully folded page, and confessed she always kept it with her. A third ex-student said that his page was framed and hanging in the kitchen; another told how the page had become part of her wedding vows. The perception of goodness invited by this teacher had transformed the heart of her students in ways she might only have dreamed about.

Welcome and Check-In (5 MINUTES)

Welcome all participants to the class. Ask people to introduce themselves and offer one sentence about how their practice is going.

Introduction to Affectionate Body Scan (5 MINUTES)

It is very easy for a passionate teacher to get caught up in enthusiastically explaining all that will happen with self-compassion work, but allow the practices to be the teacher. Briefly review a few of these teaching points before launching into the practice:

- We aim to develop a strong and nurturing connection to our own sense of self-compassion. We want to incline to our own experience like we would attend to a best friend who was having a hard time. (If there are any questions about what this is, defer the discussion to later in the session.)

- We aren't doing anything completely new here. We have already introduced the Body Scan and the Loving-Kindness practices. Now we combine these instructions by noticing the felt parts of the body and sending friendly wishes to each part.

- The first few times doing the Affectionate Body Scan practice can feel a bit silly or even ridiculous when we wish, for example, that our feet be happy. That's completely fine. Keep at it. Try to hold the stance of nonjudgmental, kind curiosity in the practice.

- We are simply allowing the space for whatever is going on in our body to be just as it is, and then we are sending affectionate wishes to each body part.

After these brief instructions, the group leader can immediately begin the practice.

Affectionate Body Scan (15 MINUTES)

We first learned a version of this practice from the work of Trudy Goodman.

It is essential that the facilitator understand the aims and potential complexities of the Affectionate Body Scan practice. As a facilitator, you will be specifically asking participants to bring potential discomfort and suffering into their awareness and holding it with affection while sending friendly wishes or goodwill to the body. Strong emotions and judgments about the body, even resistance to the practice, are possible. Be prepared to address and normalize any backdraft that occurs.

This meditation can be done while lying down or in a comfortable seated position. As you lead this practice, please make sure that you allow the students to first simply feel into a body part and then, as a second step, to wish it well.

AFFECTIONATE BODY SCAN SCRIPT

Taking a moment to arrive fully into the felt sense of the body. Allowing the eyes to softly close if this is comfortable for you. Perhaps taking a few slow, deep breaths and feeling into the entire body.

[Pause]

Now letting go of the breath as best you can and just allowing it to be natural and easy. In this practice, you will first pay attention to different parts of your body in turn, just like we typically do in the Body Scan practice. You might notice many distinctive sensations and experiences including tension, relaxation, warmth, discomfort, or even pain. Noticing whatever else might be happening in an area of the body at the moment. Just notice it and invite it in. And then send a friendly wish, an intention, for that part of the body to be happy and at ease. Feel free to swap out "happy and at ease" for another phrase that resonates more with you, if you like. It's fine if this feels awkward or even silly at first. Do it anyway.

[Pause]

Starting now by noticing the feet. Inviting in whatever sensation is present in this moment and allowing it to be.

[Pause]

Now sending some affection to the feet for all they do on your behalf. Repeating silently in your mind, "May my feet be happy. May my feet be happy and at ease."

[Pause]

Shifting your awareness to your ankles and calves and noticing whatever sensations are present. "May my ankles and calves be happy. May my ankles and calves be happy and at ease."

[Pause]

Bringing your attention to your knees. Start out by just feeling into the knees. Maybe noticing any tiredness, any ache, or any sensation at all. Inviting them all in.

[Pause]

"May my knees be happy. May my knees be happy and at ease."

[Pause]

Whenever you're ready, shifting your attention to your thighs. Feeling into the thighs. Letting go of any judgments you may have about your thighs, and noticing the sensations that are present. Allowing the breath in the body to fill the thighs.

[Pause]

"May my thighs be happy. May my thighs be happy and at ease."

[Pause]

Shifting to the buttocks, the pelvis, and the pelvic organs. Feeling into this area now. Taking a moment here to send friendly wishes to the different areas of your body here.

[Long pause]

Whenever you're ready, moving your kind attention to the lower back. Allowing yourself to be with whatever sensations are present, be they discomfort, tension, numbness, or nothing at all.

[Pause]

"May my back be happy. May my back be happy and at ease."

[Pause]

Noticing if you can maybe feel the breath in the belly. Identifying any sensations that are present in this moment. Sensations on the surface of the lower torso where perhaps you can feel your shirt, and the sensations deeper within the body in the digestive system. Allowing these sensations to be just as they are.

[Pause]

Again you might want to take a moment here to send kindness to your belly and all the internal organs.

[Pause]

"May my belly and internal organs be happy. May my belly be happy and at ease."

[Pause]

Shifting your awareness now into your chest. Noticing how the chest rises and falls with each breath. Getting as close as possible to whatever chest sensations are available to you in this moment. Any tension or tightness, any pressure, any lightness or sense of ease. And letting it all be just as it is.

[Pause]

"May my chest be happy. May my chest and heart and lungs be happy and at ease."

[Pause]

When you feel ready, take your attention to your hands. Sensing the fingers, the palms, and the backs of the hands.

[Pause]

"May my hands be happy. May my hands be happy and at ease."

[Pause]

Feeling into the wrists and forearms now. What sensations are here to feel?

[Pause]

"May my wrist and forearms be happy and at ease."

[Pause]

Now moving on to the elbows and upper arms. Sensing whatever is present in the body here in this moment.

[Pause]

"May my elbows and upper arms be happy. May my elbows and upper arms be happy and at ease."

[Pause]

As best you can, taking your awareness to your shoulders and the upper back. Noticing any sensations. Maybe there is tension present in this moment.

[Pause]

"May my shoulders be happy. May my shoulders and back be happy and at ease."

[Pause]

Noticing the sensations of the neck. "May my neck be happy. May my neck be happy and at ease."

[Pause]

Now moving on to your head, feeling into your head.

[Pause]

Checking in with the sense organs—the eyes, the ears, the tongue and lips, the skin on your face—noticing the sensations of this moment.

[Pause]

Then sending friendly wishes to the different areas of the head, including the sense organs.

[Long pause]

"May my head be happy. May my head be happy and at ease."

[Pause]

When you feel ready, opening your awareness to include the entire body again. Noticing how the entire body is alive, breathing, and filled with sensation.

[Pause]

"May my entire body be happy. May my entire body be happy and at ease."

[Long pause]

"May I be happy. May I be happy and at ease."

[Long pause]

[Ring bell]

Small Group Check-In (5 MINUTES)

Divide the group into pairs for a brief check-in about the practice. If there is an odd number of participants, consider groups of three or any combination of small group pairings.

Group Process (5 MINUTES)

In the large group, spend a few minutes asking, "Would anyone like to share his or her experience of the practice?" Look for opportunities to validate noticing whatever arises with the practice. Be curious.

Theme: Finding Compassion Within
(20 MINUTES)

This is an introduction to a complex and powerful practice. It is insufficient to explain *what* self-compassion is; the key to teaching about self-compassion is to describe *why* it is an important quality to nurture, and to dispel any barriers or preconceived notions about it. We recommend teachers briefly define self-compassion and distinguish it from other concepts, directly address some of the common barriers to embracing self-compassion, and perhaps even mention some of the research into self-compassion.

This can be a lot of information to deliver in a short amount of time. Participants may have many questions, and facilitators are sometimes understandably seduced into spending more time on this topic than the framework allows. Facilitators are well served keeping the introductory nature of the topic and the time frame in mind. Here are a few talking points in each of the areas below. Not all this information can be shared in the time allowed but is included here for background. As always, allow the practice to be the primary teacher.

Definition of Self-Compassion

Self-compassion, as defined by Kristin Neff (2003a), is composed of three elements: mindfulness, common humanity, and self-kindness. *Mindfulness* is active in the moment when we acknowledge that pain is present in our experience. It's also the ability to hold a painful moment in balanced awareness rather than overidentifying with it. *Common humanity* is our collective experiences, particularly our shortcomings and struggles. When we accept our common humanity, we see ourselves as part of a larger human experience. Instead of feeling isolated due to perceived defects, we understand defects are part of being human. We notice, for example, that "this is what heartbreak is like for all of us" or "this is what it feels like to worry about a sick child...for everyone." *Self-kindness* is being kind to yourself in the presence of hardship or failure instead of being self-critical.

Addressing Barriers and Misconceptions

Some participants will find the concept of self-compassion a wonderful idea for everyone else but will hold themselves to a different standard. It can be helpful to review common barriers; identifying, normalizing, and resolving a barrier can give people permission to try a practice they might not otherwise be inclined to try.

"I've got to be hard on myself, to be tough, or I'm never going to get it." There is a frequent misconception that harsh internal dialogue is needed to motivate ourselves and help us to achieve our goals. Harsh self-criticism actually undermines motivation (Breines & Chen, 2012). Self-compassionate people actually have less fear of failure and have greater intrinsic motivation to master the task at hand (Neff, Hseih, & Dejitthirat, 2005). We have found this harsh drill sergeant approach to be common among those in early recovery. A powerful way to diffuse this faulty belief is to ask, "If this harsh internal critic was that effective, would you be here? Isn't it time to try something different?"

We can only take so much harsh internal criticism; after a while, someone enduring all those snide internal comments may resort to a less adaptive coping strategy such as emotional avoidance, distraction, or numbing. In other words, a relapse.

"Self-compassion gets in the way of my plan to be CEO [or some other high-level achievement]. That tough internal critic drives me toward success." This is another version of the above misconception—a twist on the motivation issue, but related to success this time instead of failure. Some people believe the harsh internal critic is their primary driver of accomplishment. But is this true? "Sometimes our inner critic wants something good for us (like professional success); sometimes it is just an old tape from childhood full of doubt. But good or ill, ultimately the method of the internal critic is harsh, judgmental language. This can be dispiriting. And it isn't the critic that makes us succeed—it's our innate skills and efforts. Self-compassion supports us rather than derails our plans."

"This is too soft for me. Are you trying to turn me into a wimp?" "We are frequently socialized to believe that compassion in general is soft, unmanly, and somehow weak. Sharon Salzberg acknowledges this degradation of compassion and kindness into 'secondary virtues' in our competitive culture and instead describes compassion as a potent tool for transformation and connectedness. Compassion can also be fierce. Think of Mother Theresa or Martin Luther King, Jr. Or think about what you would do if your friend is ready to get drunk after three years of sobriety because her boyfriend dumped her. You would probably drag her to an AA meeting. That is compassion, not being weak or soft. You could call it 'tough love' or 'fierce love.'" Use an example that your participants can relate to. "Ultimately, self-/compassion isn't about turning you into a doormat, it's about relating to your own experience with kindness. If you aren't kind to yourself, who will be?"

"This is just about feeling sorry for yourself, isn't it? I don't want to wrap myself in self-pity." We often hear from students that they are reluctant to take up the practice of self-compassion because it feels so self-centered. Some might say, "I don't want to wallow in my pain." We have found that there is a lot of confusion between *self-pity* and *self-compassion*. Here is the difference: "When we are lost in *self-pity*, the sense of self is much enhanced. We feel contracted, tense, often immobilized. The whole world seems to collapse around *my* pain and what it means to *my* life and to *me*. The self-talk is usually along the lines of: 'Why me?' 'This is unfair. This shouldn't have happened—to *me*.' 'Nobody understands what I'm going through,' and so on. We feel sorry for ourselves: the 'poor me' state.

"*Self-compassion*, on the other hand, is actually the exact opposite. Through the second aspect of self-compassion, the common humanity, we let go of the tight sense of self and connect with and open into the vast universal human experience. We feel what it feels like for anybody who is experiencing this or ever has experienced this. When we can feel into the brother- or sisterhood of shared emotions, something softens and opens. We see that it's not just us, but simply what it is like to be alive. We can allow the vulnerability in the knowledge that nobody can and will escape suffering and pain—this is part of being human. For example, if you are laid off work and worried about paying rent next month, the internal talk of self-pity is 'I can't believe this happened to me! This isn't fair. I don't deserve this. What am I going to do?' On the other hand, the dialogue of self-compassion might be, 'This is hard and even a little scary. This is what it feels like for everyone who is struggling and loses a job. I can have an intention to be particularly kind to myself during this time.'"

"This is so indulgent. Isn't it like stuffing yourself with chocolate cake?" "Self-indulgence wants short-term pleasure, while self-compassion is fundamentally interested in your long-term health and well-being. So self-compassion is more like leafy green vegetables than chocolate cake!"

Self-Compassion and Research

Self-compassion is relatively new as an operationalized research construct in the West. Research has exploded in the past decade since Kristin Neff (2003a) defined for Western academics what has long been understood through an Eastern practitioner's lens. In a review of findings, Barnard and Curry (2011) summarize the many positive correlates of self-compassion including greater equanimity, happiness, optimism, social connectedness, positive affect, and life satisfaction. All of this sounds pretty good, right? Self-compassion is also negatively correlated with some less desirable traits. As self-compassion increases there are related decreases in depression, anxiety, rumination, emotional avoidance, and anger. For more research, have a look back at the self-compassion section of chapter 2.

Practicing Self-Compassion with Ease

Facilitators should encourage meditators to practice self-compassion with a sense of ease. While this is true for mindfulness in general, it is particularly so for self-compassion. Why is this so? Self-compassion is the emotional resource we use to endure our difficult emotions. It is the resource we bring to bear to meet our toughest experiences and moments of suffering. So our practice of self-compassion can bring into our awareness a variety of emotional struggles. We want to do this with kindness and ease.

Capable facilitators give their class permission to use skillful means and move away from hard spots as needed when it is just too much. Noticing when you are "opening" to the practice and when you are "closing up" is part of the work of self-compassion. *Opening* is a sense of spaciousness and a curiosity about meeting your challenges, whereas *closing* is a tightening up while avoiding or turning away from what's happening in the moment. Opening isn't always preferred, as closing up to something that is too difficult in the moment might be a skillful choice.

The goal is simply to infuse warmth and kindness into your formal practice. We do this with ease and by respecting our capacity in each moment.

Introduction to Supportive Touch and the Self-Compassion Break (5 MINUTES)

Here are two self-compassion exercises that are well suited to be taught together. Spend about 5 minutes describing and exploring Supportive Touch. Then transition immediately into the next practice, the Self-Compassion Break. While the simple "a hand on your heart" practice has been taught for a long time, we appreciate the deepening and elaboration done by Christopher Germer and Kristin Neff.

Begin by explaining to the class that "a simple touch can be a powerful way to support yourself during times of suffering. The comfort of touch is an important part of nurturing and is seen in all mammals. Just as a baby responds to being cuddled in her mother's arms or we appreciate the hug of a friend or a supportive hand on the shoulder in a hard moment, touch is the physical manifestation of warmth and caring for all of us. A simple touch can trigger a cascade of hormones and neuroendocrine signals such as oxytocin that support health and provide a sense of security in multiple body systems.

"What follows are two new practices. The first exercise is intended to take advantage of the power of touch, which will transition into another exercise designed to bring more compassion into your life. These are separate exercises but they work very well together."

Supportive Touch and the Self-Compassion Break (20 MINUTES)

Begin by saying, "It might feel silly or awkward at first to touch yourself in a compassionate way. But give it a try a few times each day for a week and see the impact soothing touch can have on self-compassion. The Supportive Touch exercise can be used any time you face a struggle or simply any time at all when you want to feel a little extra support." Plan on 10 minutes for the Supportive Touch exercise.

The Supportive Touch exercise can be done with the eyes open or closed.

SUPPORTIVE TOUCH SCRIPT

Take 5 mindful breaths. Notice if there is anything going on for you now that is difficult or painful, such as physical discomfort or hurt feelings. If not, that's just fine. Simply noticing what is here for you in this moment.

[Pause]

Gently place your hand on your chest. Feeling the gentle pressure on your chest and waiting until you begin to feel the warmth of your hand. Try two hands and see if you notice a difference.

[Pause]

Noticing the natural rising and falling of the chest as you breathe in and out.

[Pause]

Savor this feeling of support for as long as you like.

[Long pause]

Different gestures for supporting touch work for different people. Explore the gestures that feel the most soothing to you.

[Give about 30 seconds for each]

Both hands on the heart

One hand on the heart and the other on the belly

One hand on your cheek

When at a desk or table, cradle your face with both hands

Cross your arms and give yourself a gentle squeeze

Gently holding one hand in the other in your lap

Now transition immediately into the next practice, the Self-Compassion Break. It's taught here as a 10-minute formal meditation practice. But it can also be used as a brief exercise like the STOP technique (see Session 3). This is an excellent meditation to practice when you are feeling emotional pain, stress, or other difficulty. The following script is adapted with permission from Mindful Self-Compassion (Neff & Germer, 2013).

SELF-COMPASSION BREAK SCRIPT

Sitting in an upright and dignified posture. Allowing the chair to support you completely just as you are. And allowing the eyes to gently close if that feels comfortable to you. And taking a few moments to find your breath.

[Pause]

Scan your experience and bring into your awareness any emotional distress or other difficulty or strain you're experiencing in your life right now. Notice if you can find this discomfort in your body. Where do you feel it?

[Pause]

As you bring this discomfort into your awareness, if you wish, now adding the supportive touch that feels right for you. Perhaps this is placing one hand over your heart. Perhaps it is two hands on your heart. Or maybe it is simply holding one hand in another in your lap. Taking a moment to feel the warmth of your own hand.

[Pause]

The first step in the Self-Compassion Break is simply to notice whatever difficulty is here for you right now. To acknowledge that this is a moment of suffering. Mindfully allowing it to be fully here in your experience.

[Pause]

Perhaps saying something to yourself to acknowledge this moment like, "This hurts" or "This is what stress feels like in my body."

[Pause]

Shifting now to connect with your deep sense of knowing that suffering and hardship are part of life for everyone. This is, in fact, part of our common humanity. This is what connects all of us.

[Pause]

Maybe saying to yourself "I'm not alone" or "Other people feel this way too" or even "This is what it feels like when anyone is heatbroken...or lonely...or in grief."

[Pause]

Noticing again your supportive touch on your heart or wherever feels right to you. Sense the warmth and the gentleness of this touch.

[Pause]

Now asking yourself what kind words do I most need to hear right now? Perhaps you can say, "May I give myself the compassion and kindness I need" or "May I accept myself just as I am" or "May I be strong."

[Pause]

Finding whatever words are most nourishing to you. If you can't seem to find the right words, what might you say to a close friend who is struggling with the same issue? Giving yourself whatever kindness you need in this moment. Even if the words don't come easily, allow the feeling of kindness to be fully here.

[Pause]

Allowing whatever kind words come to mind to resonate. Sensing the self-compassion of this moment. And breathing in and breathing out just as you are.

[Long pause]

[Ring bell]

Group Process (5 MINUTES)

Invite the class to share their experiences with both the Supportive Touch exercise and the Self-Compassion Break meditation. It is worth mentioning that the Self-Compassion Break can be both a meditation and a brief, three-step technique they can use anytime.

Wrap-Up and Homework (5 MINUTES)

Practice Affectionate Body Scan at home. Use the Self-Compassion Break to meet difficult moments in your life with kindness.

Enhancing Resilience

In optional Session +2, we explore resilience and our capacity to bounce back from life's inevitable potholes, particularly in light of our mindfulness and compassion practices (*what*). We define resilience and explore the factors that allow some people to overcome adversity while others get stuck. And we introduce the Compassionate Breathing practice to build internal resources (*how*). We can't change our inherited predisposition that establishes our vulnerability to certain physical and mental conditions. And we have only limited control over the intensity of the environmental stressors we all experience in life. But we can intentionally develop the compensating resources we need to weather life's storms (*why*).

OBJECTIVES OF SESSION +2

- Define resilience.

- Challenge preconceived notions that we are at the whim of our particular life circumstances; shift responsibility for our well-being from the hands of fate to how effectively we engage our internal resources, particularly the key resources of mindfulness and compassion.

- Explore other factors and strategies to enhance our resilience.

- Introduce the Compassionate Breathing practice and the Drawing on Strength Reflection.

Session +2 Outline

Time (in minutes)	Cumulative Time	Activity
5	5	Welcome and Check-In
5	10	Introduction to Compassionate Breathing
15	25	**Compassionate Breathing**
5	30	Small Group Check-In
5	35	Group Process (Q&A; follow-up from last week)
20	55	Theme: Enhancing Resilience
10	65	Reflection: Drawing on Strength
5	70	Group Process
10	80	**Mindfulness of Breathing**
5	85	Group Process
5	90	Wrap-Up

Materials: Bell, watch or timer, Session +2 outline, handouts, whiteboard and markers

Poems: "Dropping Keys" by Hafiz

Story: "It's Our Broken Places That Let the Light Shine Through"

Gary was diagnosed with early-stage liver cancer. This was, understandably, a devastating blow to a hard-charging accountant on the partner track at a big firm who regularly worked more than eighty hours a week. He had a wife and two school-age children. He was worried about how this illness would impact his family and forever change their lives. The five-year survival rate for his type and stage of cancer was about 40 to 50 percent, if he was lucky enough to receive a liver transplant.

The early months of treatment were difficult. Gary stopped working, the chemotherapy infusions were demanding, and he was consumed with his family's future. He began a mindfulness practice and struggled to sit with how broken he felt, both physically and emotionally.

Gary began to align his behaviors with his core values. He started dropping off and picking up his kids from school, something he had never actually done. He returned to painting, a passion he never felt he had time for when he was working. He reported that his relationships with his family and friends were more authentic and satisfying than they had ever been.

After many months of aggressive cancer treatment and uncertainty, Gary was matched with a donor liver and successfully had a transplant. He would sit on his back patio at dawn each morning for his meditation. As the sun floated up over the horizon, rays of light would shine through the broken parts in the brick wall of the patio. This light became a metaphor in his life. It was through his illness that he began to lead a values-driven life. His fears of death created opportunity for a deeper connection to his family and himself. In a silver-lining moment, Gary began to paraphrase the Leonard Cohen song "Anthem."

Welcome and Check-In (5 MINUTES)

Spend a few moments greeting everyone and settling into the group. Consider a brief name introduction and a one-sentence check-in with each participant about how his or her practice is going.

Introduction to Compassionate Breathing (5 MINUTES)

Introduce the new practice of Compassionate Breathing, which we have adapted from the Mindful Self-Compassion program developed by Christopher Germer and Kristin Neff. "This practice is very similar to Mindfulness of Breathing, as we use the felt sense of breathing as our anchor to the present moment. Each time your mind wanders, as it certainly will do, we simply bring it back to the physical sensations of the breath with kindness and without judgment. But in a Mindfulness of Breathing practice, we are allowing whatever is present to be just as it is. In this practice, we are actively trying to 'warm it up' a bit. We do this by inviting our awareness to explore the nourishing qualities of the breath, if this is available to you in the practice. We also bring an awareness of the compassion and kindness that surround us each day, starting with the kindness in the room."

Compassionate Breathing (15 MINUTES)

As with all practices during which we are trying to illicit a particular feeling or mood state, there is a potential for backdraft (see "Dealing with Backdraft" in chapter 4). You need not explain this before the practice, but it can be helpful for new facilitators to understand that this is a normal response. Allow the practice to be the teacher. As the facilitator, try to use language that is as inclusive as possible. Not every student can access or identify compassion when he or she begins this practice.

COMPASSIONATE BREATHING SCRIPT

Beginning by sitting in a comfortable yet dignified posture and allowing the eyes to gently close. Taking a few deep and easy breaths. In and out. Bringing awareness into the body—into the felt sense of the breath in the body. Allowing yourself to drop into awareness of being alive—of breathing.

[Pause, allowing time for the group to establish regular Mindfulness of Breathing for a couple of minutes]

Checking in with your body to notice any tension or stress. If you find physical discomfort or stress, simply making note of it. If there isn't any, make note of that too.

[Pause]

When you feel ready, check for the presence of any difficult or stressful emotions you might be experiencing. Explore your chest or heart space and see what's there. Meeting either physical or emotional distress is the occasion for our compassion practice. We have a tendency to want to avoid that which is difficult, but in this practice we actively meet any suffering or discomfort with compassion. If there is no suffering in this moment, simply noticing that experience.

[Pause]

Now take a nice, deep breath. Now take another. Notice how the body is being nourished with this breath.

[Pause]

Shifting the focus of your attention to the inhale part of the breath cycle. Feeling the air coming into the body. Perhaps you can sense how this feels nourishing and replenishing.

[Pause]

If that works for you, imagine breathing in compassion, as if the oxygen molecules were carrying compassion into the body.

[Pause]

Or it could be a word with each inhalation, like "love" or "ease." You could also imagine inhaling light or warmth, whatever works for you. Whatever you need in this moment.

[Pause]

If you have a hard time connecting to compassion or kindness, see if you can imagine what it would feel like to be surrounded by love and compassion.

[Pause]

Allowing yourself to be nourished if possible.

[Pause]

Taking in the kindness that's around you.

[Pause]

Breathing in the kindness and the compassion with each inhale as much as possible.

Allowing yourself to be soothed with each compassionate inhale. Taking it all in. Just for you.

[Long pause]

When you feel ready, shifting your attention to the exhale portion of the breath cycle. Feeling the air leaving your body. Allowing any tension to melt away with each exhale.

[Pause]

Now with each exhale, imagining exhaling compassion with each breath. You can extend this compassion to someone you know who might be suffering and needing some compassion. Or perhaps you might prefer sending out compassion to everyone around you.

[Pause]

With each exhale, allowing some of the abundant compassion that is within you to be transmitted to those in need.

[Pause]

Continue to exhale with ease. Extending all the kindness and compassion so plentiful in you out into the world.

[Pause]

When you are ready, shifting your attention to now notice the entire breath cycle. Noticing both the inhale and the exhale. Breathing deeply in and completely out.

[Pause]

With each inhale, taking in some compassion that is just for you. With each exhale, sending it out to everyone else.

[Pause]

Allowing yourself to savor all this kindness and compassion coming into and leaving your body. Finding a sense of ease and balance. Taking in compassion just for you. Sending out compassion for everyone else.

[Pause]

Now allowing the breath to find its own natural rhythm. Breathing in and breathing out gently and with ease. Compassion breathing in just for you. Compassion out for others.

[Pause]

With each inhale and exhale, feeling a sense of ease, feeling the compassion all around you. Feeling whole, just as you are. Breathing compassion in and compassion out.

[Pause]

One for you and one for everyone else.

[Pause]

Allowing the soothing sense of compassion to penetrate every organ and every cell. Allowing the care and comfort to be felt in the body and then sending it out for everyone else.

[Pause]

Inhaling care and exhaling care.

[Long pause]

[Ring bell]

Small Group Check-In (5 MINUTES)

Split the class into groups of two or three. Consider encouraging group members to meet with someone with whom they haven't previously shared in a small group setting. Once again, the topic is simply whatever a participant noticed during or immediately after the practice.

Group Process (5 MINUTES)

Back in the large group, invite participants to share any experiences with the practice. Validate a variety of experiences and inquire about any barriers or issues that come up. As always, maintain a stance of curiosity, kindness, and nonjudgment.

If a student brings up backdraft, or noticing a strong experience during the practice that is the opposite of compassion, let the class know that this can sometimes happen. As a facilitator, normalize the experience and encourage students to just observe it and let it be. Those new to a compassion practice don't always connect to those feelings. This is fine. Stay with the intentions of the practice and advise patience. It will unfold in time.

Commonly, the reactions from students are typically ones of surprise and revelation. In simply resting in the field of sensory awareness of the body and with the breath, and having an orientation toward compassion, a felt sense of it can be revealed.

Theme: Enhancing Resilience (20 MINUTES)

Begin introducing today's theme by saying something like, "In Session 3 we talked about stress and how a mindfulness practice can help with it. Today we want to explore the topic a bit more in depth. Let me start by asking, 'What is resilience?'" Once participants answer this question, pose a few more: "What makes one person more resilient than another?… Can we each enhance our own internal resources and enhance our resilience profile?" You could write down answers on a whiteboard.

"*Resilience* is the ability to withstand stress and overcome catastrophe. It means bouncing back from hardship. Resilience is *not* about enjoying a charmed life free of challenges. Everyone goes through tough times now and again. This is an important part of the teachings: It's not a mistake if painful events happen to us; that is just how things are supposed to be." It can be helpful to bring in a bigger, nonpersonal perspective to the situation (see "Dharma Teacher Perspective: On the Three Marks of Existence" in chapter 4). Our measure of resilience is how much and how fast we bounce back.

It is also important to frame that resilience is *not* a dichotomous variable, something you either have or you don't. "It is something within each of us and involves thoughts, behaviors, and attitudes. Resilience is something we can improve upon and enhance. A regular mindfulness practice that includes self-compassion enhances resilience.

"We can't change our genetic predisposition (at least not yet, anyway). And we can't do all that much to control every event in our lives and avoid every pitfall. But we can augment our internal resources. And we can make a conscious effort to use these resources to support us when we need them."

"Shit happens" is crude but common slang to describe the existential reflection that life is full of capricious events. But with resilience, when we get hit with "shit happens," we have an opportunity to transform this into "shift happens." Through a mindfulness and compassion practice, we shift from being caught up in the particular story of the moment to noticing our experience with compassionate attention. This shift is also a shift in our neural pathways. A shift from our lower brain structures, or reactivity and fear-based emotional processing, to our higher brain structures of abstract reasoning and executive function. It also strengthens a more regulated emotional processing.

"Shit happens" is actually an opportunity! It is an opportunity to let all your habits of rumination and irritability come to the surface. It is an opportunity, each time, to practice engaging and strengthening inner resources.

Strategies for Resiliency

There are a number of proven strategies for enhancing resilience (APA, 2014). Some of these approaches directly relate to the fundamental teachings of a mindfulness practice. This is one area where the rivers of knowledge between modern Western psychological research and ancient practice converge so beautifully:

- **Accept that change is inevitable and part of living.** Impermanence is a central tenet of mindfulness practice. We notice everything is changing moment by moment, and we learn to accept this gracefully or as best we can in each moment.

- **Cultivate a positive view of yourself.** This is trust as self-reliance, learning to listen to your own instincts and develop confidence. Self-compassion is highly supportive.

- **Create and maintain connections.** Accept help when needed and offer help to others, when possible, while staying engaged with family and community.

- **See crises as challenges for growth rather than insurmountable problems.** Stressful events happen to everyone. With our practice we learn to surf life's waves. And mindfulness gives us the confidence that we can do that—that everything is workable!

- **Keep perspective.** Don't collapse and contract when problems happen. Use your practice to stay open and flexible while keeping an eye on the big picture. The big picture also contains the truth that this not only happens to us but to many people, so we can use practices like the Mindful Self-Compassion Break to focus on the shared humanity part, the connection with all other beings who are experiencing or have experienced that same thing.

- **Take care of yourself.** Attend to your own feelings and needs. Pay attention to the demands of the physical body and rest, nourish, or meditate as needed. Self-compassion is also supporting that.

Share the story for this week: "It's Our Broken Places That Let the Light Shine Through." Consider reviewing which of the strategies Gary used to promote resilience in his life.

After the description of resilience and a brief review of some of the strategies we can use to enhance our resilience, transition to a brief reflection for individual exploration.

Reflection: Drawing on Strength (10 MINUTES)

The Drawing on Strength reflection is an opportunity for participants to listen deeply to their own, supportive voice. It is a chance to tap in to deeper reservoirs of resilience and healing. The guided practices has two parts:

1. Reflecting on areas of strength and support in the past

2. Reflecting on how the newly learned skills of mindfulness and compassion can be part of (additional) support

DRAWING ON STRENGTH SCRIPT

Sitting in an upright and dignified posture and allowing the eyes to softly close, if that feels okay to you. Maybe taking a few long, slow breaths in and out. Allowing the body to release any tension that is ready to be released.

[Pause]

Now letting go of the breath and just trusting the body to breathe just right.

I will be making a few comments for reflection. Just listen deeply and see what comes up for you.

Remember a time in your life or maybe different times that were challenging or hard for you. Perhaps a time in your past you felt overwhelmed.

[Pause]

Take a moment and reflect on what had been helpful back then. What resources were available to you?

Maybe your family or friends? Maybe your street smarts? Maybe a book or something you heard on the radio?

[Long pause]

Now sense into how your practices of mindfulness and compassion could have supported you, too. How could they have helped you in that situation or those situations?

[Long pause]

How could these practices help you in the future to help you to surf life's waves?

[Long pause]

[Ring bell]

Group Process (5 MINUTES)

After the Drawing on Strength reflection, spend a few minutes discussing the exercise in the large group. Listen for any insights into the factors that support resilience. If you have the time, you could also list them on the whiteboard, or at least repeat them out loud.

Mindfulness of Breathing (10 MINUTES)

Complete a Mindfulness of Breathing practice. See script from Session 2.

Group Process (5 MINUTES)

After a moment of reflection, explore the experience of the practice with the group.

Wrap-Up (5 MINUTES)

Offer a recording of the Compassionate Breathing practice for participants to listen to at home if they wish. Or they can choose any other practice that they have found helpful during the course of all sessions. Encourage them to try to use their resources, and mindfulness and compassion in particular, in the next difficult situation and shift to notice the experience rather than getting lost in it. "Appreciate how your own internal resources can help you to bounce back from hard times."

References

Abba, N., Chadwick, P., & Stevenson, C. (2008). Responding mindfully to distressing psychosis: A grounded theory analysis. *Psychotherapy Research, 18*(1), 77–87.

Allen, A., & Leary, M. R. (2013). A self-compassionate response to aging. *The Gerontologist, 52*(2), 190–200.

American Psychological Association (APA). (2014). The road to resilience. http://www.apa.org/helpcenter/road-resilience.aspx#

Arch, J. J., Brown, K. W., Dean, D. J., Landy, L. N., Brown, K. D., & Laudenslager, M. L. (2014). Self-compassion training modulates alpha-amylase, heart rate variability, and subjective responses to social evaluative threat in women. *Psychoneuroendocrinology, 42*, 49–58.

Barnard, L. K., & Curry, J. F. (2011). Self-compassion: Conceptualizations, correlates, and interventions. *Review of General Psychology, 15*(4), 289–303.

Beach, M. C., Roter, D., Korthuis, P. T., Epstein, R. M., Sharp, V., Ratanawongsa, N., et al. (2013). A multicenter study of physician mindfulness and health care quality. *Annals of Family Medicine, 11*(5), 421–428.

Bishop, S. R., Lau, M., Shapiro, S., Carlson, L., Anderson, N. D., & Carmody, J., et al. (2004). Mindfulness: A proposed operational definition. *Clinical Psychology: Science and Practice, 11*(3), 230–241.

Breines, J. G., & Chen, S. (2012). Self-compassion increases self-improvement motivation. *Personality and Social Psychology Bulletin, 38*(9), 1133–1143.

Breines, J. G., Thoma, M. V., Gianferante, D., Hanlin, L., Chen, X., & Rohleder, N. (2014). Self-compassion as a predictor of interleukin-6 response to acute psychosocial stress. *Brain Behavior and Immunity, 37*, 109–114.

Brion, J. M., Leary, M. R., & Drabkin, A. S. (2014). Self-compassion and reactions to serious illness: The case of HIV. *Journal of Health Psychology, 19*(2) 218–229.

Brooks, M., Kay-Lambkin, F., Bowman, J., & Childs, S. (2012). Self-compassion amongst clients with problematic alcohol use. *Mindfulness.* doi:10.1007/s12671-012-0106-5.

Brown, S. L., Smith, D. M., Schulz, R., Kabeto, M. U., Ubel, P. A., Poulin, M., et al. (2009). Caregiving behavior is associated with decreased mortality risk. *Psychological Science, 20*(4), 488–494.

Campbell, T. S., Labelle, L. E., Bacon, S. L., Faris, P., & Carlson, L. E. (2012). Impact of mindfulness-based stress reduction (MBSR) on attention, rumination, and resting blood pressure in women with cancer: A waitlist-controlled study. *Journal of Behavioral Medicine, 35*(3), 262–271.

Carlson, L. E. (2012). Mindfulness-based interventions for physical conditions: A narrative review evaluating levels of evidence. *ISRN Psychiatry*. http://dx.doi.org/10.5402/2012/651583

Carlson, L. E., Garland, S. N. (2005). Impact of mindfulness-based stress reduction (MBSR) on sleep, mood, stress, and fatigue in cancer outpatients. *International Journal of Behavioral Medicine, 12*(4), 278–285.

Carlson, L. E., Speca, M., Patel, K. D., & Goodey, E. (2004). Mindfulness-based stress reduction in relation to quality of life, mood, symptoms of stress and levels of cortisol, dehydroepiandrosterone sulfate (DHEAS), and melatonin in breast and prostate cancer outpatients. *Psychoneuroendocrinology, 29*(4), 448–474.

Centers for Disease Control and Prevention (CDC). (2014). Leading Causes of Death. Retrieved from http://www.cdc.gov/nchs/fastats/leading-causes-of-death.htm.

Chiesa, A., & Serretti, A. (2009). Mindfulness-based stress reduction for stress management in healthy people: A review and meta-analysis. *Journal of Alternative and Complementary Medicine, 15*(5), 593–600.

Costa, J., & Pinto-Gouveia, J. (2011). Acceptance of pain, self-compassion, and psychopathology: Using the chronic pain acceptance questionnaire to identify patients subgroups. *Clinical Psychology and Psychotherapy, 18*, 292–302.

Crane, R. S., Kuyken, W., Williams, J. M. G., Hastings, R. P., Cooper, L., & Fennell, M. J. (2012). Competence in teaching mindfulness-based courses: Concepts, development and assessment. *Mindfulness, 3*(1), 76–84. http://www.ncbi.nlm.nih.gov/pmc/articles/PMC3395338/#!po=65.6250

Creswell, J. D., Irwin, M. R., Burklund, L. J., Lieberman, M. D., Arevalo, J. M. G., Ma, J., et al. (2012). Mindfulness-based stress reduction training reduces loneliness and proinflammatory gene expression in older adults: A small randomized controlled trial. *Brain Behavior and Immunity, 26*(7), 1095–1101.

Creswell, J. D., Way, B. M., Eisenberger, N. I., & Lieberman, M. D. (2007). Neural correlates of dispositional mindfulness during affect labeling. *Psychosomatic Medicine, 69*, 560–565.

Davidson, R., Kabat-Zinn, J., Schumacher, J., Rosenkranz, M., Muller, D., Santorelli, S. F., et al. (2003). Alterations in brain and immune function produced by mindfulness meditation. *Psychosomatic Medicine, 65*(4), 564–570.

Decety, J. (2010). Mécanismes neurophysiologiques impliqués dans l'empathie et la sympathie. *Revue de neuropsychologie, 2*(2), 133–144.

Di Pellegrino, G., Fadiga, L., Fogassi, L., Gallese, V., & Rizzolatti, G. (1992). Understanding motor events: A neurophysiological study. *Experimental Brain Research, 91*(1), 176–180.

Emmons, R. A., & McCullough, M. E. (2003). Counting blessings versus burdens: An experimental investigation of gratitude and subjective well-being in daily life. *Journal of Personality and Social Psychology, 84*(2), 377.

Epel, E., Daubenmier, J., Moskowitz, J. T., Folkman, S., & Blackburn, E. (2009). Can meditation slow rate of cellular aging? Cognitive stress, mindfulness and telomeres. *Annals of the New York Academy of Sciences, 1172*, 34–53.

Fortney, L., Luchterhand, C., Zakletskaia, L., Zaierska, A. & Rakel, D. (2013). Abbreviated mindfulness intervention for job satisfaction, quality of life and compassion in primary care clinicians: A pilot study. *Annals of Family Medicine, 11*(5), 412–420.

Fredrickson, B. L., Grewen, K. M., Coffey, K. A., Algoe, S. B., Firestine, A. M., Arevalo, J. M., et al. (2013). A functional genomic perspective on human well-being. *Proceedings of the National Academy of Sciences, 110*(33), 13, 13684–13689.

Glaser, R., & Kiecolt-Glaser, J. K. (2005). Stress-induced immune dysfunction: Implications for health. *Nature Reviews Immunology, 5*(3), 243–251.

Goldstein, E. (2014). The Power of Lovingkindness: An Interview with Sharon Salzberg. *Mindfulness & Psychotherapy with Elisha Goldstein, Ph.D.* (blog). PsychCentral, July 10. http://blogs.psychcentral.com/mindfulness/2012/07/the-power-of-lovingkindness-an-interview-with-sharon-salzberg/

Goyal, M., Singh, S., Sibinga, E. M., Rowland-Seymour, A., Sharma, R., Berger, Z., et al. (2014). Meditation programs for psychological stress and well-being: A systematic review and meta-analysis. *JAMA Internal Medicine, 174,* 357–368.

Grepmair, L., Mietterlehner, F., Loew, T., Bachler, E., Rother, W., & Nickel, N. (2007). Promoting mindfulness in psychotherapists in training influences the treatment results of their patients: A randomized, double-blind, controlled study. *Psychotherapy and Psychosomatics, 76,* 332–338. doi:10.1159/000107560

Hebb, D. O. (1949). *The organization bf Behavior: A neuropsychological theory.* New York: Wiley.

Hepach, R., Vaish, A., & Tomasello, M. (2013). A new look at children's prosocial motivation. *Infancy, 18*(1), 67–90.

Hofmann, S. G., Sawyer, A. T., Witt, A. A., & Oh, D. (2010). The effect of mindfulness-based therapy on anxiety and depression: A meta-analytic review. *Journal of Consulting and Clinical Psychology, 78*(2), 169–183.

Hölzel, B. K., Carmody, J., Vangel., M., Congleton, C., Yerramsetti, S. M., Gard, T., et al. (2011). Mindfulness practice leads to increases in regional brain gray matter density. *Psychiatric Review: Neuroimaging, 191*(1), 36–43.

Jacobs, T., Epel, E. S., Lin, J., Blackburn, E. H., Wolkowitz, O. M., Birdwell, D. A., et al. (2011). Intensive meditation training, immune cell telomerase activity, and psychological mediators. *Psychoneuroendocrinology, 36*(5), 664–681.

Jain, S., Shapiro, S. L., Swanick, S., Roesch, S. C., Mills, P. J., Bell, I., et al. (2007). A randomized controlled trial of mindfulness meditation versus relaxation training: Effects on distress, positive states of mind, rumination, and distraction. *Annals of Behavioral Medicine, 33*(1), 11–21.

Kabat-Zinn, J. (2011). *Mindfulness for beginners: Reclaiming the present moment—and your life.* Boulder, CO: Sounds True.

Kelly, A. C., Zuroff, D. C., Foa, C. L., & Gilbert, P. (2009). Who benefits from training in self-compassionate self-regulation? A study of smoking reduction. *Journal of Social and Clinical Psychology, 29,* 727–755.

Keltner, D., Marsh, J., & Smith, J. A. (Eds.). (2010). *The compassionate instinct: The science of human goodness.* New York: WW Norton & Company.

Khoury, B., Lecomte, T., Gaudiano, B. A., & Paquin, K. (2013). Mindfulness interventions for psychosis: A meta-analysis. *Schizophrenia Research, 150*(1),176–184.

Killingsworth, M. A., & Gilbert, D. T. (2010). A wandering mind is an unhappy mind. *Science, 330*(6006), 932.

Kim, S. H., Schneider, S. M., Bevans, M., Kravitz, L., Mermier, C., Qualls, C., et al. (2013). PTSD symptom reduction with mindfulness-based stretching and deep breathing exercise: Randomized controlled clinical trial of efficacy. *The Journal of Clinical Endocrinology & Metabolism, 98*(7), 2984–2992.

Klimecki, O., Ricard, M., & Singer, T. (2013). Empathy and compassion: Lessons from the 1st and 3rd person methods. In Tania Singer and Matthias Bolz (Eds.), *Compassion: Bridging practice and science.* Munich, Germany: Max Planck Society. http://www.compassion-training.org/en/online/index.html?iframe=true&width=100%&height=100%#272.

Konrath, S., Fuhrel-Forbis, A., Lou, A., & Brown, S. (2012). Motives for volunteering are associated with mortality risk in older adults. *Health Psychology, 31*(1), 87.

Kornfield, J. (2009). *The wise heart: A guide to the universal teachings of buddhist psychology.* New York: Random House.

Lazar, S. W., Kerr, C. E., Wasserman, R. H., Gray, J. R., Greve, D. N., Treadway, M. T., et al. (2005). Meditation experience is associated with increased cortical thickness. *Neuroreport, 16*(17), 1893–1897.

Lerman, R., Jarski, R., Rea, H., Gellish, R., & Vicini, F. (2012). Improving symptoms and quality of life in female cancer survivors: A randomized controlled study. *Annals of Surgical Oncology, 19*(2) 373–378.

Lewis, T., Amini, F., & Lannon, R. (2000). *A general theory of love.* New York: Random House.

Linehan, M. (1993). *Cognitive behavioral therapy for borderline personality disorder.* New York: Guilford Press.

Luders, E., Toga, A. W., Lepore, N., & Gaser, C. (2009). The underlying anatomical correlates of long-term meditation: Larger hippocampal and frontal volumes of gray matter. *Neuroimage, 45*(3), 672–678.

MacBeth, A., & Gumley, A. (2012). Exploring compassion: A meta-analysis of the association between self-compassion and psychopathology. *Clinical Psychology Review, 32,* 545–552.

Maguire, E. A., Gadian, D. G., Johnsrude, I. S., Good, C. D., Ashburner, J., Frackowiak, R. S., et al. (2000). Navigation-related structural changes in the hippocampi of taxi drivers. *Proceedings of the National Academy of Sciences of the United States of America, 97*(8), 4398–4403. April 11.

Matousek, R. H., Dobkin, P. L., & Pruessner, J. (2009). Cortisol as a marker for improvement in mindfulness-based stress reduction. *Complementary Therapies in Clinical Practice, 16*(1), 13–19.

Neff, K. D. (2003a). Self-compassion: An alternative conceptualization of a healthy attitude toward oneself. *Self and Identity, 2,* 85–102.

Neff, K. D. (2003b). Development and validation of a scale to measure self-compassion. *Self and Identity, 2,* 223–250.

Neff, K. D., & Germer, C. K. (2013). A pilot study and randomized controlled trial of the mindful self-compassion program. *Journal of Clinical Psychology, 69*(1), 28–44.

Neff, K. D., Hseih, Y., & Dejitthirat, K. (2005). Self-compassion, achievement goals, and coping with academic failure. *Self and Identity, 4,* 263–287.

Rossini, P. M., & Dal Forno, G. (2004). Integrated technology for evaluation of brain function and neural plasticity. *Physical Medicine and Rehabilitation Clinics of North America, 15*(1), 263–306.

Segal, Z. V., Williams, J. M. G., & Teasdale, J. D. (2012). *Mindfulness-based cognitive therapy for depression*. New York: Guilford Press.

Seppala, E., Rossomando, T., & Doty, J. R. (2013). Social connection and compassion: Important predictors of health and well-being. *Social Research: An International Quarterly, 80*(2), 411–430.

Serpa, J. G., Taylor, S. L., & Tillisch, K. (2014). Mindfulness-based stress reduction (MBSR) reduces anxiety, depression, and suicidal ideation in veterans. *Medical Care.* doi:10.1097/MLR.0000000000000202

Shapiro, S. L., Brown, K. W., & Biegel, G. M. (2007). Teaching self-care to caregivers: Effects of mindfulness-based stress reduction on the mental health of therapists in training. *Training and Education in Professional Psychology, 1*(2), 105–115.

Simon, N. M., Smoller, J. W., McNamara, K. L., Maser, R. S., Zalta, A. K., Pollack, M. H., et al. (2006). Telomere shortening and mood disorders: Preliminary support for a chronic stress model of accelerated aging. *Biological Psychiatry, 60*(5), 432–435.

Speca, M., Carlson, L. E., Goodey, E., & Angen, M. (2000). A randomized wait-list controlled clinical trial: The effect of a mindfulness meditation-based stress reduction program on mood and symptoms of stress in cancer patients. *Psychosomatic Medicine, 62*(5), 613–622.

Spiegel, D., Sephton, S. E., Terr, A. I., & Sittes, D. P. (1998). Effects of psychosocial treatment in prolonging cancer survival may be mediated by neuroimmune pathways. *Annals of the New York Academy of Sciences, 840*, 674–683.

Szalavitz, Maia. (2012) Mind-Reading Q&A: Jon Kabat-Zinn Talks about Bringing Mindfulness Meditation to Medicine. *Time*, Jan. 11. http://healthland.time.com /2012/01/11/mind-reading-jon-kabat-zinn-talks-about-bringing-mindfulness-meditation -to-medicine/.

Tang, Y. Y., Lu, Q., Fan, M., Yang, Y., & Posner, M. I. (2012). Mechanisms of white matter changes induced by meditation. *Proceedings of the National Academy of Sciences, 109*(26), 10,570–10,574.

Taylor, J. B. (2007). *My stroke of insight*. New York: Viking Adult.

VA National Center for PTSD. (2014). Mindfulness practice in the treatment of traumatic stress. http://www.ptsd.va.gov/public/treatment/therapy-med/mindful-ptsd.asp.

Woods-Giscombé, C. L., & Gaylord, S. A. (2014). The cultural relevance of mindfulness meditation as a health intervention for African Americans: Implications for reducing stress-related health disparities. *Journal of Holistic Nursing, 32*(3), 147–160.

Wren, A. A., Somers, T. J., Wright, M. A., Goetz, M. C., Leary, M. R., Fras, A. M., et al. (2012). Self-compassion in patients with persistent musculoskeletal pain: Relationship of self-compassion to adjustment to persistent pain. *Journal of Pain and Symptom Management, 43*(4), 759–770.

Yalom, I. D. with Leszcz, M. (2005). *The theory and practice of group psychotherapy* (5th ed.). New York: Basic Books.

Photo by Mark Koberg

Christiane Wolf, MD, PhD, is a physician turned mindfulness teacher, teacher's trainer, writer, and speaker. Her mindfulness practice started in the late 1980s. Before becoming a full-time mindfulness teacher, she was a board certified OB/GYN at the Humboldt University of Berlin, Germany. She also holds a PhD in psychosomatic medicine from Humboldt University. Dr. Wolf is a certified senior mindfulness-based stress reduction (MBSR) teacher and supervisor for the Center for Mindfulness at University of Massachusetts Medical School. She is the director of MBSR programs at InsightLA, a Los Angeles–based nonprofit, and the director of the VA CALM program at the VA Greater Los Angeles Healthcare System, training staff and clinicians in mindfulness and how to teach it. Dr. Wolf received Dharma transmission from Trudy Goodman, her heart teacher, in 2011, and has undergone master Insight meditation teacher training under Jack Kornfield (Spirit Rock Meditation Center, CA) and Joseph Goldstein (Insight Meditation Society, MA). She teaches meditation retreats and workshops in the United States and internationally, and lives in Los Angeles with her husband and their three children. To learn more about Dr. Wolf, please visit www.christianewolf.com.

J. Greg Serpa, PhD, is a clinical psychologist for the US Department of Veterans Affairs at the VA Greater Los Angeles Healthcare System. He is honored to teach mindfulness to America's veterans and is the first full-time mindfulness teacher and trainer in the federal system. Serpa is an associate clinical professor in the psychology department at the University of California, Los Angeles, and an associate visiting clinical scientist at the David Geffen School of Medicine at UCLA. He teaches intensive mindfulness-based stress reduction (MBSR), mindful self-compassion (MSC), and introductory level mindfulness classes at four area hospitals, and serves as a trainer, supervisor, and consultant to clinicians at the VA and UCLA. He is currently the director of interprofessional mental health education at the West Los Angeles VA, where he trains psychology postdoctoral fellows, psychiatry residents, social work interns, and nurses in mindfulness and integrative modalities of health and well-being. Serpa is a national mindfulness content expert for the VA's Office of Patient Centered Care and Cultural Transformation, where he and Christiane Wolf are preparing mindfulness toolkits for national dissemination. He is also an active researcher with a number of projects expanding on the evidence basis of mindfulness interventions. This includes a National Institutes of Health–funded biomarker study examining the impact of meditation on brain structure in combat veterans from Iraq and Afghanistan who have traumatic brain injury and post-traumatic headache.

Foreword writer **Jack Kornfield, PhD**, is cofounder of the Insight Meditation Society in Barre, MA, and a founding teacher of Spirit Rock Meditation Center in Woodacre, CA. He is author of many books, including *A Path with Heart* and *The Wise Heart*.

Foreword writer **Trudy Goodman, PhD**, is a senior Vipassana teacher in Los Angeles, cofounder of the Growing Spirit program, and contributing author to several books, including *Compassion and Wisdom in Psychotherapy*, *Clinical Handbook of Mindfulness*, and *Mindfulness and Psychotherapy*.

Index